Fassadinin:
Land, Settlement and Society in Southeast Ireland 1600-1850

William Nolan B.A., Ph.D.

Fassadinin: Land Settlement and Society in Southeast Ireland 1600–1850

by
William Nolan B.A., Ph.D.,
Lecturer in Geography,
Carysfort College of Education,
Dublin.

Foreword by T. Jones Hughes,
Professor of Geography,
University College Dublin.

Geography Publications, Dublin.

ISBN 0 906602 009

Geography Publications,
24, Kennington Road,
Templeogue,
Dublin 12,
Republic of Ireland.

Typeset by Joe Healy Typesetting, Dublin.
Photography by Gerry Deegan, Kilkenny Design Workshops Ltd.,
Kilkenny, Ireland.
Printed by Folens & Co. Ltd., Airton Road, Tallaght, Co. Dublin.

ACKNOWLEDGEMENTS

In writing this book I have been helped by very many people in a great many ways. Professor Tom Jones-Hughes of University College Dublin has given me guidance and inspiration. Sister Benvenuta MacCurtain O.P., Ph.D. read earlier drafts of the work and made helpful suggestions on content and layout. Dr John Andrews of Trinity College Dublin gave encouragement by word and example. Without libraries and record offices books about the past would be impossible to write. The staff of the National Library Dublin and, in particular, Mr. Michael Cleary, Mr. Michael Hewson and Mr. Christy Hyland were particularly helpful.

I should like to acknowledge the help of one of our younger geographers, Mr. Kevin Whelan, for the care and scholarship with which he read and corrected the book in its earlier stages. I wish to thank Dr. Timothy O'Neill and Miss Josephine Lynch for reading the proofs. I would like to record a special indebtedness to Mr. Tom Hoyne, Webbsboro, Co. Kilkenny and Mr. Tom Lynge, Noremount, Kilkenny for their encouragement and practical help.

My debt is also great to the many people of Fassadinin and Slieveardagh baronies for whom farming and mining have been ways of life rather than something to write about. This book would never have appeared without the many sacrifices made by my mother and late father to educate a family under the trying economic circumstances of the fifties in Ireland. Neither would books of this kind be possible to produce without financial subventures.

Therefore I would like to thank Sister Regina Durkan, President of Our Lady of Mercy College of Education, Blackrock, Co. Dublin and the Senate of the National University of Ireland for their kind assistance. I wish to record the encouragement and practical help which I received from Mr. Jim Gibbons T.D., Minister for Agriculture. Acknowledgement is made to Irish Clay Industries Ltd., Castlecomer, Co. Kilkenny for their generous financial assistance. The input of Kilkenny Design Workshops Limited should not go unrecorded and I wish to thank them for help in publicising the book and, in particular, for their contribution to design and photography. To all other geographers and friends whose work has helped to make this book possible I should like to record my thanks and especially to the following, P. J. Carty, P. O'Connor, P. O'Flanagan, P. J. Duffy William Smyth and John Hunt.

My greatest debt is to my wife Teresa, who has endured patiently the historical geography of Fassadinin for over ten years.

iii

For Teresa, John and Sadhbh

CONTENTS

LIST OF FIGURES

Except where specified the figures refer to the barony of Fassadinin. These figures are reproduced from Kilkenny 6" 1843 and 1" Townland Index No. 21 and are based on the Ordnance Survey by permission of the Government (Permit No. 3136).

LIST OF PLATES

Plates I, VI, VIII are reproduced from the Cambridge University Collection (copyright reserved) by permission of the Committee for Aerial Photography, University of Cambridge. Plate X is reproduced from the Lawrence Collection in the National Library of Ireland by kind permission of the Director of the National Library of Ireland.

I wish to thank the following residents of Fassadinin barony for permission to photograph their properties: Messrs. Holland (Ballyragget), Delaney (Castlecomer), Conway (Moyhora), Lennon (Swiftsheath), Ward (Moyhora), Dunphy (Kiltown).

LIST OF TABLES

FOREWORD

This study is concerned with one of the central themes of human existence, namely the ownership, occupation and working of the land. It is based on a small, cohesive and little known territory in north county Kilkenny. The author was himself brought up in a similarly endowed area in south Tipperary and as an undergraduate in University College Dublin, he pursued joint degree courses in geography and history. In this way, he had qualifications which enabled him to undertake a detailed analysis and interpretation of the changing patterns of landholding over long periods of time in this part of the south midlands. Administratively, the northern extremity of county Kilkenny was in the past known as Fassadinin *(Fásach an Dinin)*, a name which may refer to the physically less desirable qualities of the environment of the Dinin river basin, especially as these are compared with the maturely fertile flanking lowlands and foothill country that lie immediately to the south. Be this as it may, this book is essentially a detailed study of the evolution, in juxtaposition, of communities in two contrasting environments.

The bleak, inhospitable and remote Castlecomer plateau had never attracted colonists in large numbers until the advent of the exceptional social and demographic circumstances that prevailed in rural Ireland from the middle of the eighteenth century. Until then, it appears only to have acted as a refuge area for the dispossessed and the disowned. By contrast, the attractive and more easily accessible lowlands of the middle Nore and Barrow river basins have experienced a variety of colonising movements and associated cultural upheavals. Thus, whilst the plateau landscape displays few prestigious monuments from the past, the lowland immediately to the south, which forms the territorial core of the Ossory diocese, is sprinkled with the remains of some of man's finest achievements in material culture in Ireland. At present the most conspicuous of such remnants are those of early churches and monasteries as these are seen intermingled with the shells of great mansions and parklands, the latter marking the climax phase of the estate system of land organisation in the eighteenth century. Such lowlands in Leinster have also long known rather sophisticated forms of urban living for their time and Kilkenny city itself lies immediately to the south of the study area. The town of Castlecomer, on the other hand, the present administrative centre for much of Fassadinin, is indisputably of landlord origin. Similarly, the surrounding plateau surfaces and hill slopes, at an elevation of between about 150 and 300 meters, display evidence of swift and hasty settlement by smallholders and landless peoples, many of whom had initially come to participate in coal mining.

One simple method of demonstrating the contrasting history of colonisation and settlement of lowland and upland in Fassadinin is provided by a study of the surviving place–name elements, most of which appear to have originated in the medieval period and earlier. Fortunately William Canon Carrigan, the author of *The history and antiquities of the diocese of Ossory* (1905), collected a selection of field names for the whole of the county, which was later published in a book by Owen O'Kelly called *Kilkenny, a history of the county* (1969). On the plateau surface and the adjoining hill slopes, it appears that the numerically dominant name elements refer only to the most obvious of topographic features, as these were used at an early stage in the history of settlement for detailed territorial identification and demarcation purposes. The most numerous of these include *cnoc* ('hill'), *móin* ('bog'), *cúl* ('hill-back'), *currach* ('marsh', 'moor'), *gleann* ('glen'), *poll* ('hollow'), *clais* ('ditch'), *druim* ('ridge'), *leaca* ('slope') and *tulach* ('mound') In the foothill country and the skirting lowlands of Fassadinin, on the other hand, whilst the topographic features are still the most numerous, one finds a greater range and variety of name elements and many of these specifically refer to units of enclosure and settlement. Some of the latter are clearly of English origin and they are important because they represent the only detailed evidence that is available to illustrate the extent of the Anglo-Norman transgression into the foothill country. The most numerous of such lowland elements listed by Canon Carrigan are *páirc* ('field'), *gort* ('field'), *garrdha* ('garden', cultivated plot'), *ráth, baile* ('place', 'farmstead') and the suffix-*town*.

It is relatively easy to construct mental images of the differing life styles that still prevail in upland and lowland Fassadinin. The plateau surface, for example, may be epitomised by an elderly man, wandering solitary among small, wet and rush-infested fields. Alternatively, in this church-centred community, the image may take the form of groups of women attending devotions in the many tall and antiquated-looking structures erected early in the last century to serve the needs of much larger congregations. The fields and the churches are among the most striking items in a landscape which is cluttered with small dwelling houses and a variety of building styles and décor that is unusual in rural Ireland. Occasionally, these houses are huddled together haphazardly around road intersections. From the early nineteenth century, such grouped settlements came to offer, and for the first time, rudimentary services for extensive upland neighbourhoods in the form of national schools, medical dispensaries, police barracks, post offices, public houses and a variety of tiny retail stores. Clogh, on the boundary with county Laois, remains a fine example of such an amorphous development.

Moving westwards from Clogh towards the edge of Fassadinin barony, one can look down the spectacular scarp slope which overlooks the middle section of the Nore valley and the small town of Ballyragget. In front are the landscape frameworks of parishes, townlands, farm units and fields which are representative of lowland south Leinster. These the author of this book identifies with the former manorial lands of great Anglo-Norman families such as the Purcells, Archers, Mountgarretts and Butlers. Tillage is the hallmark of this region and today its farmers are avidly competing for the sale of their produce in European markets. For this purpose, the splendid landlord–induced parklands, such as those of the Butler family in Dunmore, are once more being refurbished and transformed. Ballyragget is the most substantial local example of a tradition of village and small town development which in this part of Leinster goes back to the fourteenth century. In the eighteenth century, these essentially medieval nucleations throughout Ireland came to be formalised and compartmentalised to suit landlord requirements. Ballyragget remains today a model of propriety to the extent that even its old fair green has been converted into a public park. In this way one can assert that Clogh and Ballyragget together represent the extremes of the two differing traditions of village development as these are encountered in Fassadinin.

The author of this book has been fortunate in his choice of area of study. Kilkenny is among the best documented of Irish counties and for the former manorial areas, in particular, sources such as the Ormonde papers stretch back well into the medieval period. By contrast, little detailed information is available for the hill peoples until the eighteenth and nineteenth centuries. Even then, the evidence, thorough and comprehensive as it surely is, tends to be alien in origin and temper. One is, for example, constantly astonished at the alacrity and the energy that appear to have been expended on concocting anglicised forms for Irish place-names. Nevertheless it is to such data—reports of government enquiries and pioneer social investigations, as well as the massive statistical accumulations that appeared to form such an essential part of the paraphernalia of early nineteenth century attempts to achieve more effective local administration—that the author eventually turns to with relish. And this is as it should be, for these data relate in a most intimate fashion and for the first time in their long history to his own people and his own countryside. The hill world of Fassadinin early came to be focussed on the ancient territory of Idough *(O Duach)*, the medieval O'Brenan lands which fell into the hands of the Wandesforde family in the seventeenth century at the time when the coal resources of the plateau surface were beginning to be exploited. The Wandesforde papers have survived and are now available for examination. These papers enable the author to bridge the important gap between the Cromwellian surveys of the seventeenth century and the state-sponsored reports of the nineteenth century. He is thus in a position to identify some of the important decision-making processes of that time, such as for example those governing urban development in landlord country.

This book is an impressive piece of work. Dr. Nolan has handled with great skill and confidence complex documents from seventeenth century land ledger books, to estate papers relating to the eighteenth century, as well as the massive reports of government surveys and investigations carried out in Ireland in the nineteenth century.

Using such comprehensive data, he has been able to reconstruct, in great detail and in a manner never attempted before, the changing spatial patterns relating to land working units within his chosen area. Some of the conclusions that he has arrived at appear to be of the greatest significance in the understanding of the general nature of the rural geography of modern Ireland.

T. Jones Hughes
University College, Dublin.

CHAPTER I

INTRODUCTION

The Scope and Purpose of the Study
  This study is divided into eight chapters on a chronological basis. The physical endowment of Fassadinin together with the evolution, spatial arrangement and function of its territorial divisions are considered in this chapter. The period circa 1600 is selected as a convenient starting point for the study, and the subsequent order of enquiry and presentation corresponds to the chronological sequence of events. Two chapters are devoted to a consideration of patterns of landownership and landoccupation in Fassadinin in the seventeenth century—chapter two, for example, examines the significance of Anglo-Norman, Gaelic and 'New-English' landowners in the barony in the first half of the seventeenth century. They are also concerned with describing the mechanisms through which land was acquired, and present an assessment of the spatial implications of changes in ownership. The beginning of a period of military conflict in 1641 marks a major break in the sequence of political events. Chapter three reviews the impact of war and political decision-making on the ownership and the occupation of land, for Fassadinin barony in the later half of the seventeenth century

  The eighteenth century is remarkably poor in documentary evidence and this explains the selection of the whole century as the period of study in chapter four. The stability of the proprietorial class in this period is suggested by the absence of detailed inventories of property which were such a common feature of the seventeenth century. The Wandesforde estate rather than the barony is the spatial unit which is now considered, and the source material utilised is mainly derived from the uncatalogued collection of papers, belonging to this family, now deposited in the National Library of Ireland.

  The year 1800 was selected as a convenient starting point for chapter five, insofar as it marked the beginning of a new century and was also the year in which the two kingdoms of Great Britain and Ireland were 'united' by the Act of Union. Because of the absence of material for other parts of the barony, this chapter again focusses on the Wandesforde property. It appraises the roles of landlord, principal tenants (or middlemen) and minor tenantry in changing the landscape. Chapter six is based on the three great bodies of evidence produced in the middle of the nineteenth

COUNTY BOUNDARIES
BARONY BOUNDARIES

N

LOUTH

LONGFORD

MEATH

WESTMEATH

DUBLIN

OFFALY

KILDARE

TINNAHINCH

PORTNAHINCH

MARY-
BOROUGH
EAST

UPPER-
WOODS

STRADBALLY

LAOIS

WICKLOW

CULLENAGH

BALLYADAMS

CLANDONAGH

CLARMALLAGH

SLIEVEMARGY

RATHVILLY

FASSADININ

CARLOW

GALMOY

IDRONE
WEST

CARLOW

FORTH

CRANNAGH

KILKENNY

IDRONE
EAST

GOWRAN

SHILLELOGHER

KILKENNY

ST. MULLINS
LOWER

WEXFORD

KELLS

KNOCKTOPHER

IDA

IVERK

0   10   20
MILES

Fig. 1.1 Fassadinin in Leinster.

2

century. These are the six inch to the mile townland maps of the Ordnance Survey, the various Censuses of Population, and the General Valuation of Rateable Property. The greater portion of the chapter is concerned with the valuation, ownership and occupation of land and buildings in Fassadinin in 1850. The demographic consequences of the Great Hunger and estate management are considered in the context of the Wandesforde property in chapter seven. The final chapter summarises the impact of these political decisions on the ownership and the occupation of land in Fassadinin barony.

2. The Physical Endowment

"Viewed from the plain, the coalfield appears to form an elevated plateau, but the interior is depressed in a basin-shaped form, the high ground forming the lip of the basin, and rising in many places to a height of more than 600 feet above the centre of the coalfield".
(*Explanatory Memoir on the Geology of the Leinster Coalfields,* published by the Geological Survey of Ireland, 5.)

"The Castlecomer plateau, or basin, which covers an area of more than 200 square miles between the Nore and Barrow valleys, is one of the most clearly marked *pays* in Ireland."
(Freeman, T. W. *Ireland a General and Regional Geography* (London 1950) 323.)

The barony of Fassadinin covers an area of 68,000 statute acres and lies between the River Nore on the west and its sister river, the Barrow, on the east. Fassadinin is the most northerly of the ten baronies into which the administrative county of Kilkenny is divided, and its boundaries on the north and east coincide with the county boundaries between Kilkenny, and Laois and Carlow respectively (Fig. 1.1.). Although the barony is affiliated to the province of Leinster, the physical landscape has close affinities with that of Northern Munster and may be classified as a transition zone between the Armorican structures of the south and the Caledonian structures of the east.

The origins of the physical landscape of Fassadinin are to be found in the Carboniferous period. Approximately 325 million years ago the Lower Carboniferous limestones were overlain by the younger deposits of Namurian grits and shales and the Ammanian coal measures. (Fig. 1.2.) The Armorican orogeny, which followed these depositional periods, failed to impose the east west alignment, so typical of the Armorican ridges of the south of Ireland, on this youthful landscape. Geologists assume that the failure of Armorican pressures to buckle the strata of the coalfield was related to the presence of the underlying buried block of the stable Leinster chain.[1] Instead, according to Whittow, the stresses were dissipated by the major faulting which crisscrosses the basin.

Significant topographic contrasts occur within Fassadinin and the barony may be broadly divided into two contrasting regions of upland and

3

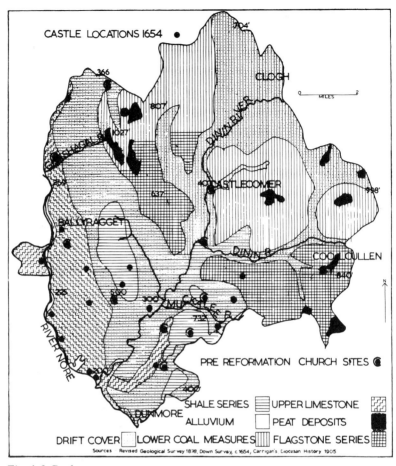

CASTLE LOCATIONS 1654 ●

PRE REFORMATION CHURCH SITES ⦿

	SHALE SERIES	UPPER LIMESTONE	
	ALLUVIUM	PEAT DEPOSITS	
DRIFT COVER	LOWER COAL MEASURES	FLAGSTONE SERIES	

Sources   Revised Geological Survey 1878, Down Survey, c.1654, Carrigan's Diocesan History 1905

Fig. 1.2 Geology

lowland. (Fig. 1.3.) The high ground forms part of the topographic region known as the Castlecomer plateau and represents a synclinal structure of Carboniferous rocks left upstanding above the plain by virtue of their sustained resistance to denudation. These hills rise abruptly and reach elevations of 1,000 feet in the townlands of Croghtenclogh, on the east and in Firoda Upper and Byrnesgrove on the west of Castlecomer town. Outward from the sandstone rim, the slopes fall rapidly away, either in steps or in high, steep escarpments, while on the inner side, the ground falls gently towards the centre, forming a basin-like depression. The term plateau is not entirely satisfactory in the context of Fassadinin, as the original flat surface has been subjected to lengthy erosional processes. The word 'Ridge' is used locally to describe the high ground on the Carlow side of the county boundary and it aptly portrays the nature of this dissected

4

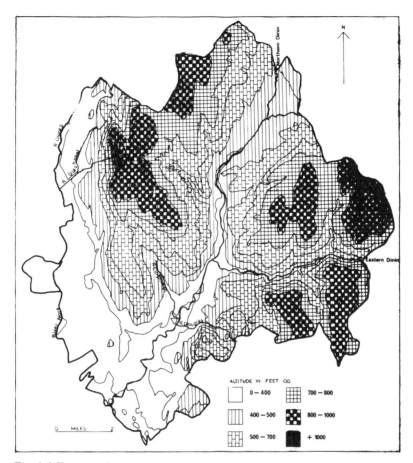

ALTITUDE IN FEET O.D.

0 – 400	700 – 800
400 – 500	800 – 1000
500 – 700	+ 1000

Fig. 1.3 Topography.

landscape. Figure 1.3 shows that a series of north-west, south-east ridges extend along both sides of the Dinin river and merge with the north Kilkenny lowlands in south Fassadinin.

The lowlying areas of Fassadinin coincide with the river basins of the Nore and Dinin and their tributary streams (Fig. 1.3). These rivers, cutting through the soft shales, have eroded broad basins which afford natural communication routes to the barony [plate 1]. It is through these accessible corridors that successive groups of immigrants have entered Fassadinin. The northern Dinin rises in the high ground on the Laois side of the county boundary. It flows westward until it joins the small Clogh river south of Clogh village. From here, it flows southwestwards for a distance of ten miles before joining the Nore north of the small settlement of Dunmore. Tributary rivers of the Northern Dinin, such as the eastern Dinin which

Plate I. The wide basin of the river Dinin one mile north of Castlecomer town. Part of the demesne townland of Ardra is in the right foreground and the slag heap of Deerpark Colliery is in the centre of the photograph.

originates in the hill country, are rapid streams and have incised deep narrow valleys in the shales. Two small tributary streams, the Cloghnagh and the Douglas, join the Dinin in Webbsborough townland.

The Nore is the great river of west Fassadinin. Apart from the townlands of Grange and Lisduff, which are located on its west bank, the Nore forms the barony boundary for over a distance of twelve miles. In this wide basin between the Slieveardagh and Castlecomer hills, the drift cover is relatively thin and patchy and the soil and drainage reflect the nature of the underlying limestone.[2] This is evident in the absence of westward flowing tributaries to the River Nore and in the development of an underground cave system to the south of the Douglas river.

3. The Territorial Framework

The purpose of this section is to briefly discuss the significance of the territorial divisions which are used throughout the study and as cadastral units in the various maps. The names of administrative divisions employed in modern Ireland have been mainly bestowed by aliens. The present

6

names of the barony, parishes and some townlands of Fassadinin are similar to those recorded in the land surveys of the late seventeenth century. The publication by Sir William Petty of his Atlas. *Hiberniae Delineatio*[3] (circa 1685) established the county framework as it is known today. Petty stated his attitude to Gaelic nomenclature in his *Political Anatomy of Ireland.*[4] In this he wrote: "the last clause of the Explanatory Act enabled men to put new names on their respective lands instead of those uncouth, unintelligible ones then upon them. And it would not be amiss if the significant part of the Irish names were interpreted, where they are not or could not be abolished." These new names have been superimposed but in many instances it was a case of putting new names on individual, or multiples of old divisions. Here an explanation is made of the significance of territorial units, such as the barony, parish, 'ploughland' or 'horseman's bed' and townland, utilised in the sources.

(a) Barony

The basic territorial division of Celtic Ireland was the *tuath* (tribe or people). Dillon and Chadwick noted the resemblance between barony names and ancient *tuath* names, but found that the *Book of Rights* in the eleventh century lists only ninety seven *tuatha* although there are today a total of 273 baronies in Ireland.[5] Goblet, one of the few writers to have assessed the impact of the land surveys of the seventeenth century on the evolution of territorial divisions, described the attributes of the *tuath* as, "territorial, political and social."[6] Butler defined the *tuath* as "the patrimony of a tribal unit having a complete political and legal administration."[7] Most commentators agree that the *tuath* was a territorial unit which also functioned in a social and political sense. In the superimposition of the barony, which was an Anglo-Norman tenure, use may possibly have been made of the existing territorial divisions as rent bearing units. A barony therefore may consist of either one or of several of the earlier *tuatha.*

The area occupied by the O'Brenans in the early medieval period was variously called 'Ui-Duach', 'Hyduach', 'Idough', 'Odough or Edogh'. It was described as, 'Ui Duach Argentross' in the Annals of the Four Masters in 850, 951, 1061 and 1156.[8] Carrigan, the diocesan historian of Ossory, maintained that the rural deanery of Odagh was co-extensive with the medieval kingdom of the O'Brenans[9] and other historians have noted that religious administrators closely followed the existing, secular divisions, when defining their territorial units. The Deanery of Odagh consisted of twenty one parishes. Of these, only Durrow and Odagh refer to the secular territorial division. Durrow, the site of a sixth century monastic establishment, is located on the west bank of the Nore, and was not recorded in Fassadinin in either the Civil Survey or the Down Survey. Neither did they record the parish of 'Achetyr'; (identified by Carrigan in the modern parish of Lisdowney to the west of Ballyragget). In 1389, the head of the O'Brenans was referred to "as captain of his own nation". In a treaty with the Earl of Ormonde, he promised to co-operate with the Earl "in controlling the Irish and English who live outside the peace and trust of the Lord King, especially in the area of March."[10] In a survey of Co. Laois completed in 1550, reference was made to "Aghtobrid lying in the March of Idowghe."[11] A Marchland was an indeterminate semi-independent area on the perimeter of civil country. In the late medieval period, the O'Brenan territory in the hill fastness north of the city of Kilkenny, and on the western edges of the Pale, was such an autonomous district.

In 1589, the greater portion of the district defined as the Deanery of Odough was described as the barony of 'Fasaghdeinyn and Idough.'[12] This designation was first applied in a survey which had its origins in the fiscal policy of the Government. During Sir John Perrot's term as Lord Deputy, a sum of money called prerogative money was levied on the freeholders of Co. Kilkenny. Along with delimiting internal units, this survey estimated that the barony contained "six ploughlands, three of mountain and three of champion ground". It further stated that "the quantity or number of acres of the said ploughlands, are not to us certainly known because said ploughlands or horsemansbedds were (as we understand) made in the beginning by view and estimation and not according to the quantity of acres." Andrews relates this ambiguity to "the fact that Ireland had no community of professional surveyors to lay down national standards of linear or areal mensuration."[13]

'Fasachlands' were defined at the Parliament held in Drogheda in 1494 as "Wastelands without the said Marches of the pale."[14] *Fásach* is an Irish word meaning 'desert', and *Deinyn* refers to the river of that name which drains the Castlecomer hills. The word 'desert' formerly meant an uninhabited place. The association of the term 'march' with the northern portion of the barony has already been noticed. It is difficult in the context of the late sixteenth century to associate the term 'Fásach' with an area of which no part was more than twenty miles from the Ormonde City of Kilkenny. The name may well have been a survival from an earlier unsettled period.

Perrot's survey suggests that the barony was evolving as the primary terrtorial and political unit at the expense of the older Gaelic division. Idough C. 1584 consisted of an undefined area in the north east of the barony and had an estimated area of two 'ploughlands' (fig. 1.4). No attempt was made to delimit the boundaries of the barony. From the names of the 'ploughlands' recorded, it appears that they were similar to those demarcated by the Down Survey almost twenty years later.

There is no evidence to suggest that the name Fassadinin, as defined in 1584, was utilised in a political or territorial sense in the early period of the seventeenth century. The weight of documentation points to the fact that, in transactions concerning land, the manor was regarded as the primary unit. Idough survived as the designation of the district in the north east of the barony. An Inquisition held in 1635 referred to the area as "the territory, precincts or circuit of Idough in Co. Kilkenny which was

Fig. 1.4 Ploughlands or 'Horsemen's beds'. Fassadinin c. 1584.

anciently called Brenan."[15] On the 16th, September, 1639 the manor of
Castlecomer was instituted and granted to Sir Christopher Wandesforde,
Master of the Rolls in the administration of his kinsman, the Earl of Strafford.[16] This grant effectively terminated the usage of Idough as a territorial or social unit.

In the Civil Survey the barony was utilised as the primary territorial
unit. Jurors appointed for each barony were to conduct the fieldwork of
the survey and report their findings to regional commissioners of the Government. The Civil Survey of Co. Kilkenny has not survived which is un-
fortunate as it would have contained a detailed description of barony
boundaries as known to the then landed proprietors. The descriptive
memoir of the Down Survey of Fassadinin barony records information on
landownership, land quality, settlement and topography for eight complete and four incomplete parishes totalling 16,309 'plantation' acres.
These parishes were further subdivided into thirty seven 'denominations'
(fig. 1.5). The survey's terms of reference excluded 'unforfeited lands', and
this explains its partial nature.

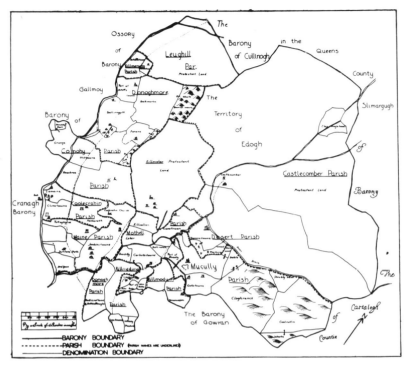

Fig. 1.5 Down Survey Map. Fassadinin c.1654.

The selection of the barony as a cadastral unit in the Down Survey reflects its importance as a territorial division in the seventeenth century. The Down Survey map of Fassadinin (fig. 1.5) delineates the outer boundaries of the barony, and also the limits of twelve parishes. It further subdivides the forfeited parishes into 'denominations' which coincided with local landowning and settlement units. The name of the district in the north east of the barony is given as the 'Territory of Edough and the parish of Castlecomer' but no attempt is made to determine the boundaries of these two divisions. The Down Survey memoir does not describe barony boundaries with the same amount of detail as is found in the Civil Survey. It merely names the baronies adjoining Fassadinin. Petty's barony map contained many of the units recorded in the 'Book of Ploughlands' c. 1584. Apart from the 'denomination' of Grange the river Nore marked the western limits of Fassadinin. For a distance of four miles north of Ballyragget, the bounds of the barony coincided with the Ouveg River. The marches of the barony in the north were similar to those of the O'Brenan lands of Idough, as laid down by the Inquisition of 1635. Topographical features in south Fassadinin are not as pronounced as elsewhere in the barony and here boundaries corresponded more to 'civil territorial divis-

10

ions' such as manors. 'Meres' were generally defined by topographic features of a permanent and outstanding nature, such as rivers which had relatively straight courses and hill crests, which were also natural drainage divides. Sacred elements such as holy wells, stone crosses and standing stones were also utilised as landmarks, as were other man-made features. The Down Survey did not superimpose new barony boundaries but utilised old ones. It was, however, the first attempt to map the barony area. A comparison of the Down Survey parish maps and the First Edition of the Ordnance Survey six inch to the mile maps c. 1843 reveals the stability and continuity of the barony bounds and subdivisions initially delimited by the Down Survey (figs. 1.6 and 1.7).

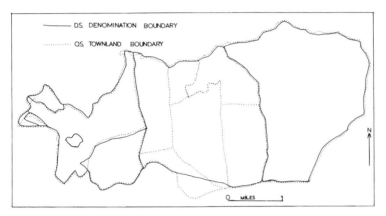

Fig. 1.6 Down Survey Map c.1654 superimposed on the Ordnance Survey six inch to the mile townland map c.1843. The parishes of Mothell (part of), Muckalee (part of).

The barony was used as one of the territorial divisions by which lands confiscated during the late seventeenth century were identified. In this way, the term acquired a legal title and was recorded in a great number of documents concerned with property and its ownership. The Books of Survey and Distribution augment one's knowledge of the internal divisions of the barony. This source gives a more comprehensive list of landholding units and landowners than the earlier Down Survey. It comprehends a total of 30,551 'plantation' acres, subdivided into seventy eight 'denominations'. County government in Ireland in the eighteenth and nineteenth centuries was the prerogative of the Grand Juries which consisted mainly of wealthy property owners. Statutes passed in 1759 and 1765 enabled the Grand Juries to levy a county rate to support road building. This cess or levy was paid by the barony in which the work was undertaken. The Grand Jury Act of 1836 authorised the holding of presentment sessions in each barony and the barony was represented at the county-at-large presentment sessions.[17]

11

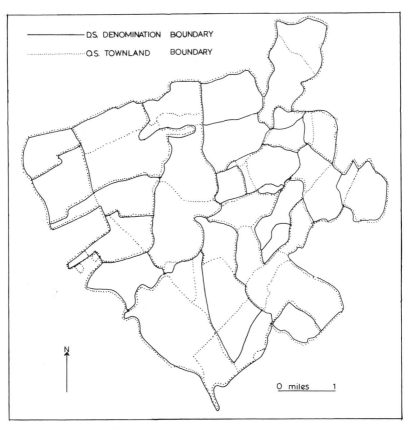

Fig. 1.7 Down Survey Map superimposed on the Ordnance Survey six inch to the mile townland map. The parishes of Dunmore, Kilmademoge, Kilmadum, Mothell (part of), Muckalee (part of), Coolcraheen, Mayne, Odagh.

Apart from its loosely defined administrative role, the barony was also recognised as a legal division in which quarter sessions were regularly held. The introduction of the Poor Law System in 1838, radically altered the existing administrative framework by establishing Poor Law unions which were further subdivided into electoral districts. The census of 1841, and earlier less reliable ones, recorded population data for townlands and towns on a parish and barony basis. This territorial classification was adhered to until the 1901 census. In that year, territorial classification was by townland, town, district electoral division, Registrar's district (dispensary district) and Poor Law union (Superintendent Registrar's district). The barony was by now almost defunct as a meaningful territorial entity and ceased to be used for administrative purposes after the Local Government Act of 1898 came into operation.

12

There is no evidence to indicate that any new maps of the barony were constructed in the eighteenth or early period of the nineteenth century. Taylor in his map of Co. Kilkenny in 1802 delineated the boundaries of each barony and recorded the names of baronies, civil parishes and some townlands. He retained the boundaries demarcated in the Down Survey map. The First Edition of the six inch to the mile Ordnance Survey maps compiled c. 1842 employed the county and townland as cadastral units. The boundaries and names of civil parishes were shown and barony names were recorded. These maps were used to delimit property units in the General Valuation of Rateable Property in 1850. Property values were recorded for each townland, parish, electoral division and Poor Law union on a barony basis.

It can be concluded therefore, that the barony of Fassadinin never gained local recognition as a territorial unit and had little meaning for the vast majority of its rural population. It was basically a term of territorial reference and was at no time the territorial basis of a social entity.

(b) The Parish

The administrative framework of the Irish Church was firmly established by the synod of Rathbreasail which met in 1111.[18] The parish was the smallest and most numerous unit in this structure and constituted an area within which a pastor or priest had care of the spiritual needs of the people. Its survival over a long period may be attributed to the existence of an institutional continuity in religious affairs. Church officials exercised spiritual power over well defined areas which in some instances were also landholding units. Their spiritual and territorial jurisdictions were carefully demarcated and frequently recorded. The Anglo-Normans were obviously familiar with the church administration they found here and made no radical alterations. Monastic orders introduced by the Anglo Normans administered parishes as adjuncts of their monasteries. These orders maintained a functional unity up to the Dissolution and, in many respects, their records are more numerous and have a greater degree of continuity than those of the secular clergy.

The church was the physical focal point of religion in the parish and was usually built of stone. Because of their spiritual associations, these churches, although often neglected, were rarely destroyed and their sites have been used as burial grounds up to the present time. The Dissolution of the monastic orders effectively shattered the spiritual and administrative structures of the Irish Church. The armed conflicts of the seventeenth century and the suppression of the Roman Catholic clergy further destroyed the continuity which had been maintained since Rathbreasail. An underground church and an emigrée episcopacy maintained elements of the old structures, but the Catholic parishes and Church sites of the seventeenth century were not those of the medieval church. The old administrative framework was adopted by the new Protestant Church, and as a civil territorial division in the great land surveys of the seventeenth century.

In 1300, the Diocese of Ossory, which was roughly similar in area to the county of Kilkenny, was divided into nine deaneries.[19] The parochial arrangements in the deanery of Odagh reveal interesting aspects of territorial organisation. Two of the twenty one parishes listed in the deanery were outside the modern barony area. Thirteen parishes were located in the lowlying area between the western edge of the hill country and the Nore and Ouveg Rivers. The parishes of Kilmacar, Castlecomer, Muckalee and Dysart embraced portion of the hill country, but in each case the parish centres were found in lowlying areas. The remaining parishes occupied the land area east of the Dinin river in the south of the barony. None of the parish centres was sited above 500' O.D., nor on the poorly drained gley and podzolic soils associated with the Coal Measures (Fig. 1.2). Medieval churchmen had a well defined preference for riverine sites which were well drained and easily accessible. Churches were built on such sites at Castlecomer, Dysart, Dunmore, Odagh and Grangemaccomb. Other churches, such as that of Muckalee, occupied elevated sites.

The taxation list c. 1300 is the earliest known record of parish names in the diocese and deaneries of Ossory. These names refer to 'cultural' items which were the products of human activity and to physical or natural features of a topographic or botanical nature. Six of the nineteen parishes listed in the modern barony area had names which referred to church settlements. In three of these the prefix, *cill* (church) was used with the name of the saint or 'holy man' to whom the foundation was attributed by tradition. Examples include, *Killcormak* (Cormac's Church); *Kilmenan* (Finian's Church) and *Killcolman* (Colman's Church). In Kilmacar, *cill* is compounded with *machair* (a level or flat place). Donaghmore *Domhnach Mór* (the big church) suggests that the foundation was ascribed to St. Patrick, patron Saint of Ireland. The ascetic nature of the early Christian Church is signified in the parish name of Dysart, *disert* (a secluded or isolated place). The district between the two Dinins was such a refuge.

Three parish names commemorate early secular settlement. These are: Dunmore, *Dún* (fort) *mór* (big); Rathbeag, *Rath* (fort) *beag* (small); and Coolcraheen, *Cúl* (corner, angle), *rathín* (small fort). The parish listed as 'Rathelo de Grangia' has been identified as the civil parish of Grangemaccomb. The c. 1300 designation refers to two separate settlement items. *Rath* refers to the double *rath* located north of the parish church and by the river Nore. *Grange* is not an Irish word but is derived from the French 'grang', which means a barn. The term suggests monastic origin: in 1300 the Cistercian monks of Jerpoint Abbey had the care of souls in this parish. In 1300 *Grange* was a relatively new addition to the name as Jerpoint Abbey was established c. 1158. Two parish names Loughill, *Léamh* (elm) *coill* (wood), and Ardaloo, *Árd* (height) *léamhach* (of the elms), depict botanical items.

Five parish names are concerned with elements which refer to physical or natural features. Mayne, *Máighín* (little plain), Mothell, *Maothail* (soft spongy land) and Muckalee, *Mágh* (plain), *tulaí* (of the mound), indicate lowlying topography. Rosconnell, Rosc (a promonotory), *connel* (Conal) and Comer, *cumar* (a river confluence) also refer to natural features, Attanagh in the north west the barony is a corrupt form of the Irish, *Ath Tanaí* (thin or narrow ford). Nine of the parishes were dedicated to 'saints' identified with early Irish Christianity and ten of the dedications were to saints of the universal church. This may imply that churches were being rededicated and also founded by the Anglo-Normans, through the provenance of the monastic orders who administered the greater number of the parishes in the deanery of Odagh.

In the Civil Survey, parish boundaries are described in detail and the tithes payable are recorded. The parish was utilised by Petty as a cadastral unit (fig. 1.5). The terms of reference for the Down Survey included the enumeration of church lands and the utilisation of the parish unit facilitated their identification. Petty's decision to employ the parish as a territorial division was related to the fact that the earlier Civil Survey had done so. In the Down Survey memoir, only three churches are listed, at Donaghmore, 'Mucully' and Grange, and these are described as 'old' and 'in little repaire'. In the Barony map, an additional three churches at Coolcraheen, Rosconnell and Kilmacar are shown (fig. 1.5). This relatively low church density suggests the impact of the Reformation and the changing function of the parish. In the Book of Survey and Distribution, all but three of the thirteen parishes recorded existed as church divisions in 1300. The 'monastic' parishes of Ardaloo and Grangemaccomb had become obsolete as ecclesiastical units at the Dissolution and were returned in the Survey as portions of Mayne and Connahy parishes. The two small parishes of Killcolman and Killcormack had also failed to survive.

Neither the Down Survey nor the Book of Survey and Distribution are complete records of parish units in the seventeenth century. The parish was utilised to make the surveys more manageable and meaningful and because, in many instances, the estates of individual landowners were coextensive with parishes. The townland, barony and county were the territorial units by which property was identified in the late seventeenth century and the parish accordingly became increasingly obsolete as a reference term.

The existence of divided religious loyalties was paralleled by the existence of separate administrative systems. The Catholic Church was a proscribed organisation and because of the absence of funds and trained personnel had drastically revised its territorial units. The identification of the older parish centres with the Protestant Church ensured that the new Catholic parishes would not be based on these ancient focal points. The great poverty of the Catholic population necessitated large units to pay for the upkeep of the clergy. Therefore up to 1751, the parish of Castlecomer comprised the present parishes of Castlecomer, Muckalee, Clogh and part of Connahy. In 1751, the two separate parishes of Muckalee and Castlecomer were created. In 1831, Clogh was constituted a parish and in the following year, the parish of Connahy was established. The Established Church controlled old parishes and collected parish tithes. Only in the parishes of Mothell and Castlecomer were the congregationists sufficiently numerous to ensure continuity of the spiritual community. During the eighteenth century the great majority of old churches fell into decay.

When Emancipation was granted, the spate of new church building occurred in the towns and villages and not on the pre-Reformation sites. Four major surveys in the nineteenth century used the civil parish as a territorial division. The proposal to substitute payments of tithe in kind by a fixed monetary charge necessitated the holding of a survey to determine the amount of tithe payable. The parish was an ideal base unit insofar as tithe was paid by both the Catholic and Protestant population to the incumbent. The Tithe Composition Books (c. 1830) are not uniform in standard or presentation and vary greatly from parish to parish.[20] They give the names of parishes and townlands in the decade before the taking of the Ordnance Survey. The parishes enumerated in Fassadinin barony

Fig. 1.8 Civil and Catholic parishes. Fassadinin, c.1838.

were similar to those delineated in the Ordnance Survey six inch to the mile maps published in 1842. The same parish units were recorded in the census of 1841 and in the General Valuation of Rateable Property in Ireland in 1850. A total of nineteen civil parishes are listed in Fassadinin by the various surveys and census documentation (fig. 1.8). Nine of these parishes are incomplete and embrace portions of adjoining baronies. This transgressing of barony boundaries suggests that the parish was a much older unit, and had been stabilised before the barony was introduced. Fifteen parishes listed in the nineteenth century were ecclesiastical units in the Deanery of Odagh in 1300. Parish names were invariably the name of the townland in which the old parish church was located.

Civil parishes in Fassadinin barony varied in size from 21,576 to 354 statute acres. There is an obvious correlation between parish size and land quality. The largest parishes, for example, Castlecomer, Dysart and Mothell, all contained much hilly or marginal land. The civil parish was rarely used in a secular administrative capacity. Damages for malicious injuries were sometimes assessed on parishes and for the collection of county cess the parish was part of the barony. The names and boundaries of the old parish units have survived, primarily because of their use as cadastral and territorial units. The loss of its earlier function rendered the civil parish meaningless to the great majority of the rural population.

(c) The 'Ploughland' or 'Horseman's Bed' and the Townland

"As to their town-lands, ploughlands, colps, gneeres, ballibos, balligetaghs, two's, horseman's beds, etc., they are at this day become unequal both in quantity and quality'"
(Petty, William, *New Edition of William Petty's tracts relating to Ireland* c. 1680 (Dublin, 1789) 372

"The Meares and bounds of the sayd parish att large sett forth with the several Towneshipps and parcells of land therein contayned". (*The Civil Survey,* Vol. I, Co. Tipperary, 126)

One is not here concerned with the origins of these territorial divisions but with their usage in the period covered by this study. Although the terms by which land units were known varied on a regional basis, it would appear that divisions originated as units of economic input or output and were rarely based on any process of measurement on the ground. Knowledge of territorial divisions and their social and economic significance is severely limited for this period. There is, for example, no evidence concerning the ways in which the O'Brenans partitioned their lands. What exists is a list of these partitions compiled by civil servants and Ormonde officials who were in the process of standardising indigenous units by superimposing acreage values.

Very little is known about the origin or precise meaning of the term 'ploughland'. Dineen translates *Seisreach* (the Irish word nearest in mean-

17

ing to ploughland) as "the land of the plough team".[21] Coughlan assumed that the *Seisreach* was the extent of land which occupied one plough and was similar to the carucate or ploughland utilised in medieval England.[22] Fassadinin was subdivided into ploughlands in 1584 to facilitate the taxation of freeholders (fig. 1.4). Ploughlands were, therefore, both fiscal and landowning units. The ploughland values together with the acreage of denominations in the parishes of Castlecomer and Dysart were recorded in the Book of Survey and Distribution. A comparison of these returns with an earlier, undated manuscript survey of profitable land in these parishes shows that divisions which contained roughly the same amount of arable land were allocated similar ploughland values.[23] Smythestown and Killdergan were both assessed as ⅛ th of a 'horseman's bed' in the Book of Survey and Distribution, whereas their acreage was given as 250 and 800 acres respectively. In the undated survey, 'Smythestowne also Ballygoan' has 360 acres divided into 288 arable and pasture and 12 wood. In the same survey the 740 acres in 'Kildergan also Uskerty' were classified as 263 arable, 327 wood and 150 mountain and bog. The jurors who conducted the assessment of Fassadinin were unable "to lay down particularly into acres the quantity of mountain or other waste land ... the most parts whereof are unprofitable for the sowing of corn". This also suggests that ploughlands were a measure of arable land rather than of land quantity which is understandable when one remembers that one is dealing with a community of farmers. The barony was partitioned into thirty four divisions. Thirty three of these were given fractional ploughland values whereas the O'Brenan lands of Idough were not subdivided but returned as two ploughlands. This does not mean that the Gaelic territory had no other internal divisions. The evidence of seventeenth century Inquisitions disproves this and shows that Idough had a more complex landholding system and more territorial subdivisions than the remainder of the barony.

This section deals with the emergence of the townland as an important territorial division in the countryside. As the progress of confiscation quickened, documentation concerning land acquired a new dimension of thoroughness. Changes in ownership necessitated surveys and inquisitions, and from the surviving documentation, it is possible to chronicle the development of the townland. Twenty nine of the thirty four 'ploughland' names recorded in 1584 are found in modern townlands names. Similar names may not, however, relate to similar areas having similar functions. The existence of cartographic evidence from the middle of the seventeenth century makes it possible to suggest spatial and functional continuity. It can be said, with some degree of certainty, that the divisions which corresponded to the lands of freeholders in 1584 are the precursors of the modern townland. It should be remembered, however, that the 'Book of Ploughlands' deals with the part of the barony in which the Anglo Norman influence was most pronounced. The increased contact between the Ormondes and the O'Brenans from then onwards provides more detailed information about the internal sub-divisions of the Gaelic lands.

In 1614, the lands of Idough were subdivided into eighteen "townes or hamlets".[24] Because some of the divisions had one or more alternative names, twenty-six placenames were recorded. Eighteen of these twenty six names are now found on modern townlands and some of the remaining eight names are used locally to designate townland subdivisions. In 1635 an Inquisition held at Kilkenny to discover the owners of Idough listed a total of eighty four territorial divisions.[25] It is in effect a fairly comprehensive inventory of 'vills', subdivisions of 'vills' called 'parcells' and a third category of divisions which were neither 'vills' nor 'parcells' of 'vills'. For example, "Edm McOwen O'Brenan est possessionat de vil ter de Ballygowne al' Smithestowne" whereas "Wil' Walsh est possessionat' de Dromshane McOwly pcell' de Coolebane". The third category may have been the 'lands' which are frequently referred to in the early seventeenth century. The Inquisition recorded twenty five 'vills', thirty nine 'lands' and twenty 'parcells'. A comparison of the names of these partitions with townland names C. 1840 shows that the names of twenty two 'vills', eleven 'lands' and one 'parcell' have survived as territorial designations. A distinction appears to have been made in the survey between 'vills' which were settlements and 'lands' which may have been empty areas. This distinction is repeated in all of the land grants in the first half of the seventeenth century. Thus, for example, Sir Charles Coote was granted the "townes, hamlets and parcells of land in Idough"[26] while Walter Archer received, among other units, the "towne and lands of Inchebrede also Inchibride".[27] It is significant that, in most instances, it is the names of 'vills' rather than 'lands' or 'parcell' designations which have survived. This suggests that the primary purpose of the territorial divisions which preceded the townland as divisions of the countryside was to name settlements and their associated lands.

Changes in land ownership through the process of inheritance or through purchase or confiscation sometimes led to conflict between new neighbours over boundaries. Sir Christopher Wandesforde purchased the Gaelic lands of Idough c. 1636. Shortly after taking possession, Wandesforde and his neighbour, the Earl of Ormonde, were in conflict over boundaries in eight different areas involving in all about 1,000 plantation acres.[28] These properties were contiguous in several places, due mainly to the great fragmentation of Ormonde's lands. No boundaries were defined in the "600 acres of waste, rough, mountain ground between the lands of Clonefylye belonging to the Earl of Ormonde and the lands of Gortnicluffe belonging unto the Master of the Rolls." On August 4th 1637 a 'Commission of Perambulation" was directed to Patrick Weymes and Bartholomew Peisley Esqr., empowering them "to perambulate, distinguish and set forth the true meares limits and bounds of certain lands in controversy . . . etc." By the 21st of September in the same year, the Commissioners and the parties involved agreed "that all the said lands shall be surveyed by the first day of May next ensuing and every one of the aforesaid parcells to be equally divided between them after the said survey". The major areas of dispute lay in the hill country which consisted of mainly marginal land devoid of human settlement. The Commissioner's decision demonstrates that new territorial divisions were rarely created in this period of great change.

Sir William Petty was highly critical of the territorial divisions he found in use in Ireland. "The limits of their land divisions", he wrote, "were no lines geometrically drawn but if the rain fell one way, then the land whereon it fell, did belong to A, if the other way to B". He considered that townlands and the English tythings were similar units insofar as they were, "divisions of land by what certain societies of men held."[29] The term townland was first used to define landholding units in Fassadinin in the Down Survey. Petty employed the townland as his basic cadastral unit and the smallest subdivision of land (fig. 1.5). The survey was preoccupied with landownership and no distinction was made between the terms 'towns' and 'lands'. The survey's terms of reference and the rapidity with which the survey was concluded precluded this. The townland now had a standardised meaning which had little to do with settlement. It identified areas of land and consequently landowners. Acreage values were superimposed and a number of townlands were reasonably well mapped. These factors combined to make the townland an eminently suitable division for the great land transfers about to commence.

The Down Survey is informative about the shape and size of townlands in Fassadinin barony. Thirty seven townlands comprising 16,309 plantation acres were delineated in the barony map (fig. 1.5). Because of the incomplete nature of the survey, a large portion of central, east and north Fassadinin was not subdivided. The average size of units recorded was 440 plantation acres. Size variation was mainly related to differences in land quality. 'Cloghranke' and 'Coolecullen' in the south east of the barony and Ballymartin in the western hill country which were in excess of 1,000 acres contained a high proportion of rough unprofitable land. Townlands were of a smaller size in the dry, drift covered lowlands close to and between the rivers Nore and Dinin. Placenames and settlement features signify that this district was a favoured living place of both Celt and Anglo-Norman. Petty's list of townlands was not a full inventory of the territorial divisions of forfeited lands in the barony. It is known that the Earl of Ormonde's lands of 'Jenkinstowne' and 'Donoghmore' (Dunmore) were not delimited into townland units. When the same proprietor owned contiguous townlands, the Down Survey sometimes delineated the 'out meares' of the property only.

The shape of townlands varied according to topography and size. In the hill country in the south, east, and south-west of the barony, townlands were large and irregularly shaped. The north and south boundaries in the townlands of 'Coolecullen' and 'Cloghranke', for example, were transverse to the contour pattern and were relatively straight (fig. 1.5). On the other hand, the 'natural' east and west boundaries which in this instance followed the course of the Dinin River were more oblique. Townlands on the east bank of the Dinin had irregular, circle-like shapes and some, such as 'John Rothestowne', were fragmented (fig. 1.5). On the west bank of the Dinin and in the lowlying area between this river and the Nore, townlands were much more regular and compact in shape. This is true of the townlands of Esker and Kilcollan which had a rectangular-like form.

The Books of Survey and Distribution cover all of Fassadinin barony. Seventy eight townlands comprising 30, 250 plantation acres were recorded. The additional townlands were mainly in the parishes of Castlecomer, Dysart, Loughill and Kilmacar, which were not included in the earlier Down Survey. Sixty two of the seventy eight placenames listed have survived as the modern townland names. In legal transactions concerning land in the early part of the eighteenth century, the separate terms 'townes' and 'lands' were still used. In 1704 Ormonde granted "in fee farm to Sir Christopher Wandesforde of Dublin Bart, the towns and lands of Clashduffe and Duntrimane."[30] Evidence in the Ormonde rentals shows that the townland was used extensively as a land 'letting' unit in the eighteenth century and earlier. Here again it was not known as a 'townland' but as a 'denomination'. The information which exists on the role of the townland in the eighteenth century reinforces earlier views on its usage. The townland was employed in the estate system of landholding to describe the lands occupied by principal tenants. In Batwell's survey of the Castlecomer estate c. 1746, the townland was used synonymously with the farms into which the estate was divided. Batwell does not use the term townland once throughout his report. Thus, he refers to the holding of Michael Brophy as the "lands of Ballyhimmin". This strengthens the assertion that the two terms 'town' and 'land' were distinct and that the 'town' referred to a settlement element, primarily. It was local, then, that the lands surrounding such a place should be described as, for example, the lands of Ballyhimmin. The usage of the townland as a means of identifying farms and consequently occupiers was one of the primary reasons for its survival. As in all ages farmers knew the area of their holdings and jealously and zealously guarded their boundaries.

The townland was used as a territorial division for a variety of administrative purposes in the nineteenth century. Improvement in estate management led to the compilation of detailed inventories of holdings and occupiers which were usually prepared on a townland basis. Estate owners commissioned cartographers to delineate and subdivide townlands into holdings. The Tithe Composition Books c. 1830 give the first detailed list of townland divisions in the barony since the compilation of the Books of Survey and Distribution. These surveys culminated in the Ordnance Survey Townland maps on a scale of six inches to the mile, the first edition of which was completed for the country c. 1842. The existence of composite maps, which consist of the Down Survey maps superimposed on those of the Ordnance Survey, makes comparison between mid seventeenth and mid nineteenth century land units feasible. Under the Poor Law Act of 1838, townlands were used to form electoral divisions into which the Poor

Law unions were divided. In 1841 and afterwards at ten year intervals, reliable census data was provided for each townland. The publication of the General Valuation of Rateable Property in Ireland, provides a key to the ownership and the occupation of land on a townland basis. The extent and depth of information available on the townland explains its choice as a cadastral unit in this study.

The Tithe Composition Books recorded one hundred and thirty one townlands in seventeen parishes. It is not a complete record of Fassadinin townlands insofar as the areas of Abbeyleix and Rathaspick parishes in Fassadinin were not included. One hundred and one of these names are listed as townlands by the Ordnance Survey. The Ordnance Survey maps delineated a total of one hundred and twenty six townlands within the boundaries of Fassadinin (fig. 1.9). The Surveyors created twenty one new townland units in Fassadinin. Because these new divisions were subdivis-

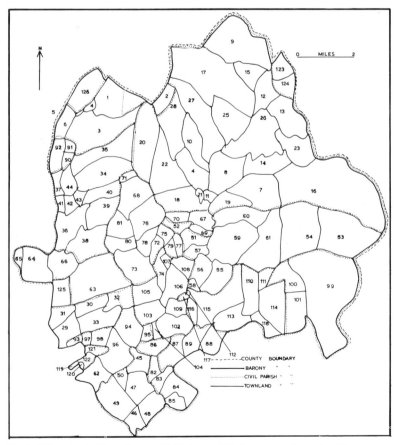

Fig. 1.9 Townlands. Fassadinan c. 1838 (see p. 259 for names of townlands).

ions of existing townlands, the new names retained the old names as prefixes and added suffixes, such as for example, 'Upper', 'Lower', 'East',
'North' 'South' and 'West'. Firoda in the west of Castlecomer parish was
subdivided into Firoda Upper and Firoda Lower. In the same way, the
townland of Dunmore in Dunmore Parish was divided into the new townlands of Dunmore, Dunmore Park, Dunmore East and Dunmore West (fig.
1.10). In some instances no new units were created: instead, new names

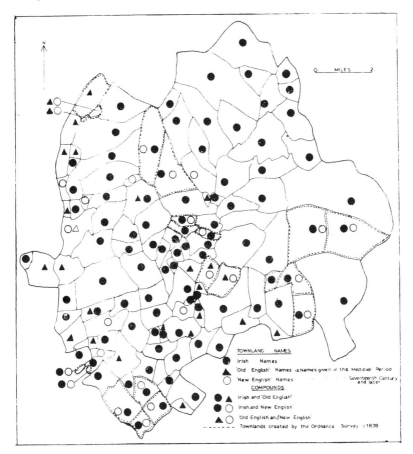

Fig. 1.10 Classification of Townland Names. Fassadinin.

were substituted for what the Surveyors considered archaic ones. The
Tithe Composition Books, for example, recorded the townlands of Coon
Webb and Coon Carter in Dysart parish. The Surveyors, aware perhaps, of
the limited span of man's earthly kingdom, changed Coon Webb to Coan
East and Coon Carter to Coan West. In the parish of Odagh, the Ordnance
surveyors created the townlands of Borris Big (41 acres) and Borris Little

(7 acres). Surprisingly enough, when they subdivided Tourney in Kilmacar parish, they retained the Gaelic prefix Tour. The surveyors added the Gaelic suffixes, Beg *beag* (little), and *Mór* (big) to form the new names of Toorbeg and Toormore.

New names did not always relate to new territorial divisions. It is known that the townlands of Swiftsheath and Webbsborough replaced the older Gaelic units of 'Ballyroe' and 'Ballinranke'. The creation of new townlands in the period from 1660 to 1840 was primarily related to changes in ownership. The subdivision of Damerstown townland in Dysart parish, for example, into the townlands of Damerstown East and Damerstown West took cognisance of the fact that Darmerstown East was held by James Kavanagh whereas the Webb family were owners of Damerstown West.

It can be concluded, therefore, that the modern townland is representative of a great variety of seventeenth century territorial divisions. Sir William Petty was the first to map and standardise the townland in Fassadinin. The longevity of the units he demarcated is clear from figs. 1.6 and 1.7. The townland did not exist in Fassadinin in the first half of the seventeenth century. The divisions that did exist were called 'towns', 'lands' and 'parcells'. It is certain that there was a distinction between 'towns' and 'lands'. In this analysis, it is asserted that 'town' referred to a land area which had settlement and that 'land' was an empty region. The Down and subsequent Surveys merged the two words to signify landholding units. There is no evidence that the term 'townland' was widely used in Fassadinin until the early nineteenth century. Nevertheless, the townland was one superimposed unit which did have meaning in the day-to-day lives of the majority of the rural inhabitants. Its survival is ample proof of this.

CHAPTER II

THE QUEST FOR OWNERSHIP 1600-1640

"Yet they never built any houses of bricks or stone, some few religious houses excepted, neither did any of them plant any gardens or orchards, enclose or improve their lands, live together in settled villages or towns, nor make any provision for posterity".
(Davies, J. *Historical tracts by Sir John Davies Attorney General and speaker in the House of Commons in Ireland,* (Dublin, 1767) 128.)

"They abhor from all things that agree with English civilty" (Moryson, Fynes. *An Itinerary containing his ten years travel through Germany-Ireland etc.* An ed. of the Itinerary, published by James MacLehose and Sons, (Glasgow 1907) 214.)

1. Introduction

This chapter is concerned with the ownership and occupation of land in Fassadinin in the first half of the seventeenth century. Impressions of the barony are derived from contemporary sources and an attempt is made to reconstruct its proprietorial geography. The Gaelic lands in the north of the barony are subjected to detailed analysis. Because of the many conflicting claims to the ownership of Idough in the period under review, its internal divisions and their owners are remarkably well documented. In the third part of the chapter, the Anglo-Norman endowment is assessed and the role of the Butlers of Ormonde in shaping the Anglo-Norman world in Fassadinin is examined. The final section is concerned with the intrusion of 'New English' politicians who were speculators in both land and iron.

2. The Barony of 'Idogh and Fasaghdeinyn' c. 1584

"The barony of Fasagh Deynin and Idogh contains six ploughlands, three of mountain and three of champion ground".
(Ormonde Deeds, V, 165.)

The placenames recorded in the 'book of ploughlands' circa 1584 should reveal how the earliest literate people viewed the landscape. They may refer to botanical and topographical features characteristic of early Fassa-

25

dinin. There is a third possibility i.e. they may identify the people who owned land or settled here in medieval times. It should be borne in mind that the 'book of ploughlands' is an incomplete record of territorial subdivisions in the barony (fig. 1.4). It deals mainly with areas of the barony below 600 feet.

Thirty five placenames are listed in the 'book of ploughlands'. Ten of these contain elements which refer to either botanical or topographical features. The remaining twenty five names are concerned with landholding units and settlement items. An examination of the topographic elements in the placenames indicate that they refer mainly to natural features found in areas of low altitude. The prefix *Má* (plain) is found in Moycully and Maine. Mothill derives its name from *Maothail* (spongy land). These 'ploughland' divisions are also names of parishes which occupy the southern portion of Fassadinin that extends from the east bank of the Nore across the Dinin valley to the barony boundary with 'The Countie of Cartalog' (Fig. 1.5). There is a mixture of topographic elements which may indicate a diversity of natural features. For example the prefixes *Ard* (height), *Drom* (ridge), *Toom* (a knoll) and Tulach (mound), are each found once. When these names are located on the map, it is found that they mainly occupy areas on the perimeter of the barony (fig. 1.4). For example *Tulleglish* (green mound) and *Ardlowe* (the height of the elms) are found directly north of the confluence of the river's Nore and Dinin. This is by no means hill country and these toponyms probably referred to easily identifiable heights and mounds which may have marked boundaries in the past. Two placenames were solely concerned with describing botanical features. *Kilcollan* (the wood of the holly trees) and *Fynnan* (the white grass), suggests that early colonists may have found these features in Fassadinin. Five of the ten topographical names are compounds of topographical and botanical elements. Examples of this are *Moycully* (the plain of the holly tree), *Dromerthyr* (the white grass ridge), and *Tomakeany* (the knoll of moss). Topographical and botanical names represent only twenty eight per cent (10) of the total names listed. They may refer to single, outstanding physical items in the landscape and in this way give a very incomplete picture. The placename evidence creates a picture of a relatively level land area, which in the past supported vegetation such as grass, elm and holly trees.

Sixty two per cent (25) of the placenames circa 1584 refer either to settlement or landholding units and also tell us more about the medieval barony than the toponymic names. The prefix *baile* (town, place, land, farm), which may have referred to a settlement and its associated lands occurs five times. *Baile* placenames are primarily found in relatively low-lying land close to, or between, the rivers Nore and Dinin. The words combined with *baile* add very little to knowledge about the barony, especially since some have become so anglicised that it is now difficult to interpret them satisfactorily. For example we get *Ballyranke* (the town of the dancing), *Ballyroth* (the red town), and *Ballymartin* (the town of Martin) in the hill country in the north west. The 'Old English' element *town* is used as a suffix four times. It is combined with Anglo-Norman personal names in Damerstown, Clintstown and Rothestown. The surname De Clynny is recorded in the Ormonde Deeds in the early fourteenth century.[1] It is perhaps interesting that a Friar Clynn survived and recorded the Black Death in Kilkenny in 1345-49[2]. There is no evidence of Damers connection with Kilkenny. The Rothes were a prominent Kilkenny merchant family who were closely associated with the Butlers of Ormonde. The fourth *town* name listed was Gallestowne. This is an interesting name as it was also recorded as *Ballynegall* (the town of the foreigners) at this period. It exemplifies a common Anglo-Norman practise of substituting their suffix *town* for the Irish *baile*. When placed on a map, the *town* names were all located in relatively level well drained land within a radius of ten miles from the city of Kilkenny (fig. 1.4). If *town* is regarded as a landholding unit, one is left with very few references to Anglo-Norman settlements in 'ploughland names'. This is surprising in view of the fact that this district was colonised by the mid thirteenth century.[3] The cultural element *achaidh* (a field) is found in the name Connahy which is translated as 'the field of hound'. *Ui Duach* (Idough), which was the O'Brenan lands in the north east of the barony, is a tribal name. In Ireland sept names were usually bestowed on the lands they possessed.

Cultural elements which referred to settlement in past times included *rath, lios, cill* and *grange*. *Rath* is the more common of these and is found in five placenames and was employed by the invader as if synonymous with their *town*.[4] The names 'Fowlkrath' and Suttonsrath are found quite close to each other in the south east of the barony (fig. 1.4). Fulk is a Christian name encountered among early Anglo-Norman families in Fassadinin[5] but the surname Sutton is associated more with north Carlow and Kildare than with Kilkenny.[6] Not alone is *rath* compounded with Anglo-Norman personal names but in the portion of a 'ploughland' called 'Graigerawe', it is combined with *Graig* or *Grange*. This monastic prefix was obviously of medieval provenance and these lands may have belonged either to the Cistercians of Jerpoint or the Augustinian Monks of Kells. Both *rath* and *baile* are combined in the placename Rathballynogly which may mean the 'fort of the town of the Nagles'. The element *lios* (enclosure) is found in two placenames.

The next most important group of 'cultural' items are those which refer to early church settlement. Three of these have the prefix *Cill* (church). 'Killmedom' and 'Killmedimocke' are the only two of this group not found as parish names circa 1300. As with the other *Kill* names, the prefix is combined with the names of the holy men to whom the original foundations were by tradition attributed.

The 'cultural' placenames yield some information on the history of the barony. Many of them were bestowed in the early Christian period and possibly before this. They therefore may be concerned with things which were of little importance in the early seventeenth century. It is known, for example, that the parish names listed circa 1300 had lost their religious significance at the Reformation, and were now used as secular divisions. Many of the settlement items referred to in the placenames did not exist in the first half of the seventeenth century. More than likely their sites were now used for tower houses, bawns and castles. Some names of medieval provenance were either compounds of Irish and 'Old English' elements, or 'Old English' placenames. These names are found close to rivers and routeways. They represent phases in Anglo-Norman colonisation and the mingling here of two cultures. It is surprising that so few of the thirteenth century settlers are commemorated in placenames. This may indicate a Gaelic resurgence in the late medieval period: alternatively, many of the Anglo Normans were possibly absentee landlords who lived in towns. The evidence suggests that in the west and south of the barony the two cultures met and intermingled. They may indeed have merged socially and economically in the same way as the diverse elements were combined in the placenames.

The 'book of ploughlands' is an example of tax assessment in the late sixteenth century. The amount levied was based on the capacity of known land divisions to produce wealth. The evidence suggests that factors other than land fertility, such as distance from the sea and susceptibility to predatory raids from rapacious neighbours were taken into account. The jurors who compiled the survey were members of prominent landowning and merchant families in Kilkenny city and county. Kilkenny was the second city in Ireland, seat of the Earl of Ormonde and an important commercial and administrative centre at this time. It can therefore be assumed that the jurors employed the commerical criteria of the day in their task of delimiting 'ploughlands' in the county.

They identified two contrasting social and economic regions in Fassadinin. The greater portion of the barony was delimited into 'ploughlands' or fractions of this unit (fig. 1.4). They returned the taxable area of Idough in the north east as two 'ploughlands' and proceeded to levy tax on the O'Brenan 'septs' who lived there rather than, as they did elsewhere, on named land units. This was an implicit recognition of two diverse, landowning systems practised by two social groupings. The jurors were more precise in their definition of economic regions. It was found that the northern portion of the barony, "doth border with Upper Ossory and Leix, and in another part thereof with the Keavanaghs". Located between two Gaelic families who were hostile to state policy, it was, "by occasion of divers spoils and preys in times of disorder" subject to waste.[7] Apart from the ravages of private armies inconveniencing commerce and agriculture, the northern district was further disadvantaged because it was "remote from the sea." The jurors asked that the hill country, which had so many geographical defects, be accorded preferential treatment in respect of tax liability. "We pray" they wrote, "that ploughlands in that Shire are not to be charged with those of such as are of far greater commodity and free from the afore specified inconveniences". The 'ploughlands' may well be a key to wealth distribution but this cannot be established, given the lack of an acreage equivalent. They give little information about landownership, as land units rather than landowners were named.

3. The O'Brenans in Fassadinin circa 1600-1640

"There is in Idough two 'ploughlands or horsemansbeddes', and thereof the sept of Clanvickconnil, Clanawly and Clanmcogillenebe are charged with the two parts, and the sept of Clanmoriertagh the third part" (Ormonde Deeds, V, 157).

The distinctive physical divisions of Fassadinin were paralleled by the existence of two diverse cultural groups. It is apparent from the evidence of placenames, settlement features and territorial organisation that the comparatively level land area to the south of the barony was Anglo-Norman in character. The Gaelic lands lay beyond the steep escarpment which marks the western limit of the Castlecomer hills. The medieval homeland of the O'Brenans was much more extensive than the hill refuge to which they had been driven by the superior force and more sophisticated technology of the invader. The historical record indicates the greater independence and autonomy of the O'Brenan in medieval times. In 1389 an O'Brenan chieftain, who made treaties with the Earl of Ormonde, was given the proud title of "Captain of his own nation", and the O'Brenan homeland was defined as the "area of March outside the trust and peace of the Lord King".[8]

The 'book of ploughlands' gives a picture of a depressed, disorderly region isolated in political and physical terms. It was a common practise among seventeenth century administrators to define tracts of country in terms of the political affiliations of their leading families. Idough was a vaguely defined hilly area in the north of the 'civil' county of Kilkenny. The district was inhabited and controlled by a semi-independent Gaelic family. It was bordered on the east and north by the two powerful Gaelic families of Kavanagh in Carlow and the Fitzpatricks of Upper Ossory. The Nore and Barrow river corridors carried the major commerical routes to the inland city of Kilkenny and the port of Waterford. It is certain that the hills and the society of those who lived in them were avoided by 'civil citizens' who lived in "walled towns or other places of strength for their securitie, saufgarde and succour."[9] Beyond the fact that it was occupied by four O'Brenan 'septs', little is known about Idough circa 1584.

(a) The Anglo-Norman Penetration

The beginning of the period under review coincides with the Earldom of one of the most able and energetic of the Ormondes. Thomas, tenth Earl of Ormonde, called from his dark complexion 'Black Tom' or in Gaelic *Tomás Dubh,* held absolute sway over the greater part of counties Kilkenny and Tipperary and a far flung collection of manors. Black Tom was

29

a particular favourite of the virgin Queen, Elizabeth. He had been brought up and educated at the Royal Court with the young Prince Edward, later to become King Edward VI. During his long earldom, from 1552 to 1614, he was a firm supporter of the monarchy, the Reformation and the Common Law. His primary ambition was to extend the *de facto jurisdiction of* the monarchy and to reclaim for the Crown Gaelic areas such as Forth O'Nolan in Carlow, Ormonde, North Tipperary, and Aughrim, Wicklow, which had reverted to the Irish in the early sixteenth century.[10] During his long life, 'Black Tom' alternated his residence between Carrick and Kilkenny, and from there his civil servants and highly skilled legalists kept a meticulous account of the transactions of this great Lordship. The Ormonde deeds document the extension of Butler influence north to the hill country. They record the mixing of two diverse peoples and the absorption and assimilation of the economically weaker and strategically exposed O'Brenans.

The policy of 'commercial plantation', which was to eventually engulf and destroy the autonomy of the O'Brenans, may have commenced in 1594. There is no evidence to suggest what initially motivated Ormonde to acquire lands in Idough but it can be assumed that it was part of his grand strategy to extend the jurisdiction of the Crown. On November 26th, 1594, four members of the O'Brenan family did "for a certain sum of money paid to them, by Thomas, Earl of Ormonde, grant to Peter Butler of Graighdowskie, Co. Kilkenny and Thomas Cantwell of Cantwellscourt in the same all the messuages, lands, tenements etc in Aghetobbir".[11] In 1595, these lands passed to Robert Roth, Henry Sheeth and Thomas Archer, all members of families prominent in the administrative and commercial life of Ormonde's city, Kilkenny. 'Aghetobbir' is the last townland in north Fassadinin and adjoined the Fitzpatrick lands of Upper Ossory. In two separate transactions in 1595, Ormonde acquired the "messuages, lands, and other hereditaments in Corryshin alias Cowrefoynshim" from four members of the O'Brenan family and Redmund Purcell of Esker. This townland is located in the east of Idough, north of the Dinin river and close to the county boundary with Carlow and the Kavanagh country. A list of Ormonde possessions in the same year reveals that he also held the 'denominacion of Cloghmoilehed' in north Idough. *Clogmoilehed* (stone of the wide plain) occupies one of the few level, well endowed areas along the upper reaches of the northern Dinin. Ormonde acquisitions were located in border regions to act as 'buffer zones' against the predatory raids of the Fitzpatricks and Kavanaghs, while at the same time providing a base in the O'Brenan heartland for the diffusion of Crown policy.

In 1614, the Earl of Ormonde applied the provisions of the policy known as 'Surrender and Regrant' to the Gaelic landowners of Idough. This policy, formulated by Elizabethan administrators, attempted to standardise legal aspects of land ownership and inheritance and to bring the Gaelic landowning classes under the Common Law of England. The 'clan' chiefs or leaders surrendered lands in their possession to the Crown and received a regrant of the same lands "to be held in tail male under the Crown."[12] In some instances customs and duties of Gaelic origin, which were attached to land, were abolished and replaced by money rents.[13] From 1614, the O'Brenan lands were to be held "of the Earl of Ormonde in socage tenure at 6/9d. a townland in lieu of all services, duties and demands previously made by Ormonde."[14] The manuscript in which the agreement was recorded shows the coming together of two diverse legal systems. It contains the names of "townes and hamlets as the gentlemen and freeholders hath in Idough" as well as "a note of the several septs of the said lands." The Earl of Ormonde agreed to "bear all the expenses and trouble of procuring the necessary grants and patents for the purpose". The manuscript is important as it identifies the four principal O'Brenan families and enumerates their holdings. The O'Brenans were becoming increasingly dependent on the patronage and protection of the powerful and influential Butlers. Military and economic dependence eventually led to loss of autonomy and identity and made the disintegration of the clan system inevitable.

'Sept' names in 1614 were similar to those listed in the 'book of ploughlands' circa 1584. The four septs listed held twenty 'townes' or 'hamlets' whose names were recorded. Twenty six placenames, which included one instance of three and four instances of two alternative names, were enumerated. This relatively high incidence of alternative names suggests that territorial subdivisions in Idough were not as strictly delineated as those in the south of the barony. It should be remembered, however, that one is dealing with the property of collections of families rather than that of single individuals. In fig. 2.1, an attempt is made to reconstruct the ownership pattern in Idough in 1614. The lands of the primary O'Brenan 'sept' of 'Clanmoriertagh' were mainly south of, or adjoining, the site of the modern town of Castlecomer. The 'seat' of this family was located close to the confluence of the two Dinins at Rathcally, which was the name of a territorial subdivision and a settlement. This site had obvious strategic advantages as it guards the approach route to Idough through the Dinin valley, while being bounded by water on the west and south. It also includes a small portion of the fertile and attractive north Kilkenny plain and probably represented the final stage of the O'Brenan retreat.

It appears that the primary 'clan' did not hold the largest area of land. It is probable that the 'septs' who occupied large portions of the hill country in north and east Idough had more territory. It is significant, however, that the primary clan held the land of greatest strategic and agricultural value. They were also more distant from the unstable border area. Sept holdings did not occupy contiguous blocks of land but neither were they greatly fragmented (fig. 2.1). Each sept had access at some point to the river Dinin. 'Sept' residences were found mainly in the southern and better endowed area of Idough. Irish as well as Anglo-Norman avoided the cold, wet lands of the hill country. The O'Brenan lands were adjoined on

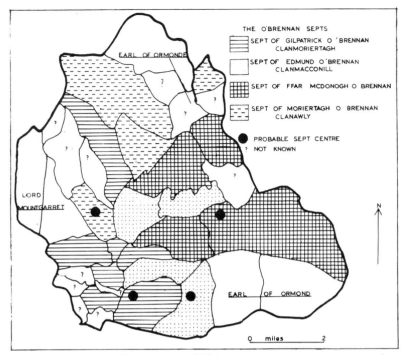

Fig. 2.1 Ownership of land. Idough 1614.

the north, south and west by the powerful Anglo-Norman families of Mountgarret and Ormonde. The contraction of their medieval patrimony and dispersal northwards symbolised their increasing isolation and impotence within the political and economic structures of early seventeenth century Ireland.

This document is not very informative about landownership in Idough. The existence of a hierarchical ownership structure is implied but not explained. It is salutory to recall that this contract was drawn up at a period when the crown administrators openly confessed their inability to comprehend the Gaelic landholding system.[15]

The relegation of the O'Brenans to the status of occupiers within their medieval homeland is an important aspect of these transactions. Henceforth, their relationship with Ormonde was mediated through a series of intermediaries such as, the Rothes, Archers, Shees and Purcells. These intermediaries, who belonged to landholding, professional and commercial families prominent in the civic life of Kilkenny city, were the precursors of eighteenth century middlemen.

(b) The 'New English' penetration

Many of the earlier transactions concerning the Gaelic lands of Idough were mere paper transfers. Despite the O'Brenan claim, the lands of Idough were granted in 1617 to Sir Francis Edgeworth, a Privy Councillor in the Government.[16] There is no evidence to suggest that Edgeworth ever occupied or attempted to occupy any portion of the territory of Idough. He subsequently transferred two thirds of the lands to the Earl of Ormonde, and the remaining third to the Earl of Londonderry. The new proprietors were refused peaceable possession of the lands. In May 1634, a Commission under the Great Seal of Ireland was directed to "the Lord Esmond and divers other Commissioners."[17] The Commissioners terms of reference were, "to inquire what are the limits and bounds of Idough, what title the King had to them and who were the occupiers and what their yearly value was".[18] On the strength of this Commission, an Inquisition was held at Kilkenny in May 1635. The Inquisition found that the title to Idough had passed from the original Anglo-Norman proprietor, Strongbow, through his descendants, to the King of England. It also stated that the "O'Brenan were mere Irish and had held the territory by force of arms, not having any rightful title".[19] They were classified as intruders into the territory and the King now represented the legal owners. The King, being informed that the territory of Idough was found to be his majesty's proper right and inheritance, and that the natives of that place had "injuriously witheld possession", confirmed Ormonde and Londonderry in possession. The lands conveyed were to be held under such "rents and reservations" as they should think "fit for the advancement of the King's profit and the civilising of that Country".[20]

The quest for ownership intensified in 1636. Between April and August of that year four transactions concerning Idough are recorded in the Records of the Rolls. On the thirteenth May 1636, the lands were granted to Sir Charles Coote by Ormonde and Londonderry. On the eighteenth May, "trepass to Sir Charles being proved", the Court of Chancery ordered the High Sheriff of Co. Kilkenny to "establish Sir Charles Coote in peaceable possession". Records dated the 24th May 1636 show that Sir Charles was confirmed in possession on payment of a £4 fine.[21] The 'premises' were transformed into the Manor of Castlecomer with power "to hold courts baron and leet and to enjoy all waifes and strayes". On the fifth of July 1636 the lands of Idough were "for valuable consideration of money, conveyed by indenture tripartite" to Christopher Wandesforde Esq., Master of the Rolls in the administration of the Earl of Wentworth.[22] The Calendar of State papers recorded that on the 15th June, "the master of the Rolls is now in Kilkenny taking possession of a great territory of land which has passed to him".[23] The Wandesforde manuscripts reveal that Wandesforde acquired the territory of Idough for the sum of two thousand pounds.[24]

(c) Idough in 1635

The Inquisition held at Kilkenny in May 1635 defined the boundaries of the Gaelic lands of Idough. It listed the names of over thirty landowners and over eighty land divisions. It may have been the first written inventory of ownership in Idough. It is important for this reason and also because it preceded a period of great change. In the Inquisition the boundaries are described in terms of an imagined journey which began at 'Downanough' in the north east and proceeded by a circular route to the place it commenced. The boundary was not delimited in the same detailed manner as in the Civil Survey. It was defined as the boundary of a collection of territorial subdivisions which were located at the ends of, or adjoining the territory of Idough. This was the system followed by the Down Survey and it facilitated the speedy conclusion of the Inquisition. It was only in the areas where the boundary coincided with well known, visible and permanent topographical features that it was delimited accurately.

The survival of the placenames listed in the Inquisition as territorial names makes it possible to identify the course of the boundary. Seventeen placenames were recorded. Twelve of these were either names of land units or identified settlements. The remaining five referred to well defined topographical or botanical features. Three of the placenames recorded were located in Co. Laois. The first of these, and the place where the boundary commenced, was *Downanough* (the small *dún* in Idough) which commemorated the tribal name of the O'Brenan territory. This suggests that the medieval *tuath* of Idough may have extended into Co. Laois in the north east. The south east boundary of Idough coincided with the "meres of Slewmarge". Slievmargy is the name of the hill range which forms the eastern portion of the Castlecomer hills. It is also the name of a barony in the extreme south east of Co. Laois (fig. 1.1). The Inquisition was more definite concerning the limits of Idough in the south. Here they followed the course of the "stream of water called Dynyn passing through the wood called Keyliffooke". In the north west the meres of Idough were identical with the "outmeares of the Earl of Ormonde's lands called Killmacar and Ballyoskill and the Lord Viscount Mountgarret's lands of Castell O'Maghan". The "stream of Glasegall" formed the boundary in the extreme north and west and from there it proceeded eastwards by *Clycoledobuy* (the broad, yellow ditch) which Carrigan claims was the traditional man-made boundary between Idough and Co. Laois.[25]

The Inquisition enumerated eighty three territorial divisions which were classified as 'vills', 'parcells' and 'lands'. The names of twenty four 'vills', thirty nine 'lands' and twenty 'parcells' were listed. These placenames complement those returned in the 'book of ploughlands' and reveal something of the topographic and botanical conditions in Idough at this time. It is significant that only thirty four 'ploughlands', or fractions of 'ploughlands', were listed for the whole barony whereas over eighty land divisions are found in the 'territory of Idough'. This suggests that land in Idough was subject to a more extreme form of subdivision than was practised elsewhere in the barony. Fifty three per cent (44) of the placenames refer to topographic or botanical items. The prefixes *cnoc* (hill), and *cúl* (hillback, corner) are each found seven times. *Drum* (ridge) is another prominent toponym and occurs in six names. Elements concerned with level land are conspicuous by their absence. For example, the prefixes *Gleann* (glen) and *má* (plain) occur only once. *Coill* (wood) was the most common botanical prefix and occurs in four names. *Skehanagh* (place of bushes) *móin* (bog) are encountered three times while *daire* (oak wood) is found only once. The great majority of toponyms refer to hill topography. Apart from the fact that woods, bushes and turf bogs were found here in the past, little is learned about the physical landscape from the placenames.

Baile (town, place, farm), is the dominant 'cultural' element and occurs ten times. Baile was compounded frequently with the adjective *sean* (old). For example, the names 'Shanballyelly; 'Shanballyio; 'Shanballysheary' and 'Shanballyrallie'. Some of these names are also found without the prefix *'sean'*. The usage of this term may imply extension of settlement to new lands or may designate tilled land. *Achadh* (field) and *Fearann* (farm) are each found three times. *Gort* (field) and *cluain* (meadow) occur twice while the unusual *acre* is encountered once.

The range of cultural items referring to settlement are limited and less numerous than in the 'book of ploughlands'. For example, only four references are found to early church settlement. The element *cill* (church) is met with twice while the name *Desert* (secluded place), which also occurs twice, aptly portrays the medieval environment in the hill country. Elements concerned with early settlement such as *dún, rath* and *cloch* (stone) are each found twice. The only reference to Anglo-Norman settlement is contained in the placename Castlecomer. It is significant that when this name was first encountered in the list of parishes in the barony of Idough circa 1300, the prefix *Castle* was missing. Placenames tell us very little about the social and economic conditions which prevailed locally at the time they were bestowed.[26]

Suffix elements used in the placenames are difficult to unravel as they were misinterpreted and anglicised to a greater extent than the more common prefix terms. The names *Acrenamucky* (the acre of the pigs), *Aghamucky* (the field of the pigs), and *Gurteenagapull* (the small field of the horses) contain references to livestock. *Kilbolyskahanagh* (the wood of the bushy booley) refers to the custom of booleying which one would expect to find in this peripheral district. *Clonalyne* may mean the 'meadow of flax'. Other placenames suggest that the early inhabitants of Idough were aware of the existence of deposits of coal and ironstone. Knowledge of their existence does not imply exploitation. Names such as *Drumgooly* (the ridge of coal), *Kildeargan* (the wood of the little forge), and *Ballygowne* (the town or place of the smiths) are found. *Clashduff* (the black pit or hollow) may refer to digging operations for coal or it may signify a topographical feature.

One looks in vain for Anglo-Norman personal names, and Castlecomer is the only example of a placename in which the Gaelic and 'old English' elements are combined. The element *town* is used once as a suffix in 'Smithestowne', but this is obviously a translation of the Gaelic 'Ballygowne' which is given in the Inquisition as an alternative name. Names

35

commemorating saints or holy men are absent and the area had a weak urban and parochial structure. The preponderance of Gaelic elements in the placenames suggest that the north east was a Gaelic refuge region avoided by colonists and churchmen.

(d) The quality of the land

In the subdivision of Fassadinin made by 'view and estimation' in 1589, the lands of the O'Brenans were returned as two 'ploughlands' and varying proportions of taxation were levied on four named 'septs'. In 1614, surveyors subdivided Idough into twenty 'townes or hamlets' the proprietors of whom were classified as 'gentlemen freeholders and septs' respectively. An undated manuscript in the Wandesforde collection shows that Idough was partitioned into sixty denominations with associated acreage values c1630 and the amount of profitable and unprofitable land in each of these divisions was quantified.[27] This survey enables one to make a more meaningful assessment of the quality of the Gaelic lands. A comparison of the form of two placenames listed in this survey and in the Inquisition of 1635 suggests that it may have been compiled before the holding of the Inquisition. Thus, for example, the placename 'Donegeelhofer' in the manuscript survey whereas the Inquisition lists the anglicised form 'Upperdownegill' In the same way the denomination of 'Ballygowne' in the survey is recorded as 'Ballegowne alias Smithestowne' in the Inquisition. If we assume that Gaelic forms of placenames are older than their anglicised versions it appears that the survey was completed circa 1630. The survey classified land type in sixty denominations, comprising 16,759 'Irish' acres. Forty five per cent (7,506 acres) all classified as arable and pasture; twenty four per cent (4,085) as wood; and thirty one per cent as mountain and bog. Figure 2.2 is based on the Ordnance Survey's one inch to the mile, Townland Index Map. The Ordnance Survey listed twenty nine townlands in the combined parishes of Dysart and Castlecomer which were co-extensive with Idough as defined by Inquisition in 1635. It was possible by amalgamating contiguous units to obtain a generalised picture of land type. Many of the subdivisions recorded in the survey were extremely small. Eight denominations were under seven acres in area. Land units such as 'Gleabe by the Mill' ($^{120}/_{160}$) acres; 'Gleabe by the Way' ($^{35}/_{160}$) acres and 'Castlecomer', 6 acres are found. The interpretation of land quality which follows uses the civil parish and the subdivisions listed circa 1630 as the territorial basis.

The district co-extensive with the Ordnance Survey parish of Dysart contained 3,587 'Irish' acres. This was classified as forty-eight per cent (1,662) arable and pasture, thirteen per cent (482) wood and thirty nine per cent (1,443) mountain and bog (fig. 2.3). Two distinct regions stand out in Dysart parish. The highest proportion of arable and pasture was found in the south west of Dysart, where land divisions were relatively small in area. For example the three denominations of 'Ballincomo' (110), 'Ballinhiman' (135) and 'Desertnimehale' (30) had their total area returned

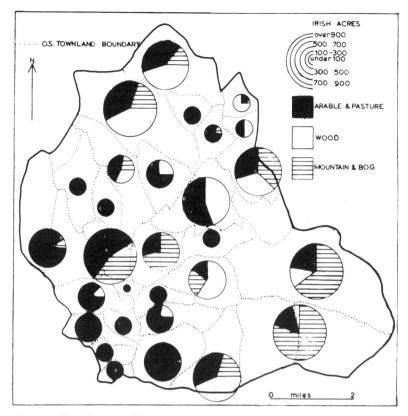

Fig. 2.2 Classification of land. Idough c.1630.

as arable and pasture. 'Rathcally,' the townland seat of the primary O'Brenan family, along with the contiguous units of 'Killrobin' and 'Knocknadogie', contained 649 acres of which ninety-nine per cent (637) was defined as arable and pasture. It was not just the Anglo-Normans who showed a liking for the well drained, sheltered lands.

It is clear from fig. 2.2 that land quality deteriorates towards the east of the parish and the boundary with the counties of Carlow and Laois. In 'Killdergan', which is roughly in the centre of Dysart, forty-four per cent (327) was returned as wood, and the relatively high proportion of twenty per cent (150) as mountain and bog. As land quality deteriorated, denomination size increased. The border townland of 'Conseely' contained 1,541 acres of which eighty-two per cent (1,293) was classified as mountain and bog. In the west and south west of Dysart parish, land was good arable and pasture. In the central area there was a noticeable increase in the acreage under wood, and the peripheral eastern district was characterised by mountain and bog.

37

The northern portion of Idough circa 1630 was co-extensive with the civil parish of Castlecomer as delineated by the Ordnance Survey. The manuscript survey estimated the area of this district as 13,172 'Irish' acres. This land was classified as forty-four per cent (5,844) arable and pasture, twenty-eight per cent (3,603) wood and twenty-eight per cent (3,725) bog and mountain. An examination of the proportion of parish lands in each of the three categories shows that both parishes had roughly the same percentage of arable and pasture. In Castlecomer twenty eight per cent of the land was under wood whereas the comparative percentage in Dysart was eighteen per cent. The proportion of land described as mountain and bog varied greatly between the two parishes. In the northern district, areas dominated by arable and pasture were intermixed with denominations containing a comparatively high proportion of unprofitable land. This variation in land quality is reflected in the great disparity between the areas of some land divisions. Extensive areas at the 'ends' of the parish were described as woodland. One finds that over fifty per cent of the large border denominations of 'Aghtoberid' (877) and 'Cruitte' (1,257) was in this category at the time of the survey.

The same pattern of land use was found in the smaller denominations of Kilbolyskehane (the wood of the bushy booley) and 'Turtane' (110) in the north east of Idough. In the south, along the barony boundary with Co. Laois, the quality of land deteriorated sharply. Approximately sixty-five per cent (692) of 'Crottnocloygh', (1,065) in the south east of the parish was non-profitable mountain and bog. In the central portion of the parish close to the site of the modern town of Castlecomer, the predominant land type was either arable and pasture or wood. Figure 2.2 indicates that the total area of the divisions 'Coolebane' (186) and Drumgoole (125) was defined as arable. North-east of the site of the modern town, woodland dominated in Ardragh (537) where it accounted for seventy-one per cent (379) of the denomination's area. Apart from Killtowne, land units in the west of the parish had a uniformly high proportion of arable and pasture.

There is no indication as to how the three categories of land were defined. The identification of woodland may indicate that the survey was related to the iron industry, then sporadically functioning in north Fassadinin. It may well have been an optimistic summary of land quality compiled by the nominal owner of Idough, Sir Charles Coote, before it was sold to Wandesforde. The 'Book of Ploughlands' presented a picture of a depressed, disorderly Gaelic region in the north of the barony. This was a political definition and an Anglo-Norman viewpoint. The undated survey was a reappraisal of the resources of the Gaelic lands based on analysis by territorial sub-divisions. The end result was a commercial evaluation and may well have been the viewpoint of the 'New English' entrepreneurial class then arriving in Ireland. The delimitation of land into 'profitable' and 'non-profitable' was a common practise of seventeenth century surveyors. If wood is regarded as profitable land, one finds that approximately seventy-nine per cent (11,591) of Idough was in this category. Three 'land type' regions may be identified in Idough c1630. The border lands in the south east coincided with the Slievmargy hills and were the most uniformly poor and infertile area in the O'Brenan lands. The high proportion of mountain and bog found here made it unprofitable by any criteria and discouraged settlement. The land divisions in the west and south west of Idough were relatively small and consisted mainly of arable land. Spatial variations in denomination size in the north and northeast mirrored landscape differences. Woodland dominated in this district.

(e) "Who were the occupiers and what their yearly value was"

The Inquisition of 1635 marks a progression from a vague, ill-defined record of 'sept' lands to a detailed inventory of individual occupiers and the land divisions they held in Idough. This document is a record of the impact of events in the early seventeenth century on the occupation of land in the O'Brenan homeland. However, the interpretation of the Inquisition presents many difficulties. It is written in Latin and much of its terminology belongs to the medieval rather than to the early modern historical period. The jurors were, according to the terms of reference of the Inquisition, required to assess the yearly value of lands in Idough but there is no evidence that this was done. Furthermore the Inquisition is an incomplete record of land occupation. The names of the occupiers of fractions of twenty-eight land divisions are not returned; neither were the acreage equivalents of the land units and their fractions used in the survey recorded. The Inquisition is basically a record of the occupiers of 'vills' and 'lands' and parts of both these units. 'Parcell', the third land partition used in the survey, was not subdivided.

The lands of Idough were held by a great diversity of occupiers whom one can attempt to classify on the basis of their assumed surname origins. The first significant factor that emerges is that by 1635 the O'Brenans were not the dominant numerical group of occupiers; neither were they the only Gaelic land-holding family. A total of thirty holdings or collections of holdings were enumerated in the Inquisitions; the O'Brenans held twelve of these; two holdings were occupied by other Gaelic families; occupiers with surnames of assumed Anglo-Norman origin, such as Purcell, Butler and Walsh, had ten farms; the remaining six holdings belonged to 'New English' occupiers. By giving acreage values found in early seventeenth century land grants to the corresponding divisions in the Inquisition, a rough estimate can be made of the quantity of lands held by the various surname groupings. According to this calculation, the Gaelic occupiers held 5,012 acres, Anglo-Norman 5,543 and 'New English' 2,435 acres respectively. Religious and secular institutions in Kilkenny city held land in Idough. Income from glebe land and other church taxes on lands were assigned for the upkeep of St. Canice's Cathedral in Kilkenny and the support of church personnel representing the deanary of Odagh. The mayor, burgesses and citizens of Kilkenny claimed possession of the lands and other privileges formerly held by the dissolved monastery of St. John in Kilkenny. This diverse list of occupiers reveals the complexity of land occupation in Idough and there is little to suggest that the district in 1635 retained the anonymity it had had in the late sixteenth century.

The Inquisition reveals some important changes in the spatial pattern of land occupation. A comparison of figs. 2.1. and 2.3. shows that the

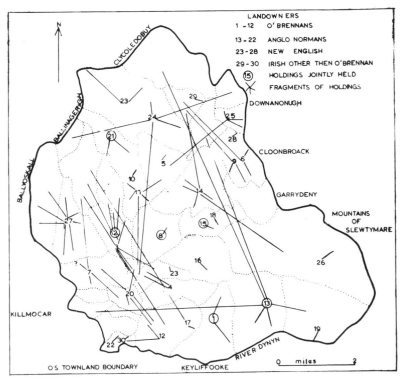

Fig. 2.3 Occupation of land. Idough C.1635.

lands held by the O'Brenans were reduced considerably in the period from 1614 to 1635. Seven of the twenty 'towns' held by them in 1614 were now in the possession of either Anglo-Norman or 'New English' occupiers and portions of four other 'towns' had also been alienated. The attractions of a financial settlement appear to have encouraged the O'Brenans to alienate parts of their property. They disposed first of the mainly empty and infertile tracts in the border country. In 1635, the O'Brenans were concentrated in the districts to the north and northeast of where the modern town of Castlecomer now stands. Their broad medieval kingdom had shrunk to a meagre heartland.

Occupiers of Anglo-Norman origin included seven Purcells, four Butlers, one Walsh and one Pooer. All of these, except Pooer whose family

40

name was usually found in County Waterford, were members of prominent Kilkenny families closely connected with the Butlers of Ormonde. Their strong presence in north Fassadinin is clear evidence of the success of the policy of 'commercial' plantation initiated by Ormonde at the close of the sixteenth century. Figure 2.3 shows that Anglo-Norman holdings consisted of widely dispersed fragments. One finds, for example, that "Ric Butler, Fil' Jac; Ric Butler Fil' Petr & Patric' Purcell possessionat sunt de vil' de Confelie, Corfinshyon, Aghtubred, Clashduffe, Dontreman & Cloghmoyleheade". Although, the O'Brenan holdings were more fragmented and consisted of smaller divisions than their Anglo-Norman counterparts (as is shown by Fig. 2.3), these fragments were usually located in contiguous land divisions. This suggests that the O'Brenans farmed their holdings whereas the weight of evidence leads to the conclusion that the Anglo-Normans were merely rent-receivers and absentees.

The identity of the 'New English' occupiers presents evidence of the involvement of state and church officials in the quest for ownership of the Gaelic lands. The lands of the Earl of Londonderry, a Privy Councillor in the administration of the Earl of Wentworth, consisted of six fragments dispersed throughout the north and northeast of Idough. Cipriam Horsfall who held "de tot' vil' de Crutt & Cooliad p'cell de Crutt" was listed with David Roothe and William Shee as a Governor of the City of Kilkenny in 1640.[28] Olyver Wheeler who was in possession of '¼ vil de Croghtenclogh' was the son of the Protestant Bishop of Ossory.[29] The spatial distribution of both Anglo-Norman and 'New English' occupiers suggests that they were not necessarily associated with the good arable land of Idough (fig. 2.3). Their perception of the value of land was related to considerations other than its agricultural potential or the monetary return from its rents. It has earlier been suggested that Ormonde was primarily concerned with extending the jurisdiction of the Crown. The acquisitions of the 'New English' are discussed in the later part of this chapter in connection with the discovery and exploitation of iron ore in Idough. If figs. 2.2 and 2.3 are compared, it can be seen that they were found mainly in the 'woodland' district.

One is now faced with unravelling what appears to have been a very complex system of land occupation in what may be termed a trihedral area. The Inquisition refers to compact holdings and to holdings which consisted of a collection of scattered land divisions. Some instances of multiple tenancies occurred. Examples of communal occupation and tenancies where each tenant had a specific share of the holding are found. This does not mean that either farming in common or the 'runrig' system of land management was practised in Idough. Little is known about how the allocation or management of the land divisions described in the Inquisition were worked out on the ground. It must also be taken into account that the Inquisition may have recorded units of taxation returns rather than actual land divisions. Furthermore there is no obvious uniformity with respect to land occupation in the groupings classified according to patronymic names. Three of the twelve O'Brenan farms were held in common without partition. For example, "Donat' McWilliam O'Brenan, Edm McLaghlin O'Brenan & Owen McShane O'Brenan sunt possessionat de vil de Kildergan & Uskurt". This appears to have been a compact farm but the second communal holding occupied by the O'Brenans consisted of the two parts of eight scattered land divisions. These survivals of communal occupation were once part of a wider social and economic system which existed within limited family groups in Idough. The Inquisition presents clear evidence that this form of landholding was now being replaced by an arrangement whereby the lands of individuals were clearly defined. The remaining O'Brenan farms were held in this fashion. Thus, for example, "Edm McOwen O'Brenan est possessionat de vil & ter de Ballygowne al' Smithestowne". The O'Brenans shared land divisions with the 'New English' and Anglo-Norman occupiers in 1635. The Inquisition records that, "Tho Evers est possessionat 'de $\frac{1}{3}$ de Loan al' Loell". Communal occupation was also found on holdings belonging to Anglo-Norman tenants. Unlike the O'Brenans however, these occupiers had not the same patronymic names. The fractional divisions of land held by Anglo-Norman and 'New-English' occupiers were obviously the recently alienated shares of 'sept' lands.

One can say very little about settlement in this society. In this context, the primary concern is the O'Brenans as there is no evidence that either the Anglo-Normans or 'New English' ever settled on their Idough lands. Clusters inhabited by kin groups have been characteristic of areas of both communal and shared occupation of land. It should be remembered, however, that one is dealing with a sparsely populated district where the rearing of cattle was the predominant agricultural activity. If one accepts that the twenty five 'vils' recorded in the Inquisition refer to some form of permanent settlement, one is obviously dealing with a system of dispersed habitations. It is significant that when these 'vils' are located on a map it is found that they are more numerous in the profitable land areas of Idough. These were also the areas which had the greater number of fractional land divisions. 'Vil' appears to have been a comprehensive term which embraced a settlement and its associated land area. This settlement may have had 'parcells' of arable land and other 'lands' which were pasture grounds.

4. The Anglo—Normans in Fassadinin 1600-1640

(a) *The distributional evidence:*

The 'Sean-Gaill' although described as "of Iryshe habyt, of Iryshe language and of Iryshe conditions"[30] were never allowed to forget their origins by English administrators. Fynes Moryson described them as the 'English Irish' whereas modern historians refer to them as 'Anglo-Normans'. By 1600, many of them had formed a community of religion, custom and language with the indigenous inhabitants. The distinction between Gael and 'Sean Gaill' was finally obscured by the Cromwellians when they divided the residents of Ireland into 'Irish Papists' and 'English Protestants'. The north Kilkenny lowlands have been described as an area of "durable, Anglo-Norman rural occupation".[31] The historian, Orpen, found that Anglo-Norman mottes were "thickly scattered throughout the lordship of Meath, Leinster, Ulster and in South Tipperary".[32] On his map, he depicts two mottes within the barony of Fassadinin at Castlecomer and Bally-ragget. It is significant that these two placenames were formed by combining Gaelic and 'old English' elements. The motte of Odough was located on the west bank of the Nore close to the barony boundary in the south west. R. E. Glasscock has classified Odough as "a shrunken rural borough" which in 1307 had 110 burgages.[33] Traces of the medieval colonisation are found in the placenames (fig. 1.10), in the more durable settlement items such as castles and mottes, and in the historical record. In 1207, Kilkenny City was granted its first charter by William Marshall, Earl of Pembroke in Wales, and son-in-law of the adventurer, Richard Strong-bow.[34] The Anglo-Normans expanded northwards through the river corri-dors of the Nore and Dinin and by 1300 they owned the greater portion of Fassadinin.[35] The extension of their sphere of influence resulted in the expulsion of the dispossessed Gaelic 'clan' from their homeland. Fassadinin was partitioned amongst families with surnames such as Archdeacon, De La Freyne, Ragged, Rocheford, Devereaux, St. Leger and Purcell. The enumeration of land divisions held by them circa 1300 suggests that they were in possession of all the western sector of Fassadinin, which stretched along the River Nore from Dunmore north to Attanagh. Figure 2.4 indi-cates that Anglo-Norman territory extended as far north as the hill fringes of the Gaelic heartland.

Apart from Purcell, the surnames of the thirteenth century colonists are not found as landowners in Fassadinin circa 1600. This may imply that the first phase of expansion was followed by a period of Gaelic resurgence and consequent contraction of the Anglo-Norman settlement, especially in the north-east sector of the barony. The demise of the thirteenth century colonists may be related to the rise in prominence of the Butlers of Or-monde who selected Kilkenny city as their primary residence in 1391. Both explanations are valid to a degree. In 1600, traces are found of the Anglo-Normans in the hill country. Any association that existed was re-lated more to the new phase of territorial aggrandizement, inaugurated by the tenth Earl, Black Tom, than to continuity of medieval settlement. It may be deduced from the surnames of the Anglo-Norman landowners circa 1600 that the majority of them had been installed by Ormonde. They included the Ormondes themselves and their kinsmen, the Mount-garrets; the Purcells who were the hereditary military allies of the Butlers; the families of Rothe and Archer who were merchants in the Ormonde towns of Kilkenny and New Ross; the O'Sheas, a family of Gaelic extrac-tion, who conducted the legal business of the Ormonde lordship.

Figure 2.4 shows that the Butler families of Ormonde and Mountgarret

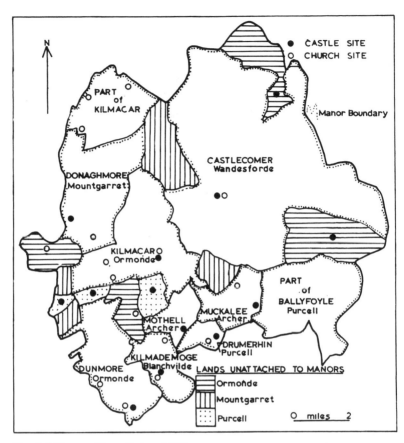

Fig. 2.4 Manors Fassadinin c.1639.

held all of west Fassadinin, part of the central area of the barony and newly acquired outliers in the Gaelic lands. The primary Ormonde manor was located at Dunmore in the south-west of the barony (fig. 2.4). Its physical centre probably occupied a site directly south of the confluence of the Rivers Nore and Dinin and close to the old parochial church of Dunmore. Ormonde rentals in 1690-91 record that this building was damaged in the military campaigns of that period.[36] Today, portion of the old building is embodied in the house which stands there. The name *Dunmore* (the big dún) signifies that the place was a settlement previous to its acquisition by the Anglo-Normans. Buildings, as well as the administrative divisions for which they served as physical focii, were often new structures on old foundations. It is a recurrent feature of Irish settlement history that the same site has served different cultural groups in similar ways over the centuries. Dunmore was ideally located as an administrative centre. It controlled the routes which led to the upper regions of Fassadinin through the

44

Nore and Dinin river basins. In 1581 Dunmore consisted of "the town of Dunmore with its appurtenances with the towns of Ballyraghtane, Sheahanagh, Ardlowe, Ravallynogly and Tulloglahse".[37] All these denominations are listed as fractions of 'ploughlands' circa 1589 and, apart from 'Skeahanagh,' are delineated as townlands in the barony map of the Down Survey (fig. 1.5). The manor lands contained all of Dunmore parish and part of the parish of Maine. They also included the territorial division of *Ardlowe* which in 1300 was listed as a monastic parish held by the priory of the Canons Regular of St. Augustine, whose house was located at Kells, in the barony of the same name. Ardlowe was part of the monastic property which passed to Ormonde at the Dissolution.

Kilmacar, the second Ormonde manor in Fassadinin, was listed as a parish in the rural deanary of Odagh circa 1300. It is known from the Ormonde Deeds that the manor of Kilmacar was not a stable territorial division but was augmented by various land transfers from time to time. In 1572, Kilmacar consisted of the "towns of Kilmacar, Tomecheny, Kisalyn and Warigy alias the Market Castle".[38] The manor estate was augmented in 1575 by the addition of "Coolraheen and Singanagh" which lay to the south.[39] In 1581 "Ballynroshalegh alias Russellstown and Kilmenan"[40] were conveyed to the tenant of Kilmacar. An examination of fig. 2.4 shows that Kilmacar manor circa 1639 consisted of two fragments. The focal point of the manor was found in the southern sector, which was obviously the original core area. It is significant that this 'castle' or tower house was located close to the parish church which served the medieval parish of Kilmacar. All Ormonde lands did not belong to manors. These unattached lands included the territory recently acquired by Ormonde in Idough, the denominations of Grangemaccomb and Oldtown in the mid west of the barony and Jenkinstown in the south. Grangemaccomb and Oldtown were part of the property of the dissolved Cistercian monastery of Jerpoint in the Barony of Gowran.

In 1580, Richard Butler, youngest son of Piers Rua, ninth Earl of Ormonde, was raised to the peerage and given the title Viscount Mountgarret.[41] This junior branch of the Ormonde family had their seat at Ballyragget in the Nore valley and in 1639 Richard, Viscount Mountgarret, held the manor of 'Bealaragged alias Donaghmore'. These alternative names reveal the strong association of church and Anglo Norman with this fertile and attractive part of the Nore valley. The name *Bealaragged* (the ford of Raggett) commemorates the family who established a settlement at a bridging point on the river Nore sometime in the thirteenth century. Carrigan, the ecclesiastical historian of the diocese of Ossory, claimed that the Anglo-Norman motte of Ballyragget was in fact the *dún* of *Tulacbarry*, (the green hill of the Ui-Barrche) and that the settlement here was of Gaelic provenance. The denomination 'Tullaghbarr alias Mountetullaghbare' is listed in Mountgarret records up to 1638.[42] The motte is now commemorated in the townland name of Moatpark, north of the modern town of Ballyragget. The Mountgarret lands as defined by

Inquisition held at Rosbercon on October 30th 1621 were found mainly in the vicinity of Ballyragget and in the adjoining segment of west Idough. Figure 2.4 indicates that this family also held fragments further south in the Nore valley and to the east of the Ormonde manor of Kilmacar. Mountgarret is not returned as holding any lands in Idough in the Inquisition of 1635. Neither are his Idough lands listed in 1638 when Mountgarret was confirmed in his estate on payment of a fine of £200. It is probable that the royal grants of Idough to Wandesforde obliterated Mountgarret's claim to ownership here. The complex nature of landownership in the seventeenth century is indicated when Mountgarret is found returned as proprietor of west Idough in the Books of Survey and Distribution. The Mountgarret seat and the functional centre of the manor was the impressive square castle standing on the east bank of the river Nore. This building, erected within a rectangular stone enclosure, was protected by a network of rounded turrets located at wall junctions (Plate II).

Figure 2.4 shows that manors in south east and south Fassadinin were smaller and more compact than those in the western and northern sectors.

Plate II. Ballyraggart castle, seat of the Mountgarret family, was built c.1500.

The size of manors was related to the political status and influence of their proprietors and not to land quality as other territorial divisions were.

The Anglo-Norman families of Purcell, Archer and Blanchvilde owned the great manors here in the first half of the seventeenth century. Of these, the Purcells were the more numerous and probably occupied the greater territorial area (fig. 2.4). Historical evidence and local tradition testifies to the strong and long association of the Purcells with the land of south Fassadinin. A Walter Purcell attested the charter of foundation given to Kilkenny city by the Earl of Pembroke in 1207, and was the first Sheriff of the newly created Shire of Kilkenny in 1215.[43] The primary seat of the Purcell family was not in Kilkenny, but in Loghmore, Barony of Eliogarty in the east of county Tipperary. In 1639 five Purcell families held estates of varying sizes in south east Fassadinin and in the level lands between the Dinin and Nore rivers. An examination of sources suggests that the Purcell property in south east Fassadinin had been more extensive and at one time embraced the "manor of Muckalee'. One finds, for example, that Phillip Purcell of Ballyfoyle in Gowran barony was confirmed in possession of lands in Fassadinin under the provisions of the Commission for Defective Titles. These included the manor of "Muckilly" and the denominations of "Gallestowne alias Ballynigawle, Cloghranke, Drumerhir, Kilmadum and Coolcullenduffe".[44] An examination of fig. 1.6 shows that these land divisions were delineated as townlands in the Down Survey map of Fassadinin barony. In 1639 Phillip Purcell was granted permission by special Crown license to convey to Henry Archer, gentleman, of New Ross, Co. Wexford the "manor townes and lands of Muckilly". Carrigan has linked the decline in Purcell family fortunes to the succession of a minor to the property in 1606. During this period, the estates were mismanaged and subsequent piecemeal alienations of property were necessary to avoid bankruptcy and ruin. Both Gaelic and Anglo-Norman landowners were experiencing the effects of commercial plantation in the decade from 1630 to 1640. Cloghranke castle the probable administrative and settle-ment core of the "manor of Muckilly", occupied a high site overlooking the Dinin valley. Local tradition associates the castle with the O'Brenans and this may suggest that it was one of the strongholds acquired and utilised by the invader.

There is no indication when Drumerhin manor was created but it is known that it was held by a branch of the Purcell family of Ballyfoyle. The manor may have been coextensive with the parish shown in the barony map (fig. 1.5). The remaining Purcell holdings in Fassadinin had not the status of manors but were held of "the chief lords of the fee". These estates were invariably smaller than manors and were, in all probab-ity, the areas effectively farmed and inhabited by individuals. An Inquisi-tion post mortem held at Gowran in January 1622 defined the land of the deceased William Purcell of Esker. It was found that he "died seized of the castle, town, lands of Esker, Castlanabolan, Tullepishane, Kilcollan, Ballincomo, Cowlebane and Dromgoile where Castlemander has been lately built".[45] The last three divisions named in the Inquisition are located in Idough close to the site of the modern town of Castlecomer. This implies that the Purcells as well as the Ormondes were expanding northwards in this period. Seven Purcells were listed as occupiers in Idough in 1635. The centre of Purcell property in this area seems to have been the castle of Esker located on the west bank of the Dinin. In 1638 Edward Purcell, proprietor of the Esker property, received a new title to his lands on payment of a fine of £2.13.4[46] Figure 1.6 indicates that the two separate Purcell farms of Foulksrath and Lismaine were located in the mid-west sector of the barony, close to the river Nore. The Purcells have left material evidence of their existence in the form of the strong tower-house erected here in the early sixteenth century (plate III). Historical records prove that as early as 1382 the Purcells occupied Lismaine, which guarded the passage of the Nore, and a mill located there.[47] This territorial division contained a castle and mill in 1635 and was in the possession of Richard Purcell.

Plate III. Foulksrath castle. This Purcell castle located in the townland of Foulksrath dates from the early fifteenth century.

In a list of administrators of Kilkenny City from 1325 to 1620, the Anglo-Norman surname, Archer, occurs sixty seven times.[48] Two distinct Archer families occupied adjoining estates in south Fassadinin circa 1639. The "manor of Muckilly" had been acquired from the financially weak Purcells by Henry Archer, a merchant from the Ormonde town of New Ross, Co. Wexford. The Archers of Mothill had a longer connection with the barony and it can be assumed that they resided on their lands here. An Inquisition post mortem, extant for Archer lands in 1618, details a complex system of landholding and inheritance and reveals that families like the Archers held lands from various overlords. Thus, for example, John Archer held "Ballyranke" of the manor of Dunmore; he occupied "John Rothestowne" and "Rathomane" as tenant of the Purcell manor of Drumerhin; "Byragghes" (subdivision of John Rothestowne) as parcell of the Blanchfield manor of Kilmademoge and also Lisclevan of the manor of Mothill.[49] An examination of the Down Survey Parish map (fig. 1.6) reveals that these four divisions were all recognised as distinct territorial entities circa 1654. The Blanchvilde manor of Kilmademoge was not the subject of any Inquisition in the first half of the seventeenth century. From the Ormonde records, it is known that it was roughly coextensive with the parish of Kilmademoge (fig. 1.5). By allocating the "ploughland" value listed in the "book of ploughlands" circa 1584 to the known territorial divisions of manors, one gets a rough indication of the ownership hierarchy of the barony circa 1639. The Gaelic lands of Idough are not included in this reckoning. One finds that the Earl of Ormonde held approximately one ploughland; the Archer family three quarters; the Mountgarret Butlers two thirds; the Purcells four sevenths and the Blanchvildes one seventh. These figures indicate the families varying status at this time.

(b) *The manorial system.*

The manor was part of the system of central and local government superimposed on those parts of Ireland in which the Anglo-Normans had become entrenched. These feudal freehold estates were held in fee simple without restriction on inheritance. The greater number of Fassadinin manors were created by Ormonde through the process of sub-infeudation which was commonly practised by tenants-in-chief. By 1639 Fassadinin had a complement of eight manors ranging in size from 20,000 to 500 acres (fig. 2.4). Manor names were also parish names and castles and churches, the central sites of this dual system, were usually found in conjunction. These buildings occupied contiguous sites in Castlecomer, Kilmacar, Kilmademoge and Dunmore. The granting of elements of an urban constitution to manors made an important contribution to the development of town life in Ireland. Urban growth in Castlecomer and Ballyragget was stimulated by royal grants of weekly markets and annual fairs in the early part of the seventeenth century.

The manor was a legal entity and the lord of the manor had jurisdiction over manor tenants through three separate courts. The 'court baron' was for free men, the 'court customary' for unfree men and the "court leet" was authorised by a special royal grant. An examination of the royal grants of manors in Fassadinin shows that they were all empowered to hold 'courts baron' and 'courts leet' and to create tenures. Apart from a reference to boundary disputes being brought before "Therle of Ormond's Seneschiall holding his Barron Court at Donmore".[50] There is no documentary evidence that these legal institutions were functioning in the seventeenth century. The grant of the 'manor of Bealaragged alias Donaghmore' empowered Richard Viscount Mountgarret, "to create tenures, 500 acres at least for a demesne to each manor, to hold courts baron and leet, to enjoy all waifes, strayes, wrecks and deodands, to make parks not exceeding 2,000 acres with free warren and park and to build and keep tan houses".[51]

Extant manorial inventories for Ormonde lands contain precise information about classes of tenants, their landholdings and corresponding rents and services.[52] The six classes of tenants recorded were free tenants, farmers, gavillers, cottiers, betaghs and burgesses. This hierarchy was based on the occupation of varying proportions of the manor lands: tenants were also differentiated in respect of tenure and services. There is a striking similarity between this form of land occupation and the estate system which succeeded it. The nature and distribution of settlement in this society is more ambiguous. Otway-Ruthven assumed that the betaghs lived "in what seem to have been family groups in distinct townlands".[53] She also held the opinion that "the betaghs no doubt cultivated their own lands on the native system, but there is adequate evidence of the dispersed strip holdings of the English open-field system all over the area, which, as we have seen, was populated by English settlers". Aalen also placed great emphasis on the dual elements in Norman-Irish society.[54] He differentiated between a native, irregular open field system with associated settlement and the Anglo-Norman village with its tower house, church and regular fields.

Is it possible to outline the nature of society and settlement in Fassadinin at this time? The evidence is quite fragmentary and surviving documents are concerned with matters other than the internal structure of manors. The Ormonde deeds detail services and rentals payable by tenants and this enables one to build up a faint picture of the transactions concerning land in this period. A surviving deed, which records the grant of the manor of Killmacar to Donyll McShane in 1572, reveals the services and money payments demanded from the chief tenants of manors.[55] "All eyries of hawks, and all conies, pheasants, partridges, deer and the main wood upon said premises" were reserved for the use of the Earl of Ormonde. The tenant was allowed "fire-lot, house-lot, hedge-lot, car-lot, plough-lot and car-lot". The term of tenancy was twenty one years and the rental was comprised of a money payment, a payment in kind, a share of the profits of the manor courts and the "customs and labours due of said premises". The deed also stipulated that the "caterers and purveyors" of Ormonde were to be allowed to enter the premises and purchase provisions. The terms of an earlier deed, dated 1565, suggest that conditions written into contracts of this kind may have been responsible for generating landscape change.[56] In the grant to Blanchvilde of the manor of Dunmore, the terms of tenure required that "the tenant shall cause the farmers of the villages to trench and enclose around about their principal farm houses and dwellings". The 'villages' in this contract may have been the six places named in the grant of the manor of Dunmore in 1581. The manor of Dunmore may have consisted of the principal settlement at Dunmore, which was held by the chief tenant, and a complementary group of five settlements occupied by farmers. Another such example is contained in the deed which confirmed John Archer Fitzwalter in possession of the lands of "Jenkynstown and Mayne" in south Fassadinin. The deed stipulated that Archer was to extend the castle of 'Jenkynstown' vertically; to cover it with "oaken timber and slates" and to "build a bawn near said castle within four years".[57]

Anglo-Norman rural society was preoccupied with land, its contents and its boundaries. It is fortunate that an account of the proceedings of the Commission instituted in 1589-94 to confirm "the bounds of the Earl of Ormonde's ancient estates" has survived.[58] Although the Commission was concerned with the delimitation of land boundaries, some of the evidence given by the thirty seven deponents describes the social and economic life of the barony. The areas in dispute in Fassadinin were described as the "great parcell of arable and wood of Kilmenan" in the north west and the "ten acres of the Country measure being by estimacion two hundred burgess acres of land" between the Ormonde manor of Dunmore and the Blanchvilde manor of Kilmademoge. The witnesses to the Commission came from the districts in Fassadinin owned by Ormonde. Sixteen were from Killmacar, nine from 'Connehie', six from Dunmore, three from Marketcastle, two from Ballyesker and one from Rosconnell. All of these places were referred to as 'towns' in inventories of Ormonde property in Fassadinin in the early seventeenth century. This suggests that 'villages' or house clusters dispersed at roughly regular intervals were the dominant settlement items along the western flank of the barony. If it is assumed that the surnames recorded by the Commission were representative of this part of the barony, then one is dealing with a society in which the strongly dominant numerical group were of Gaelic origin. One finds, for example, that thirty of those who testified were of Gaelic stock and the remaining seven were of Anglo-Norman descent. The heterogeneous nature of Gaelic society in this part of the barony is reflected in the great variety of Gaelic patronymic names recorded. The surname Brenan occurs twice and the remaining names include Bolger, 'Mulchahell', 'Deagin', O'Kelly, Delaney, Meagher and McShane. Four of the seven Anglo-Norman deponents were, predictably, called Purcell. Richard Purcell Fitzpatrick of Killmocarr is an interesting example of a hybrid name, which one would expect to find in an area where Irish and Anglo-Norman lived side by side.

In order to illustrate aspects of society and settlement, it may be appropriate to examine the manor of Kilmocarr in some detail. Figure 2.4 shows that Kilmocarr consisted of two detached parts which were separated by the Mountgarret manor of Donaghmore. The evidence presented to the Commission suggests that trespass by adjoining landowners, such as Mountgarret and Shortall, was common in the detached northern fragment. The witnesses hoped to show that these lands belonged to Ormonde. In this document the country men of the late sixteenth century are heard speaking. These were "the divers aged persons who knew the meares and marks" of the Earl's lands". Their testimony was based on knowledge transmitted to them by their ancestors and on observations that they had made in their own life time. The undisturbed possession of the fruits of the land and its occupation from "time immemorial" were the factors on which they based claims to ownership. It is ironic that the Anglo-Norman overlord depended on the communal memory of his Gaelic 'husbandmen' to define his estate boundaries for him. The chief tenant of Dunmore was described as "constable and Tenaunt" whereas the occupant of Killmocarr manor was referred to as 'tenaunt' and 'fermour' (farmer). All rights apertaining to the lands of the manor, apart from those reserved in the instrument of tenure to the Earl of Ormonde, were vested in the chief tenants and their supervisory role is evident from this document. Under-tenants (commonly referred to as 'husbandmen') were allocated grazing rights and access to timber on payment of money. 'Doneghe O'Hoen of Connehie' stated that he was "born at Killcolman near Killmocarr where he bought pasture for his cattell and wood for his provision of Patk. Fitzpatrick Purcell and Donyll McShane". Another witness asserted that he had "cutt tymber for a house and som wood upon Falskehen, by the lycence of Donyll McShane". There is no reference to arable farming in the context of Killmocarr and the emphasis on cattle suggests their significance in the pastoral economy of the manor. Apart from specialists such as studkeepers, tithe proctors, tithe collectors and cowherds, there is no indication that the inhabitants of Killmocarr manor were divided into the classes found in early inventories of Ormonde lands. The majority of husbandmen had the status of tenants only, although John Purcell of Kilmocarr was described as "servant and Tenaunt to the sd. persons at Tommecheny part of the demeaynes of the sd' Kilmocarr". Individuals such as Purcell together with the specialist workers provided the labour force for the working of the demesne. Although there appears to have been a distinction between the demesne lands of the manor and the out-lying areas, there is no evidence that this led to the dual system of land tenure and land utilisation outlined by Aalen and others for other inter-mixed areas. The residents of outlying villages shared the tenancy of manor lands with their overlord. The evidence of Teige O'Deagin of Connehie supports this contention. He stated that he was "cowherde to said Donill and sawe the sd. Donill and his tenauntes cattell pasture uppon the sd. lands without interrupcion". The occupation of land may have been based on the capacity of tenants to pay rent or to provide other services. Other sources seem to suggest that this practise was widespread. In the Dowdall Deeds which are concerned with lands near the town of Dundalk in Co. Louth, one finds that tenants were charged rent for specified numbers of livestock or specific produce rather than for defined areas of land.[59]

5. The Nua Gaill (New English) in Fassadinin 1600-1640.

"It was an age of adventurers and Projectors, the general taste of the world ran in favour of new discoveries and plantings of countries, and such as were not hardy enough to venture into the remote parts of the Kingdom fancied they might make a fortune near home by settling and planting in Ireland." (Carte, T. *Life of the Great Duke of Ormonde*, (Dublin), 1736 1, 10.)

The 'New English' in Fassadinin c. 1639 were found in that part of the barony which had been described as depressed, disorderly and Gaelic in the late sixteenth century. This section attempts an explanation of their presence here. The Earls of Ormonde and Londonderry were confirmed in possession of Idough in 1635 "for the advancement of the King's profit and the civilising of that country." The Wandesfordes, affected by the spirit of their time, began their colony here "for the good of the Church and the Commonwealth". This was a dynamic period in Irish history. A new class of administrators-cum-entrepreneurs who had recently arrived from England were involved in a great variety of activities which merged private enterprise and state policy. In 1637, for example, Edmund Spiring of Malahide, Co. Dublin, petitioned the Government for financial assistance to develop an ironmine in the south west of Ireland.[60] He claimed that "he had discovered iron ore on the sea coast between Cork and Kerry, in a rock between land and high water, also lymestone a thing necessary for a furnace". He asserted that the state would be doubly recompensed if they financed the project as "it will pay double custom on exportation from Ireland and importation into England and furthermore will effect an English plantation by erecting ironworks in that barren place".

If the names of the ironmasters in Ireland at this time are examined one finds that they were a small group of wealthy 'New English' landowners, who apart from Sir Richard Boyle, Earl of Cork, had participated in the administration of Thomas Wentworth. Sir Charles Coote, who acquired Idough in 1630, erected an iron furnace in partnership with Boyle in Co. Leitrim close to Arigna on Lough Allen in 1629.[61] Coote was also involved in an iron furnace at Mountrath, Co. Laois.[62] The Earl of Londonderry, who acquired a third part of Idough c. 1620, had interests in an ironworks at Ballinakill to the north west of the barony. The Lord Chancellor, Sir Adam Loftus, worked iron at Mountmellick on the Barrow and manuscript sources reveal that Sir Christopher Wandesforde, the eventual purchaser of Idough, had, in partnership with Sir George Radcliffe of the

Privy Council, acquired an interest in ironworks at Macroom, Co. Cork, Killeshin, Co. Carlow and Graig, Co. Kilkenny c. 1635.[63]

Boate claimed that "all the mines which to this day are found out in Ireland have been discovered by the English, that is, such as have come over since the time of Elizabeth." However, placename elements found in land divisions close to the modern town of Castlecomer suggest that the Gaelic people, who named them, knew of the existence of ironstone and coal deposits in the district. Another factor which may have attracted the adventurers was that twenty-four per cent (4,088 'Irish' acres) of Idough was classified as woodland in a survey compiled c. 1635. A comparison of figs. 2.2 and 2.3 reveals that it was in the districts in the north and north east of Idough where the woodlands were located that the 'New English' landowners are found in 1635. To the much travelled adventurers, Idough, with its underexploited timber resources and unknown quantity of iron ore, had many attractions. They had the political patronage necessary to obtain a 'legal' grant of the lands here. They also possessed the technology and knowledge of the world of commerce necessary to exploit the reserves of iron. These were probably the factors which led to the increased interest in Idough in the decade from 1630 to 1640.

The Wandesforde manuscripts chronicle the course of iron mining in Fassadinin. An indenture, concerned with the transfer of property from Walter Archer, merchant, of the city of Kilkenny to the Baron of Limerick, contains a reference to a "furnace at Killdroyn in Idough."[64] 'Killdroyn' was possibly the same place as 'Killdergan' listed in other property transactions.[65] The only physical structure mentioned in the Indenture was a furnace. It may be assumed that the preliminary melting of the ironstone took place here and that the unfinished material was transported to one of the Laois ironworks for further refining and casting. It is probable that this ironworks was at Ballinakill which is approximately eight miles north west of Killdergan. Transportation overland, though time consuming, was a usual feature of the ironwork industry and did not necessarily retard its growth.[66] The Indenture drawn up in 1635 reveals that mismanagement and financial malpractices were a feature of the iron industry in south east Leinster. It also records that at this period Belgians from the city of Liege were working the furnace and forge of Ballinakill. This works had acquired the Royal patent for "the casting of iron ordinance within the Realm of Ireland." The Indenture detailed the grant by the Earl of Londonderry of "an ancient furnace and one forge anciently used for the making and raising of iron at Ballinakill in the Queens County together with a forge called Clonmagought lately erected in Co. Kilkenny" to Richard Blacknell of Macroom, Co. Cork. The grant included the castle called "Castlemander, alias Myners Castle and one bawn adjoining it." This castle was held by the Purcells of Esker in 1622 when it was described as "newly built".[67] It was located in the townland of Drumgoole east of the site of Castlecomer town. The deed listed many of the tools used in the iron industry. These included hammers, anvils, bellows and bellow leathers. It referred to the 'liberty' given to the tenant, "to digge iron-myne, hearthstone, lymestoen" and "of felling, cutting, clearing, cordinge and carrying away of all manner of wood or underwoods." Blacknell appropriated the sum of £480 belonging to the ironworks, which by 1635 had passed to Christopher Wandesforde and George Radcliffe, both Privy Councillors.

The last reference to ironmining in this period was concerned solely with regulating the working of a newly erected furnace in Idough.[68] This Indenture was drawn up in 1637, approximately one year after Wandesforde had taken possession. The principals involved were Wandesforde, Sir John Browne of Spolmaldine in Kent in the 'Realm of England' and a Captain Richard Steele. The transactions recorded in the Indenture included the letting of a furnace and provisions for the erection of houses for workmen in "such parts of the territory of Idough alias Brenan as the said Christopher Wandesforde shall think fit." The tenure was for a period of twelve years at the rent of £300 per annum. The furnace was licensed to manufacture "iron potts, kettles, chimney tops, salt pannes, sope pannes and the manufactures of soft iron mentioned in the patents granted to John Brown in 1637, ordnance and Shott excepted."[120] As in the other deeds, the tenants were granted permission to mine whatever material and cut whatever timber required for the ironworks. The indenture concluded with the admonition that before the tenants embarked on the digging of new pits they were to make sure that the old workings were properly secured so that "no men or cattle may fall therein." This contract implies that the physical structure at Castlecomer included a furnace, forge and finery or casting work. In the later part of the century, such complexes had a wide range of equipment and large numbers of employees. The smelting process required a continuous fire which was fed with alternate layers of limestone, ironstone and charcoal. Some works, such as those in the Barony of Dunkerron in south west Kerry visited by Molyneaux towards the end of the century, utilised water power to drive the bellows and to rotate the large hammers in the forges.[69]

There is a tradition in the Castlecomer district that Wandesforde introduced the art of haymaking and manufactured scythes here in the early days of the colony. A lease of the Castlecomer property in 1640 refers to the "quarries, maynes, coales, wood, mills or furnaces, forges, scythe mills" in the district. Comber, the biographer of Wandesforde, made the claim more strongly when he wrote: "he (Christopher Wandesforde) erected a mill in which he wrought scythes in such abundance that the Irish, who had hitherto barbarously suffered their grass, which their cattle could not eat, to rot on the ground, now imitated the English manner of mowing and preserving hay".[70] There is no indication whether Wandesforde exported any of the finished iron. The Nore, by which Coote sent his iron to Waterford, runs by the west of the barony and the river Barrow is only four miles distant from the barony boundary on the east.

The English colony of Castlecomer and its subsequent development in the latter half of the seventeenth century is examined in greater detail in the next chapter. The motivation for 'New English' involvement in Fassadinin has been explicated in this section. It appears from the available evidence that it was the presence of large quantities of virgin woodland and unknown amounts of ironore which attracted them. It may also have been that seventeenth century adventurers felt a sense of duty towards their church and king, which was manifested in their quest for a spiritual and temporal empire. Despite these altruistic notions, however, the economic motivation seems to have been paramount. Perhaps they assumed that the other things would follow in its wake. If it was the ironstone which initiated colonisation, it was not iron but coal which was to shape the future geography of north-east Fassadinin.

CHAPTER III

SURVEY AND DISTRIBUTION 1641-1700

"Do mheasadh a Stát is tá ar láimh na meirlach
Is táid a mbailte faoi bhastaraibh Bearla
Is táid a gceartacha daingean le tréimhse
Ar laimh na nGall nach ceannsa céadfa
Is a ndúnta faoi a mhúnlach lucht céirde
Is gan dá ndaingeanacha acha le féachain
Ach príosúin dhubha nó tithe na ngéibheann."
(Lines 208-215, "Aiste Dháibhí Cúndún c. 1654" in O'Rahilly, c. (ed.)
Five Seventeenth-Century Political Poems (Dublin, 1952) 44-45).

"Upon the whole the Irish may justly blame themselves for whatever they have or shall suffer in the issue of this matter, since it is apparent that the necessity was brought about by themselves, that either they or we must be ruined." (King, William, *State of Protestants in Ireland under the late King James's Government* (London, 1691) 63).

1. Introduction

The primary aim of this chapter is to examine the impact of two wars and three land settlements on the patterns of ownership and occupation in the barony. The termination of the Confederate Wars and the victory of the radical protestants under Cromwell led to wholesale confiscation and the settling in Ireland of soldiers and adventurers. Various Acts of Parliament which included the Act for the Reduction of the Rebels 1642, the Act for Settling Ireland 1652 and the Act for Satisfaction 1653, provided the political and legal terms of reference. The enactment of this legislation involved the Commonwealth government in massive schemes of transportation, plantation and transplantation which had important repercussions in the landscape.

The Restoration of the monarchy did little to modify the land settlement. It was almost impossible to derive any single formula of retribution and reward which would satisfy all the competing claims to Irish land. The Act of Settlement passed in 1662 took account of the changing political situation but in 1665 the Cromwellian grantees were confirmed in their estates by the Act of Explanation. It is estimated that by 1670 only some 8,000 soldiers and adventurers had their estates confirmed by Charles II and of these approximately 500 were adventurers.[1] The new reorganisation of ownership proposed by the 'patriot parliament', convened by James II in 1689, would have re-established a Catholic proprietorial class. The military defeats suffered by the Jacobites at the Boyne and other provincial centres ensured that the Restoration Land Settlement was to remain the basis of ownership in Ireland for the following two centuries. Confiscation alone did not satisfy the victors. New legislation, with the well defined purpose of preventing the development of a Catholic landowning class in the future, was enacted. This final redistribution of property and political power in the seventeenth century laid the basis for the development of a minority, Anglican, landed oligarchy, which in the course of time became known as the Protestant Ascendancy. It is indeed fortunate that a great variety of documentation concerning land has survived from this period. The range and detail of the source material suggests the thoroughness of the conquest. The redistribution of land was a corollary of confiscation. Land was identified, mapped and valued, its contents enumerated and described. The chapter is based on an analysis of this rich documentation.

2. Survey

"The Barony of Fassaghdining in the County of Kilkenny is bounded on the North with the Barony of Cullinagh in the Queene's County, on the North East with the Barony of Slimargagh, on the East with the County of Catherlogh, on the South with the Barony of Gowran, on the West with Barronyes of Cranagh and Galmoy and on the north west with the Barony of Ossory in the Queene's County aforesaid."

(Ms 720. N.L.I.).

(a) *Political Strife in Kilkenny*

The political affiliations of Fassadinin landowners during the Wars of the Confederacy determined ownership in the second half of the seventeenth century. Landowners from the barony were actively engaged in the war and this factor must be taken into account in any consideration of land use, settlement, ownership.and occupation. Apart from the prolonged siege of the city of Kilkenny by Cromwellian forces in 1650, there is no record of any major military confrontation in the vicinity of the barony. Involvement of landowners led to the neglect of land and buildings and the imposition of levies to support the war effort deprived the district of manpower and capital. In a society where military organisation was a mixture of Gaelic and feudal practices, the tenant was expected to follow his lord into battle.

Phillip Purcell of Ballyfoyle, Gowran barony and Robert Shee of Kilkenny city, both of whom owned lands in Fassadinin (fig. 3.1) sat in the General Assembly of Confederate Catholics held in Kilkenny city in 1644.[2] The Archers and Rothes, merchant landowners of Kilkenny and New Ross, were also actively involved. The O'Brenans, deprived of

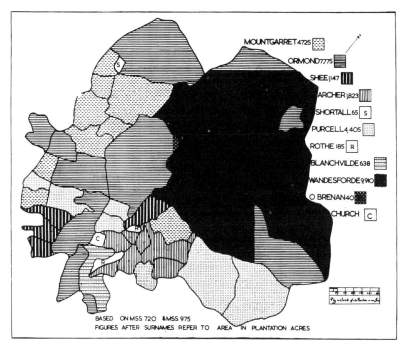

MOUNTGARRET 4725
ORMOND 7775
SHEE 1147
ARCHER 1823
SHORTALL 65 [S]
PURCELL 4,405
ROTHE 185 [R]
BLANCHVILDE 638
WANDESFORDE 9910
O BRENAN 40
CHURCH [C]

BASED ON MSS. 720 & MSS. 975
FIGURES AFTER SURNAMES REFER TO AREA IN PLANTATION ACRES

Fig. 3.1 Ownership of land. Fassadinin 1641.

their homeland in 1635, regained Castlecomer and expelled the 'New English' settlers. Edmund Butler, son of the fourth Viscount Mountgarret, Garret Blanchvilde, whose family held lands in south Fassadinin, and Captain Bryan, principal tenant of the Earl of Ormonde, took part in the attack on Kilkenny city in 1641. The Earl of Ormonde and Lord Mountgarret, who were the principal landowners in Fassadinin circa 1639, played a major role in the conflict. Ormonde, a Protestant Royalist, was Lord Lieutenant of Ireland from 1642-48 and Commander-in-Chief of the Confederate army defeated by Cromwell. Mountgarret, united through marriage with the O'Neills of Tyrone, was President of the Supreme Council of the Irish Confederation: on the defeat of the Royalist army, he followed his kinsman, Ormonde, into exile in France. The absence of exiled or executed landlords, the great uncertainty about the future, and the ravages of war disturbed the pattern of living and led to a marked deterioration in the quality of the landscape.

(b) *Land quality*

According to his instructions from the Surveyor General, Sir William Petty was "to describe the barony by its meets and bounds, by the soile, by the nature of the soile in general; rivers running, rising, meeting; by the several cities, towns and passes".[3] He was also to measure the height of "all notorious high hills and mountains" and to describe their "manner of rising". The Down Surveyors were mainly concerned with the location, ownership and valuation of forfeited lands. The terms of reference of the survey and the political pressures for its rapid conclusion precluded any detailed description of topography. "Fassadining", the compilers of the survey noted, "is very conveniently watered, the rivers of Dian and Dinine running through the middest thereof and joyneing together discharge themselves into the famous River Nore which passeth by the west side of the barony".[4] These three rivers are shown on the barony map but only the River Dinine which flows west from the hilly ground on the Kilkenny-Carlow border is named (fig. 1.5). Two prominent areas of high ground stand out on the map. A large area of upland is depicted in the denominations of 'Coolecullen' and 'Cloghranke' in the south east of the barony. The western edges of the Castlecomer plateau, which project as a prominent escarpment overlooking the Nore valley, were shown as "waste barren mountains" in the north east of the barony map.

The lands of Fassadinin were subject to the general division of profitable and non-profitable. Land was classified according to the categories arable, pasture, meadow, wood and waste mountain. Meadow, arable and pasture were defined as profitable and the natural waste of mountain was the only category of land regarded as unprofitable by the surveyors. Six different types of pasture were identified. Lands were described by the general term pasture or the more particular terms heathy, shrubby, moorish, furzy and mountain pasture. These distinctions were not applied consistently throughout Fassadinin and the surveyors seem to have regarded "heathy", "shrubby" and "moorish" as synonymous terms. The differentiation made between wood "fitt for timber" and "shrubby" wood was a response to the contemporary demand for timber and timber products. The Civil Survey shared this interest in timber and recorded the distance of "wood fitt for timber" from ports and navigable rivers.

Figure 3.2 shows the spatial distribution of profitable and unprofitable land in the part of the barony surveyed. Approximately ninety seven per cent (15,804) of the 16,309 plantation acres evaluated was returned as profitable. Arable accounted for more than sixty per cent (9,789) of the profitable land and was found in every denomination apart from 'Coolecullen' in the remote south east borderlands. The highest proportion of arable was recorded for the parish of Mayne, which adjoined the River Nore. Over ninety two per cent (1,595) of this division, which formed part of the Ormonde manor of Dunmore, was estimated as arable. Land suitable for tillage was particularly important along the western flank of the barony where colonisation had left its mark in the pattern of settlement and townland nomenclature. The carefully selected demesne lands of manors such as Connehy, Ballyragget and Kilmademoge, had a uniformly high proportion of arable. Local concentrations of upland were responsible for the deterioration of land quality in the comparatively large territorial divisions of Ballymartin, 'Cloghranke' and 'Coolecullen'. The belt of land

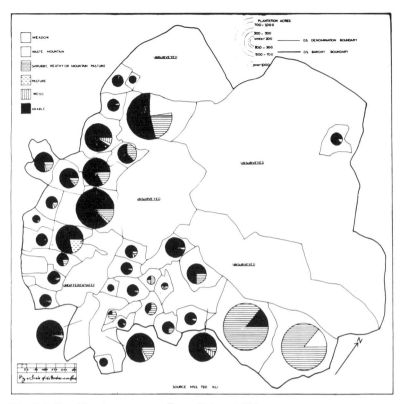

Fig. 3.2 Classification of land. Fassadinin c.1654.

at the eastern end of Mothell parish, which was divided into small denominations, was the only other area where arable was not conspicuous.
This high ground consisted of a southern projection of the coal bearing
rocks of the Castlecomer plateau; the participation of local landowners
such as David Roothe and Walter Archer FitzJohn in the Confederate wars
may also have had some bearing on the quality of land c. 1654. The widespread distribution of arable land was a reflection of the inherent fertility
of the soil rather than an accurate measure of cultivated land. Nevertheless, the impression derived from contemporary documentation is of a
society with an overwhelming pastoral character.

Pasture of some kind occupied approximately twenty-two per cent
(3,633 plantation acres) of surveyed land. In figure 3.2 grazing lands are
differentiated into the two categories of 'Pasture' and 'shrubby, heathy,
mountain and moorish pasture'. It is difficult to understand the reason for
the surveyors elaborate classification of pasture as they regarded all these
lands as profitable. The small amount of "pasture" (which presumably referred to grassland clear from any noxious vegetation) returned in the survey suggests that one is dealing with the marginal lands of the barony. The

61

distribution of the second category of pasture, which amounted to twenty-two per cent (3,460) of surveyed lands, was influenced by variations in topography. 'Pasturable mountain' was confined to the hilly country. In the townland of 'Cloghranke', for example, seventy-eight per cent (1,200) was described as 'mountain and heathy pasture'. "Moorish pasture" was not distributed widely but one location is significant enough to detail. Twenty per cent (90) of the denomination of Grange on the west bank of the Nore was classified as 'Moorish pasture'. Grange was in the possession of the Cistercian monks of Jerpoint up to the time of the Dissolution when it passed to the Earl of Ormonde. The neglect of monastic lands may well have been a widespread effect of Reformation policy in Ireland. Shrubby pasture was recorded in seventeen, and heathy pasture in six, of the twenty seven townlands assessed by the surveyors. Lands in these categories rarely exceeded 100 acres in extent and probably marked a temporary regression. This land type was found in small quantities in the west and central districts of the barony which were characterised by level, arable land. Less than one per cent (111 plantation acres) was described as meadow. Natural water meadow was found in very small quantities in fifteen denominations. The division of 'Cloghmoylehed', which was part of the Ormonde Idough lands, had the comparatively high proportion of nine per cent (20) of its area described as meadow.

It seems that the preservation of grass for winter feeding did not have any great significance in Fassadinin. This viewpoint is strengthened by the inclusion of the admonition, "to mow yearly all the meadow ground belonging to the said manor," in the terms of the Identure which granted the manor of Dunmore to Leonard Blanchfield in 1565.[5] Woodland amounted to approximately two per cent (477) of the Down Survey area. Only 37 acres of wood in Ballyragget townland was "woodd fitt for timber". It can be assumed that this plantation had been established by the Mountgarret family. The other area of 'shrubby woodd' occurred along the middle reaches of the eastern Dinin. The Down Surveyors found little unprofitable land in Fassadinin. The three per cent they did return was found in the hill summits of 'Coolecullen' and Ballymartin where the process of sub-aerial denudation had exposed the Namurian flagstones, shales and grits at the surface.

(c) *The Network of Settlement.*

"In every village is a castle, and a church, but both in ruyne. The baser cottages are built of underwood, called wattle and covered some with thatch and some with green sedge, of a round forme and without chimneys, and to my imaginacon resemble so many hives of bees about a country farme".

(Luke Gernon, A discourse of Ireland (1620), Quoted in C. L. Falkiners *Illustrations of Irish History and Topography* (1904) 355).

The Down Survey contained a selective inventory of settlement items found in each parish, with a brief description of their physical shape and condition. The survey was not a complete record of barony settlement. Additional buildings were depicted on the barony map, both in the unforfeited land areas and in districts that came within the terms of reference of the Survey. The surveyors were concerned mainly with the more durable items which housed the principal landowners.

The victors were primarily interested in regulating ownership and paid little attention to the lesser tenantry. The Books of Survey and Distribution incorporated the Civil Survey summaries of settlement for the three unforfeited parishes of Castlecomer, Dysart and Kilmacar. Ten settlement items were enumerated in the Survey. These included castles, bawns, churches, cornmills, tucking mills, houses with chimneys, stone houses, thatched houses and thatched cabins. Fifteen castle sites were recorded by the Down Survey. A comparison of figs. 3.2 and 3.3 reveals that castles were mainly found in the areas with a relatively high proportion of arable land. The physical shape of castles were described by the terms 'round', 'little' or 'stump'. The phrases, 'in repaire' or 'in little repaire' defined the structural condition of these items circa 1654. Surprisingly nine of the fifteen castles were in repair. These included Ballyragget (Mountgarret), Connahy (Ormonde), Foulksrath (Purcell), Tulleglass (Shee), Kilmademoge (Blanchvilde), Corbetstowne (Archer), Clintstowne (Mountgarret), Jenkinstowne (Ormonde) and Cloghranke (Purcell).

Castle stumps were recorded at Drumerhin (Purcell), Gallstowne (Archer), 'Cloghmoylehed' (Ormonde), Kilcollan (Purcell), Esker (Purcell), 'Clonsely and Clonfunction, (Ormonde). The existence of only part of the original edifice did not always lead to abandonment; in the Civil Survey of Co. Tipperary many such items continued to function as settlement centres. Desertion and consequent dereliction may have been due to a variety of factors. The Purcells of Drumerhin, for example, were in financial difficulties in the early half of the century and were mortgaging portions of their estates. Gallstowne held by the Archer family of New Ross was one such property. The Archers were absentees and probably allowed the castle to decay but they did retain the mill which in the Down Survey was 'in repaire'. 'Cloghmoylehed' and 'Clonsely and Clonfunction' were Ormonde properties located in former Gaelic lands. The Down Survey map and parish memoirs show that Kilcollan and Esker were adjoining denominations in central Fassadinin and were held by the Purcells. Figure 3.3 indicates that no other settlement was recorded for Kilcollan circa 1654, but a 'house' was listed in Esker. This may suggest that the family had erected the more conventional English type dwelling which was soon to replace the damp, uncomfortable castles.

The castles of Clinstowne (Mountgarret), Tulleglass (Shee) and Kilmademoge (Blanchvilde) were described as 'little'. It was also noted that Kilmademoge was a 'round' castle. Two castles from this period have survived relatively intact. These are at Ballyragget the centre of the extensive Mountgarret property, and Foulksrath (Plate III), the residence of the Purcell family who farmed over 500 acres in the fertile land between the

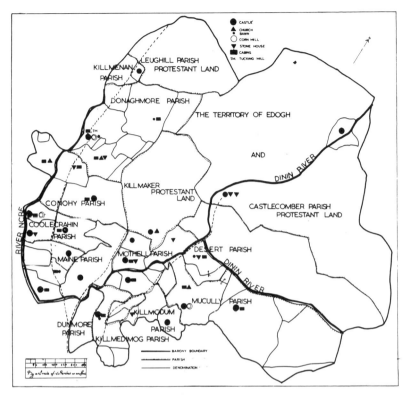

Fig. 3.3 Network of Settlement. Fassadinin c.1654.

Nore and Dinin in south Fassadinin. Both buildings had a roughly similar rectangular shape and tall angular appearance. Ballyragget Castle was surrounded by a much more extensive wall system which included circular turrets at wall junctions. The greater proportion of castles in the barony were probably similar in shape to that of Foulksrath. These tall buildings, comprised of dark grey limestone and roofed with oaken timber and slates, were conspicuous features in the open landscape of south and west Fassadinin.

Figure 1.5, which is a transcript of the Down Survey barony map, depicts three castles, at Kilmacar (Ormonde), Castlecomer (Wandesforde), and Nicholastown (Shortall), in addition to those recorded in the memoirs. In general, castles were found at regular intervals of about two miles in the west and south of the barony and closer than this in the better endowed south west (fig. 3.3). Another element of standardisation which in medieval times had a wider distribution was the church. In the parish accounts, the three churches of Donaghmore, Grange and Mucully were listed. All were described as 'old' and 'in little repair', which adequately symbolised the spiritual and material state of the Catholic Church in this period. The writer

64

of the parish memoirs omitted mention of the churches of Mothell, Mayne, Coolcraheen and Rosconnell which were depicted on the barony map (fig. 1.5). Churches and castles occupied contiguous sites in Kilmacar and Coolcraheen (fig. 3.3). They were invariably found in the same townland though not always adjacent to each other.

The existence of bawns and corn mills suggests the dual nature of the agricultural economy. *Bawns* (cow forts) were enclosures into which cattle were driven for protection at night and during periods of bad weather. The Down Survey listed six bawns in Fassadinin. They were found in association with castles at Ballyragget, Kilmademoge and Castlecomer and in conjunction with substantial houses at Suttonsrath, Ballymartin and Damerstowne. Although they naturally varied in size, the bawns had a similar structure. They are depicted in the barony and parish maps as four sided, double enclosures. The castle or other building formed the central portion of the south-facing inner wall and the vaulted castle archway was the entrance. This inner area may have functioned as a cattle enclosure and the space between the inner and outer walls may have been occupied by the habitations of the lesser tenantry. Fig. 3.3 indicates that bawns were not limited to any barony area, and their wide distribution suggests the overall dominance of cattle. Five mills were located in conjunction with castles at riverine sites in the townlands of Ballyragget, Lismayne, Gallstowne and Castlecomer. The first two of these townlands occupy areas which adjoin the river Nore. The mill at Gallstowne was located on the Douglas River, an east bank tributary of the Dinin. The Dinin provided the water force for the Castlecomer mill.

The surveyors distinguished between 'thatched' houses and 'stone' houses with chimneys, although no such differentiation was made on the barony map (fig. 1.5).). This latter class of dwellings, second in respect of size to the castles, were probably the houses of principal tenants, manor officials or clergymen. Thatched houses were returned in Ballyragget, Donaghmore, Lisnefunshin, Oldtown, Damerstowne and 'John Rothestowne.' Apart from Ballyragget these buildings were not found in association with castles. In Donaghmore, for example, the thatched house was located contiguous to the old church. In Damerstowne it was probably the building around which the bawn was erected. The placenames of these territorial divisions suggest that thatched houses were strongly associated with Anglo-Norman districts. On the other hand, stone houses were probably of more recent provenance. The term may have referred to houses with stone walls or alternatively, houses roofed with slates. In Lismayne, Clintstowne and Esker, such houses were found in conjunction with castles. The remaining stone houses were located in townlands close to Castlecomer. One of them at 'Coolbane and Drumgoyle' was described in the Civil Survey as "a little stone house with iron myne and coal" and may well have been the furnace referred to in Wandesforde indentures circa 1637.

The cabin was the most numerous settlement item found in Fassadinin circa 1654. Collections of cabins were recorded in conjunction with the

65

more substantial edifices such as castles, churches, thatched or stone houses and bawns. They were not found in isolation. These cabins were the dwelling places of the dependent tenantry. Petty estimated that Ireland had 16,000 of these "narrow, nasty cabbins in which 6 out of 8 of all the Irish live in a brutish, nasty manner with neither chimney door, stairs nor windows".[6]

The territory of Idough to the north east of the barony was unforfeited Protestant land, and as such did not come within the scope of the Survey. Settlement depicted here on the barony map included a bawne and mill at Castlecomer and two 'stone' houses at 'Coolebane' and 'Smythstowne'.

The quest for Idough continued throughout the period of the Confederate wars. Sir Christopher Wandesforde, who purchased Idough from its nominal proprietors in 1636, was elected Lord Deputy of Ireland in 1640 and died in December of the same year.[7] Idough was granted to his brother, William Wandesforde, merchant of the City of London, for a term of twenty one years. In 1653-54 this William petitioned the Commissioners of the Commonwealth for affairs in Ireland to resettle him in possession. The petitioner stated that in 1641 he possessed, "the coalpits, woods, ironworks" and "a very fair estate" in Idough. This was taken from him by the rebels and he was forced to "fly for safety". However, through God's blessing the "same is now reduced" and an English garrison planted there. Most of the lands were "lying wast and inhabited by strangers and Irish not paying any rent". Wandesforde promised that he would endeavour to "plant the same again with English inhabitants as formerly, whereby the public benefit may be furthered." Another witness before the Commission testified that the late Lord Deputy "hath laid out 14 thousand in buildings of a market towne with houses of lyme and stone and other houses, severall iron works, impounding a great deerpark and many other improvements". The petition succeeded. William Wandesforde was confirmed in possession of, among other things, a "corne and water milne, iron furnace near the said town."[8] The grants of "courts baron and leet," a weekly market and three fairs during the year, were reaffirmed. It is difficult however, to reconcile this manuscript evidence which may well have been contrived to impress the Commissioners and the testimony of the Civil Survey which records only rudimentary settlement at Castlecomer.

(d) *Ownership in 1641*

"Edm Brenan McDonagh
Jn. Brenan McGillpatrick
Owen and Jas Brenan McDaniell
      Irish papists"

Skehanaduffe $\frac{1}{3}$ pt.
of a horseman's bed   040 acre

(Ms 975 Books of Survey and distribution).

To facilitate distribution it was imperative to the Cromwellian administration that the lands of forfeiting proprietors should be identified and this objective was achieved by the Down Survey. By combining the evidence of the Down Survey and the Books of Survey and Distribution, it is possible to obtain a comprehensive picture of landownership in the barony in 1641. Because the Down and subsequent Surveys provided acreage equivalents for hitherto vaguely defined territorial divisions the amount of land held by individuals and ethnic groupings in the barony can be estimated. The Books of Survey and Distribution returned 30,551 acres for the barony. Landowners described as Protestants held fifty seven per cent (17,685) of the barony area and the remainder was held by 'Irish papists'. If one differentiates between the proprietors in terms of their origins, as these are suggested by the family names, one finds that the Anglo Normans had sixty-four per cent (19,454) the 'New English' thirty-two per cent (9,910) and the Irish four per cent (1,187). The O'Brenans possessed one third of the barony area in 1589. By 1641 their share had declined to 40 acres. This shows that policies of selective state confiscation and plantation through purchase were effective instruments of change.

'English Protestant' lands in the barony included the estates of the Earl of Ormonde and that of Sir Christopher Wandesforde. Figure 3.1 indicates that the Wandesforde lands occupied a compact block in the north east, whereas the Ormonde property was greatly fragmented. Portion of the Butler estate was scattered throughout the Gaelic lands of Idough in the extreme north-west and occupied a large central tract stretching from Kilmacar south to Dunmore. These lands constituted the hereditary estate of Ormonde in Fassadinin augmented since 1600 through the policy of commercial plantation. The Wandesforde connection originated in land trafficking by members of the Wentworth administration. Wandesforde's purchase may have been made in good faith, but the earlier transactions concerning Idough were highly illegal, abrogating the very laws that the State was attempting to establish.[9]

The Anglo-Norman family of the Mountgarret Butlers held 4,725 acres in the barony and were the primary Catholic landowners. Their estate was similar to the manor of Donaghmore and the other fragments held by the family circa 1639 (fig. 2.4). A comparison of figs. 2.4 and 3.1 shows that they had lost the western sector of Idough to Wandesforde. Ballyragget was a major defensive stronghold and had an impressive array of settlement items (fig. 3.3). Clinstowne on the Nore was the only other Mountgarret possession which had a castle. The denominations of Ballymartin, Donaghmore and Damerstowne had cabin settlements in conjunction with more substantial edifices. Figure 3.2 shows that the quality of Mountgarret land deteriorated towards the Castlecomer hills.

The Purcells held 4,405 acres in four separate farms. The Down Survey reveals little about them that is not known already. The largest Purcell holding consisted of the hill-lands in the south east. A comparison of figs. 2.4 and 3.1 indicates that this estate comprised all of Drumerhin and portion of Ballyfoyle manors. The Down Survey recorded a 'stump' of a castle in Drumerhin. Figure 3.2 demonstrates that this property consisted of comparatively large territorial divisions which had a high proportion of rough grazing and unprofitable land. Consequently it was a remote, empty district. The Purcell farms of Foulksrath (554) held by Phillip, and Kilcollan and Esker (503) owned by Edmund, were roughly similar in area. Both were inhabited. The Survey listed a castle and a collection of cabins at Foulksrath. Esker's settlement consisted of a 'stump of a castle' and a 'stone' house and cabins. The smallest Purcell holding contained 186 acres in the land division of Lismaine on the banks of the Nore. The number of settlement items recorded here suggest that it may well have been the most prosperous. Lismaine possessed a castle, mill and a "house with a chimney, in repaire". The absence of cabins indicate that this may have been a 'family' estate operated without dependent tenants. Figure 3.2 shows that the Purcell lands west of the Dinin had a relatively high proportion of arable.

The Archer-owned estates contained 1,823 acres and coincided with the manors of Mothell and Muckalee (fig. 3.1). The Down Survey differentiated between Henry Archer who held 1,359 acres and Walter Archer Fitz-John who occupied 464 acres in Mothell parish. Walter Archer Fitz John was a resident landowner whereas Henry Archer's involvement in the barony was speculative. The Blanchvilde lands of Kilmademoge were exactly similar in area to the manor held by the same family circa 1600 (fig. 3.1). The families of Rothe and Shortall completed the list of Anglo-Norman landholders in 1641. Figure 3.1 shows that David Rothe's holding consisted off two fragments in the south of the barony. The fact that one of these holdings was named 'John Rothestowne' intimates that their estate here may have been more extensive in earlier times. The Rothe family were prominent merchants in Kilkenny city and held extensive lands in the country.[10] One of their members was Catholic Bishop of the city during the Confederate Wars. The Shortall farm was at Nicholastown in the north west. The family held no other lands in Fassadinin and were primarily associated with Clomantagh, Crannagh barony to the west of the Nore.[11] The Down Survey barony map depicted a castle here (fig. 1.5), but this was not listed in the parish memoirs. The Shees (O'Sheas) originated in the Barony of Iveragh,[12] Co. Kerry and acquired considerable status and property as legal advisers to the Ormondes. Two Shee proprietors held 1,147 acres in the south west of the barony, adjoining the River Nore (fig. 3.1). It can be inferred from the evidence that one of these Shees was an absentee. Robert Shee, owner of the two adjoining dominations of Suttonsrath and 'Ardloe' containing 863 acres, may have been non-resident. No substantial settlement items were recorded here by the Down Survey. This Robert was also a member of the provisional Parliament held in the city of Kilkenny in 1644. On the other hand, in Tulleglass, the holding of Peter Shee, a 'little castle in repair' was listed in the Survey. The absence of cabins may imply that this estate was farmed by the family.

(e) *Summary of the Down Survey*

The Down Survey was concerned with the proprietorial geography of a society in which old and more recent intruders interacted with the descendants of the early indigenous inhabitants. The identification and mapping of the forfeited lands was its major achievement but it also is informative about the quality of land and the network of settlement. It is an extremely significant document because it outlines aspects of the geography of the barony at a time when medieval society was being reshaped by a dynamic and powerful group of new intruders.

Arable, according to the survey, was the most important and widely distributed category of land and only three per cent (501) of the forfeited area of the barony was classified as 'unprofitable'. The historic march-lands were now the comparatively infertile townlands along the eastern periphery of the barony. Along the river basins small territorial divisions are found and a comparatively close network of settlement. Settlement in south and west Fassadinin was associated with two separate Anglo-Norman incursions and the erection of monastic and episcopal churches in the early medieval period. The absence of wood gave the countryside the appearance of champion land and castles and ruined churches were the most conspicuous and outstanding items in the landscape. This countryside was not completely open and small well defined patches of arable and settlement were enclosed either by stone walls or earthen dykes "sett with quicksetts". Castles served both military and domestic functions and attracted the more ephemeral settlements of dependent tenants and manor servants. The distribution of corn mills reflects the importance of cereals in the Anglo-Norman economy but the rearing of livestock was the most important agricultural activity.

The foundations of town life in the barony were established in this period. The two riverside settlements of Ballyragget in the west and Castle-comer in the north-east were outstripping other centres in terms of size and function. Both Castlecomer and Ballyragget had elementary trading functions which had been extended by grants of weekly markets and annual fairs in the early seventeenth century. Both had administrative and domestic functions, associated with their rank as centres of relatively large manorial estates. The families of Wandesforde and Mountgarret who owned these settlements attained high political and social status. Smaller settlements in the south and south-west were associated with landowners of lesser political and social status and with manors of smaller size. The failure of the Ormonde manorial centres such as Kilmacar and Dunmore to develop as major settlements may be related to the fact that they were not the administrative or functioning centres of manors. The affairs of these estates were directed by the Ormonde bureaucracy resident in the city of Kilkenny, from which neither was more than 8 miles distant. The number of settlements was invariably related to the density and distribution of population. There is no reliable estimate of barony population at this time. The census of Ireland compiled in 1659 recorded an enumerated population of 1,741 in the barony and a general picture emerges of a thinly populated district with empty hill areas in the north and south east.

3. Redistribution

(a) *The Cromwellian land settlement.*
The ownership of land in the second half of the seventeenth century was often temporary and always uncertain. It was directly linked to political and religious loyalties. In the early part of the century, a confiscation policy had been formulated by the State and carried out by entrepreneurs and State officials such as Wandesforde. The policy of commercial plantation had been practised with some success by regional magnates such as the Earl of Ormonde. By 1641, over half the land of Fassadinin was held by these two Protestant families. Change in ownership was not only a feature of the later part of the century: confiscation was implemented on a sectarian basis c. 1654 and the State superceded all other agencies of plantation.

The Cromwellians divided the inhabitants of Ireland into 'Irish Papists' and 'English Protestants' and in the sectarian climate of the period, religious denominations were much more libels than labels. The bitter nature of the sectarian conflict and the excessive cruelty displayed by both sides made the thoroughness of the resultant forfeitures inevitable. The amount of land lost by individual Catholics was related to the degree of their involvement in the Confederate Wars. The four classes of 'Papists' who were to be deprived of part or all of their estates were summarised by Lodge as follows: (a) If those who had been involved in the rebellion, together with Jesuits and other priests, did not comply with the ultimatum to surrender arms, they were to be excepted from pardon of life or estate; (b) Those who had borne command were to be banished, and forfeited $2/3$ of their estates, the other $1/3$ to be assigned wheresoever the Parliament would decree; (c) Papist residents between 1641 and 1650 who had not manifested constant good affection to the parliamentarian interest were to forfeit $1/3$ of the lands and to be assigned lands to the value of the other $2/3$ where the parliament would appoint; (d) All papists who did not manifest constant good affection were to forfeit $1/5$ of the estates.[1]

There are a number of estimates of the extent of change in ownership in the seventeenth century. According to J. C. Beckett, the Recusants (i.e. Catholic interests) had about three fifths of the land in Ireland in 1641 and after the Act of Explanation, held only a little more than one fifth.[14] Sir William Petty estimated the population at 1,100,000 in 1672.[15] This figure included 300,000 English and Scotch and some 800,000 Irish. He further calculated that the British Protestants and Church had, "$3/4$ of

70

the land, $^5/_8$ of the housing, $^9/_{10}$ of all the housing in walled towns and places of strength and $^2/_3$ of the foreign trade." J. G. Simms in his study on the latter half of the seventeenth century found that in 1688, Protestant landowners held almost all of Ulster, $^4/_5$ of Leinster, all of Munster excluding Co. Clare, the whole of Co. Leitrim and the greater area of Sligo in Connaught. Catholics had retained ownership of the major portion of Connaught west of the Shannon and throughout the country a few individual Catholic landowners such as Lords Galmoy and Mountgarret had managed to keep their estates intact.[16] The Williamite Confiscations reduced the amount of land owned by Catholics by a further million acres, so that by 1700 Catholics held approximately one seventh of the country's land.[17]

A comparison of fig. 3.1 with fig. 3.4 gives the impression that the pattern of ownership in Fassadinin had remained relatively stable in the period from 1640 to 1670. Ormonde, Mountgarret and Wandesforde, whose combined estates amounted to two-thirds of the barony area were

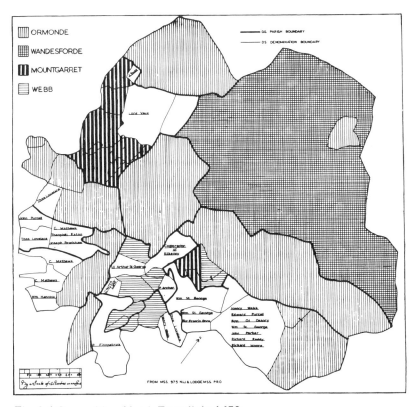

Fig. 3.4 Ownership of land. Fassadinin 1670.

still in possession in 1670, and Ormonde's property had been augmented by the addition of portion of the forfeited Purcell lands. The map shows that it was the Catholic proprietors of relatively small estates in the south and south-west of the barony who lost most. The 1641 proprietors may be classified according to those who were temporarily, and those who were permanently deprived of their estates. A further distinction may be made between proprietors who lost portion, and those who lost all of their estates. Defeat of the Confederacy forces led to the dispossession and expulsion of the Earl of Ormonde and Lord Mountgarret. The Down Surveyors were apparently unsure as to the status of Ormonde. Figure 3.3 shows that his lands in Loughill and Kilmacar parishes were listed as un-forfeited Protestant lands and consequently were unsurveyed. On the other hand, Ormonde property in the south and west of the barony was fully surveyed and returned as forfeited. The surveyor of Mayne parish listed Ormonde as an 'Irish papist.'[18] In 1660 at the Restoration, Ormonde was confirmed in possession of all "lands, honours and rights" which he held in 1641.[19]

Mountgarret was another landowner who was temporarily deprived of his property. At the termination of the war the lands of the exiled Mountgarret passed to the Cromwellian governor of Kilkenny, Daniel Axtell. The subsequent course of events portrays the complexity and instability of political structures in late seventeenth century Ireland. In 1666 Axtell was executed for his part in the death of Charles II and the Mountgarret estate were restored to Edmond Butler. In the same year Mountgarret was confirmed in possession and the denominations he held were enrolled in the Records of the Rolls under the Restoration Act of Settlement.[20] Mountgarret lands in 1670 were not exactly similar to his estates in 1641 (fig. 3.4). He had been deprived of the denominations of Bally-martin, part of Damerstowne, Knockroe and Clintstowne, which amounted to thirty-seven per cent (1,740) of his earlier estate. The map also shows that apart from Ballymartin, these townlands were detached from the manor of Ballyragget.

In 1689 the Catholic Mountgarrets went to war for the second time within fifty years. This time they fought on the side of the 'Jacobites', were defeated, and had their estates confiscated. However, through the influence of Ormonde, now Lord Lieutenant of Ireland, the Mountgarret Butlers retrieved their Fassadinin property. The rebellion of 1641 resulted in the destruction of the infant colony of Castlecomer and the dispossession of the Wandesfordes for a period of twelve years. The Wandesforde title to Castlecomer was reaffirmed by the Commonwealth Commissioner in 1653. In the course of his petition for re-entry to the lands, William Wandes-forde claimed that he "hath lost two sons in the service of the Common-wealth."[21]

The durability of the Wandesforde, Ormonde and Mountgarret connec-tions and their tenacity in retaining a foothold in a period of great uncert-ainty and change was the major feature of ownership in Fassadinin in the seventeenth century. Elsewhere in the country the impact of two wars resulted in the transformation of the proprietorial class. The Catholic proprietors of smaller estates in the south of the barony were not as fortunate. The families of Shortall, Rothe, Shee, Blanchvilde, Purcells of Esker, Purcells of Foulksrath and Walter Archer FitzJohn of Corbetstown were permanently dispossessed of land they held in 1641 (fig. 3.4). Under the provisions of the Restoration Act of Settlement, Edmond Purcell was granted 496 acres in 'Cloghranke'.[22] This amounted to twenty per cent of the lands held by his kinsman, Phillip Purcell in south-east Fassadinin in 1641. The Archer family, who held 1,359 acres in the south of the barony, were regranted ten per cent of their original estate in 1666.[23] Exclusion from the homeland either by banishment overseas or transplantation to Connaught was a corollary of forfeiture. The principal landowners such as Ormonde and Mountgarret suffered temporary exile only. One is less certain about the impact of transplantation policy on the lesser landowners.

R. C. Simington has published the results of extensive research on the transplantation to Connaught and has produced a list of the freeholders who were allocated lands in that province.[24] The names of some Fassadinin landowners are included among the 1,900 principal landowners transplanted. It is not possible, for a variety of reasons, to be certain of the number of Fassadinin owners removed to Connaught. In the lists from which Simington compiled his account, the barony of origin is not always given. This makes the identification of landowners difficult, particularly when the christian name of the transplanter is not the same as that of proprietors listed in the Down Survey. It is also true that some of the landowners who lost possession were resident outside the barony and their Fassadinin lands formed only part of more extensive estates. One finds the names of John Purcell of Lismaine, Elizabeth Purcell of Esker and Thomas Purcell of Foulksrath among the list of those transplanted. John Purcell received 124 acres in the barony of Longford and 120 in the barony of Costelloe, Co. Galway. Elizabeth Purcell was allowed "by order land worth £200 per annum in 1644 in lieu of Jointure". Her new holding, located in the barony of Longford, consisted of 2,000 acres. Robert Shee, who may have been the individual returned as proprietor of Ardloe and Suttonsrath in 1641, was allocated 500 acres in the barony of Bunratty, Co. Clare. Thomas Shortall, whose 65 acres in Nicholastowne was but part of his more extensive estate in the adjoining barony of Galmoy, received 469 acres in the barony of Tirawley, Co. Mayo and 500 in the barony of Clonderlau, Co. Clare. It may be assumed that the Richard Blanchfield who got 300 acres in the barony of Dunkellin, Co. Galway was the successor of Garret Blanchfield who held 638 acres in Kilmademoge in 1641.

Minor Catholic landowners who escaped forfeiture under Cromwell were dispossessed by the Williamite confiscations. Among the thirty five attainted were twenty O'Brenans, four of the Butler family of Ballyragget, three Purcells, four Pays, and Archer of Kilmademoge, Bryan of Jenkinstowne, Dormer of Ballymartin and Lawler of Smithstown.[25]

The families of Bryan and Pay were, according to the Ormonde Mss evidence, principal tenants of the Duke's estates in Fassadinin.[26] Within the space of fifty years, the Purcells of Lismaine had been attainted and deprived of their lands by the Commonwealth: restored by Charles II and finally attainted and dispossessed by the administration of William III.

The Cromwellian confiscation practically obliterated the Catholic landowning class, both Gaelic and Anglo-Norman. Some of these, such as, for example, Robert Shee, David Rothe and Henry Archer were absentees and representative of the commercial and legal class who had speculated in property. Ardaloo in the extreme south west part of the estate of Robert Shee was held by the Augustinian Priory of Kells prior to the Dissolution of the monastic orders. The Archers of Corbetstown, the various Purcell families and Blanchvilde of Kilmademoge must have felt a greater sense of loss in being deprived of the estates on which they resided. In many instances, these lands had been in the possession of these families over a long period, a factor which would have established a special bond between them and the barony. Forfeiture in Fassadinin may not have resulted in a major social upheaval insofar as many of the proprietors were absentees and mere figureheads. It is possible that Ormonde was never in the barony. It is known that Mountgarret lived at Ballyroe in Crannagh barony. The first Wandesforde may have occasionally visited his newly acquired estate, but he was never a resident. Therefore, if Phillip Purcell of Ballyfoyle, Gowran Barony is listed as an absentee, only eleven per cent (3,458) of the land of Fassadinin was held by resident landlords in 1641. Confiscation in the Williamite era affected many who seem to have been principal tenants. Names such as, for example, Bryan, Lawlor, Dormer and Pay did not feature in previous inventories of property owners. There is no indication how the forfeitures affected the lesser tenantry who remained largely anonymous throughout the seventeenth century. The next section of this chapter examines the spatial organisation of ownership arising from confiscation policy.

(b) *The Restoration land settlement*

The immediate task of the Commonwealth Government was to allocate eleven million acres of Irish land to 35,000 soldiers and 1,500 adventurers. It was the only feasible way of paying the soldiers and adventurers who had respectively fought and financed the Irish wars. By 1670 only 8,000 soldiers and adventurers combined had their estates confirmed by Charles II.[27] This establishes the slow and tedious nature of the redistribution. The implementation of plantation policy was hampered not only by delays in surveying the forfeited lands, but also through the reluctance of soldiers and adventurers to settle in a hostile and foreign country. The names of beneficiaries under the Cromwellian and Restoration land settlements are listed in the Books of Survey and Distribution and in the Records of the Rolls.[28] Both lists of names are roughly similar, although in some instances grantees listed in the Books of Survey and Distribution were deceased by the time the Restoration land settlement had been completed. The fact that the grantee's names and the land denominations they received were recorded is no indication that they resided in Fassadinin. In some cases lands in Fassadinin were only fragments of much more extensive estates held elsewhere. The identification of the beneficiaries of confiscation and the extent of their property in the barony should help in any assessment of the impact of plantation policy.

One should expect to find the initiation of the estate system of landownership and the social, political and economic dominance of landlords in this period. There was no large scale transformation of the proprietorial class in Fassadinin. The slight evidence that exists suggests that many of the beneficiaries of plantation never entered into possession. These absentees had no social function and only operated in an economic sense as rent receivers. In many instances, the evidence of their involvement has been obliterated by subsequent transactions concerning land. There are various ways whereby the grantee's association with the barony can be discovered. A number of them remained as landowners in Fassadinin down to the time when Griffith's Valuation, the great inventory of ownership in the mid-nineteenth century, was compiled. Descendants of other original grantees participated in the land transfers of the early part of this century and the legal evidence of their association with the barony was recorded by the Irish Land Commission. Some of the new proprietors such as, for example, the Webbs built great houses which became the functional centres of estates. They also renamed and reorganised territorial divisions. The relationship of several of the new landowners with the barony has been preserved orally. Other land owners listed in the Books of Survey and Distribution had only a temporary connection with the barony. These have left little or no trace on the cultural or physical landscape and are as anonymous and silent as the lesser tenantry of the seventeenth century.

Figure 3.4 demonstrates that the landholding units delineated by the Down Survey were the divisions on which the allocation of forfeited lands was based. New estates consisted of individual townlands or collections of townlands which were not necessarily contiguous. Figure 3.4 shows that in many instances these units were deliberately fragmented. This fragmentation resulted in the creation of new territorial divisions. 'Cloghranke', the forfeited holding of Phillip Purcell in south-east Fassadinin, was redistributed in seven divisions to seven different grantees under the Restoration Act of Settlement. Figure 1.6 shows that in 1840 the Down Survey denomination of 'Cloghranke' consisted of six townlands. The surviving inventories of grantees indicates that six of the new proprietors held military rank in the Cromwellian army. These included Captain Henry Webb, Captain William St. George, Colonel Daniel Redman, Lieutenant Christopher Mathews, Lieutenant Arthur St. George and Sir Francis Gore, Knight.[29]

Daniel Axtell, temporary proprietor of the Ballyragget estate of Mountgarret, was a Lieutenant Colonel in the army and Cromwellian Governor of the county of Kilkenny.[30] The remaining beneficiaries of the Act of Settlement may have been non commissioned army men or speculators who purchased land debentures from soldiers unwilling to settle in Ireland.

A striking feature of the spatial organisation of new estates in Fassadinin was their comparatively small size (fig. 3.4). The estates of Henry Webb and Captain William St. George were the only two in excess of 1,000 plantation acres. This suggests that Fassadinin lands were only fragments of much larger estates held elsewhere in county Kilkenny or in other parts of the country. It seems that the infertile, forfeited lands in the south east and north west of the barony were 'thrown in' with more profitable lands elsewhere to make up acreage deficiencies. This ensured that these lands were never to become the residential or functional centres of estates.

The genesis of the Webb association with the barony was embodied in two separate land grants, which were confirmed and enrolled in 1667 and 1668. The earlier grant conveyed to Henry Webb the townlands of "Drumerhin part, Kilmadum, John Rothestowne, Lisclivane, Corbettstowne, Ballynranke, Mucully next to Ballynranke, Damerstowne and Kilcollan."[31] In 1668 the same individual was confirmed in possession of 'part of Cloghranke' townland.[32] In 1641 these land divisions were portions of six different estates. This suggests that, apart from large compact properties, little attention was paid by the distributors to the existing estate framework.

In the Fassadinin 'census', no reference is found to the Webb family.[33] This suggests that the Webbs had not settled in the barony by 1659. In 1678 Henry Webb was High Sheriff of Co. Kilkenny and was returned as resident at Webbsborough, formerly called 'Ballynranke'.[34] Arthur Webb was among the Fassadinin Williamites attainted by the 'Patriot Parliament' of James II.[35] He was however restored to his Kilkenny estates by William III and the family were to continue to occupy lands in south Fassadinin until the beginning of this century. The connection of the St. Georges with the barony was tenuous. Two individuals with this surname were listed as beneficiaries of the Restoration Act of Settlement. Lieutenant Arthur St. George received the denomination of Esker (259), part of the forfeited property of Edmond Purcell (fig. 3.4). The other St. George was granted a total of 1,041 plantation acres in the eastern sector of Muckalee parish. There is no indication in the 'Census' of 1659 or in the list of Fassadinin 'Williamites' in 1689 that either of the St. Georges lived in the barony. A property transaction dated 1691 concerning the lands of Gallstown in south Fassadinin suggests that small isolated holdings were absorbed by the larger adjoining estates. The Deed transferred the property of Lieutenant Colonel Francis Gore of Artarman, Co. Sligo to George St. George of Athlone.[36] The deed stated that these lands "by reason of the distraction of the late times were now wholly untenanted and waste and yielded little or no manner of profits."

There is great difficulty in determining the connection which the majority of the grantees had with the barony. The list of 'Williamites' which should have contained the names of all Protestant landowners, records only six proprietors in Fassadinin.[37] Three of these were the Duke of Ormonde, Sir Christopher Wandesforde and Arthur Webb. The list also contained the names of Joseph Bradshaw of Foulksrath, Thomas Cuffe of Smithstown and William Smith of Foulksrath. Bradshaw was a beneficiary under the Restoration Acts of Settlement and was granted 181 acres in Foulksrath.[38] Neither Cuffe nor Smith were listed in any of the inventories of ownership in this period. Carrigan, writing in 1905, recorded that a monument in Donaghmore Church commemorated the burial there of Joseph Bradshaw.[39] The inscription on the tombstone read: "here lieth the body of Joseph Bradshaw late of Foulksrath, gentleman. Borne neare Northwitch in Chesire, deceased the 23rd of March 1693." There is no evidence to suggest that either Christopher Mathews, who received an estate of 516 acres in the adjoining townlands of Foulksrath, Tullewglass, and Suttonsrath, or Thomas Lovelace, whose grant included three detached portions, (fig. 3.4), ever took up residence in Fassadinin. Neither did Colonel Daniel Redman who was allocated 830 plantation acres of hill land in west Idough.[40] On December 10th 1668, he had a confirmation under the Act of Settlement of 14,900 acres situated in Meath, Laois, Offaly, Kilkenny, Wexford and the liberties of Kilkenny.[41] By 1670 his lands in west Idough had been conveyed to Sir Christopher Wandesforde (fig. 3.4).

(c) *New Beginnings*

By the end of the seventeenth century the ownership of land in Fassadinin was vested in a powerful, absentee minority. The concentration of property, privilege and power into the hands of a close-knit group, who were protected by partisan legislation, was a dominant feature of Irish life in the following two centuries. Cromwellian and subsequent confiscations were not spontaneously conceived policies but the culmination of half a century of theorising on the Irish problem. In the context of Fassadinin, plantation was merely the continuation of a policy which by 1641 had drastically changed the pattern of ownership in the barony. The impression derived from a consideration of the documentary and cartographic evidence is that distribution in Fassadinin was carried out in a haphazard way.

New estates were rarely big enough to sustain the kind of enterprise which would support an individual landlord establishment. The smallest estates were found in the area of poorest land quality in the south east of the barony. Lands granted in the barony were often but part of estates located as far distant as Westmeath in the midlands and Sligo in the north-west of Ireland. The reorganisation of ownership, particularly in the south and south west of the barony, did however lead to the creation of new territorial divisions. It is difficult to indicate the extent to which the changes in ownership were responsible for this, as the Down Survey parish maps did not delineate all the territorial subdivisions. The later half of the seventeenth century was the period when title to land in Ireland was confirmed. The possession of property based mainly on confiscation was always to remain uncertain, even in periods of calm and quiet.

In 1641 the Anglo-Normans held sixty-four per cent (19,454), the 'New English' thirty-two per cent, (9,910); and the Irish four per cent (1,187) of the land of Fassadinin. In 1670 the 'New English' had fifty-seven per cent (17,387); the Anglo-Normans forty-one per cent (12,566), and the Irish two per cent (638). Protestant landowners in 1670 held ninety per cent of the barony area and the remaining ten per cent (2,928 plantation acres) was owned by the primary Catholic proprietor, Lord Mountgarret. Historians have estimated that the Catholics of Ireland held approximately one seventh of the land of the nation in 1700. The proportion held by Catholics in Fassadinin was above this national estimate.

The new proprietorial class was either directly or indirectly to control and regulate the ownership and management of land in Fassadinin for the following two centuries. In the context of the barony, stabilisation of the ownership class rather than its transformation was the primary feature of the late seventeenth century. The retention of ownership by specific families did not entail continuity in estate management. In this period, one can begin to talk of the estate rather than of the manorial system. This symbolises the break from the late medieval to the early modern historical period and was associated with the reorganisation of ownership. It is difficult to determine the immediate social consequences of confiscation and distribution. Little is known about the relationship which existed between 1641 proprietors and the lesser tenantry. Many of the old and the great majority of the new grantees were absentees. The First and Second Dukes of Ormonde were Lord Lieutenants in the administrations of Charles II and William III, respectively. The Wandesfordes did not establish their principal residence at Castlecomer until c. 1694.[42]

The Cromwellian grantees were not strong enough numerically to create a self sufficient economic or religious community. The 'Census' of 1659 returned an enumerated population of 1,741 in the barony, of whom 688 were Irish and 53 English. Of the twelve 'tituladoes' listed, only five were English. John Todd was the only one of these whose name appeared in the Books of Survey and Distribution. Ballyragget had the largest English population in the barony. The English population there in 1659 was obviously associated with the fact that Daniel Axtell, the Cromwellian Governor of Kilkenny, had received a grant of the Mountgarret property. Of the twelve 'tituladoes' listed in the barony, six resided in Ballyragget. Three of these, Nathaniel Williams, Walter Thoss and Richard Makins were described as English gentlemen. Burtchaell stated that Williams was a brother-in-law of Axtell.[43] It is significant that of the three other 'tituladoes', two, Nicholas Shea and John Rothe, were described as merchants. This was a role which many of the dispossessed landowners were to fulfil in the eighteenth century. The execution of Axtell as a regicide in 1660 led to the reconfiscation of the Ballyragget property and the probable dispersion of the English colony. The comparatively high density of English here in the period immediately after the war, contrasts sharply to their absence from other parts of the barony. It also serves to illustrate the problems of a practical nature which faced other grantees in Fassadinin. Axtell's estate had an existing nucleus and was sufficiently large to maintain a dependent population. Axtell's role as military governor of Kilkenny, his close ties with Oliver Cromwell and his reputation as a soldier would have, no doubt, encouraged English colonists to become his tenants. New estates in the barony nevertheless were not sufficiently large to induce grantees to settle. Places in the south and south west of the barony most affected by the confiscations had been characterised by small estates which had maintained rudimentary settlement only.

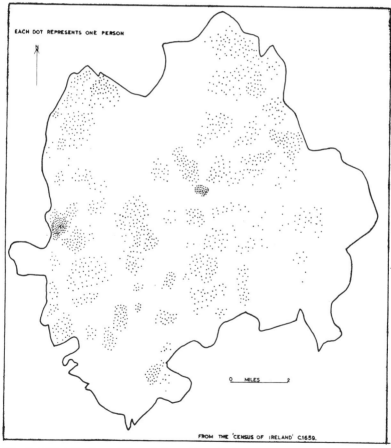

EACH DOT REPRESENTS ONE PERSON

0 MILES 2

FROM THE 'CENSUS OF IRELAND' C1659.

Fig. 3.5 Distribution of Population. Fassadinin c.1659.

The 'Census' of 1659, however unreliable, gives some indication of the distribution and density of people. If, as Hardinge assumed, it was compiled by the Down Surveyors it may, like their maps, be reasonably accurate. An examination of population density per 100 plantation acres of total land reveals that the highest densities were found in the parishes of Loughill (22), Kilmenan (12), Donaghmore (10) and Kilmacar (13) (fig. 3.5). The parishes of Donaghmore and Kilmenan had a high proportion of arable land and were held by Anglo-Norman proprietors in 1641. Kilmacar and Loughill were recorded as unforfeited Protestant land in the possession of the Duke of Ormonde. This sector of the barony was long characterised by Church and Anglo-Norman settlement, possessing manorial centres which were focal points of some importance. A wide range of settlement items were recorded in the parishes of Donaghmore and Kilmenan by the Down Surveyors (fig. 3.3). The lowest population densities in 1659 were found in the three adjoining parishes of Muckalee (3), Mothill (3) and Kilmadum (2) in the comparatively infertile and mainly derelict south east. The parishes of Connahy (5), Coolcraheen (6), Mayne (6) and Kilmademoge (7) had similar densities (fig. 3.5).

In the territory of Idough a density of approximately five people per 100 plantation acres was returned by the 'Census'. The population distribution circa 1659 reveals interesting characteristics. The old manorial nucleii, such as Ballyragget, (127) Castlecomer, (40) Kilmacar (30), Kilmademoge (36) and Corbettstown (25) had retained their importance as settlement and population centres. Townlands such as Donaghmore (54), Loughill (52) and Muckalee (32) which were ecclesiastical central places in the Reformation period were still important focal points.

By far the most significant aspect of townland population in 1659 was the comparatively high numbers found in areas held by the Mountgarret and Ormonde families. This is especially noticeable in isolated fragments of their properties which were not attached to manors. Jenkinstown, for example, in the south of the barony had approximately eighty-six per cent (67) of the population of Mayne although occupying only fifty-seven per cent (976) of the parish area. The population of the Ormonde townlands of Aughatubrid and 'Cloghmoilehed' in Castlecomer constituted twenty per cent (95) of the total parish population. This proportion is even more significant when it is considered that Aughatubrid was a relatively large, thickly wooded townland in the extreme north east. Similarly the Mountgarret townland of Damerstown in Dysert parish had approximately thirty-seven per cent (46) of the population, though constituting only fifteen per cent (480) of the total parish area.

It appears, therefore, that the dependent population was primarily attracted to the settlement centres owned by the principal landowners. This suggests that considerations other than economic ones determined population distribution in a period of great political instability. It also indicates that properties in the possession of absentees were not subject to the same rigid administration as the farms of resident owners. The absence of strict controls may have encouraged squatting by the more mobile elements in the population or those excluded from other estates. The 'Census' contained a summary of the principal Irish names and their numbers. The most common surname was O'Brenan, of which 116 were found in the barony. Surnames which occurred more than twenty times included those of: Purcell (35), Birne (Byrne) (31), Phelan (31), Dulany, (Delany) (23) and Kelly (20). Apart from Purcell, the majority of these names were rarely found in inventories of ownership.

The architects of plantation policy had hoped that while fulfilling the military objective of permanently pacifying Ireland, the confiscations would also help in converting and civilising the 'wild Irish'. There is little definite evidence of the success achieved by the colonists in the religious sphere in Fassadinin. Numerically the colonists constituted a minority community thinly scattered through the barony. The desire to promulgate the faith is only one of the many human actions motivated by religious fervour. The complex question of the influence of Protestantism on the rise of capitalism has long been discussed by historians. The Cromwellians subscribed to a particularly rigid form of Protestantism, asserting that those predestined for salvation could be identified by the success of their endeavours on earth. The inner conviction of the righteousness of their cause gave a powerful momentum to their civilian and military activities. Axtell, the Cromwellian grantee who acquired temporary possession of Mountgarret property, may have been typical of the colonists. Motivated by strong religious convictions, he had rapidly risen through the various military ranks.[44] Burtchaell stated of him that "firmly believing that it was his solemn duty imposed by the Almighty to exterminate those who opposed him in religion and politics, even as the Jews had been commanded to exterminate the Canaanites, his proceedings in Kilkenny were marked with much cruelty". It is often forgotten in relation to the Cromwellians that they were also revolutionaries engaged in a unique social upheaval. It may have been that the Cromwellians brought to land and commerce the same fanatical energy with which they won the war. This could help to explain the rapidity with which landlordism was diffused throughout the country.

Petitioners seeking the restoration of their sequestered lands emphasised their service to religion and the state. In 1653-4 the Wandesfordes petitioned the administration for the restoration of their Castlecomer property. They claimed that the sept of the O'Brenans were still very numerous in Idough and, "a great terror to the English inhabitants of that country, and did frequently commit many great robberies and murthers and were in arms for the late King". The petition also stated that "there is at this present about 500 English Protestants besides Irish who have lately been converted by the preacher." It was reiterated that, until the Wandesfordes commenced their work "there was not one of the natives a Protestant heard of among them." The petitioner complained that because of the uncertainty of the time, "their priests did say Mass frequently within

Idough and the natives have threatened our workmen from divers employments and uses of materials."[104] It is doubtful if the number of inhabitants quoted was correct. It seems however, that there was an incursion of Protestant settlers to Idough at this period. The Wandesfordes established their principal residence at Castlecomer in 1694. In confirming the Wandesforde claim the administration specified that it was, "in consideration of the manifold good and great services done unto us and our Crown by our well beloved subject and for the better strengthening and supporting the English Protestant interest within the country of Idough."[106] This claim, by placing emphasis on the idea of service for the sake of the Church and State, reaffirmed the classical concept of colonisation. Personal enrichment was supposedly incidental and secondary to the main military and religious obligations.

Sir William Petty catalogued to an extent the dereliction caused by the Cromwellian wars but he was more concerned with recording the 'profitable' elements of the landscape. The Ormonde manuscripts of the late seventeenth century detail the reorganisation of a great Lordship, wasted by war. They paint a graphic picture of a derelict landscape and chronicle the final destruction of the Catholic gentry. Eight of the nine denominations owned by Ormonde in Fassadinin were untenanted.[45] The house and garden held by John Mackie in Dunmore were waste. The house was "pulled down many years since lyeing in the parke near the Barne." Captain John Purcell, tenant of the lands of Dunmore, asked for an allowance for monies paid, "to King James collector for rent and subsidies." The rental explained that Purcell was in Limerick when the account was made up and therefore the earlier payment was overlooked. Purcell had total arrears of seventy seven pounds. A footnote at the bottom of the page stated simply "the tenant gone to France, estate and effects seized into the Kings hands." The tenant of the paddock of Dunmore, William Comerford was "not to be found". It was further observed that Lord Galmoy who "is gone to France kept his troope horses in the paddock." The observations made in relation to Captain James Bryan, tenant of Aughatubrid, are interesting insofar as the Bryan family were the only Catholic landowners to retain their property down to the twentieth century. Bryan had arrears of sixty seven pounds. The rental recorded that "he went to Limerick at ye rout of the Boyne and continued there till ye surrender by reason whereof no allowance of the payments made in King James time were given him, he not being here to crave it." A footnote stated that Captain Bryan was restored to his estates under the articles of Limerick. Mr. George Green the tenant of 'Lewhill' in north west Fassadinin was "very poore and absconds", and Mr. Pat Walsh and wife, tenants of 'Coolecullenduffe' in the north east were likewise "poore and gone".

In 1698 Dunton described Dunmore as the "finest house in Ireland".[46] On some of the floors he found 24 rooms and described how the staircase was "hung with curious landscapes". The house required but another branch to become a "perfect H", but even without this additional space it had more rooms than "are to be found in some whole towns."[47] By 1709 when Thomas Molyneaux visited the district the house was "pulled down and the furniture and pictures all carried to the castle." The destruction of the Ormonde house in Dunmore symbolises the collapse of the medieval Anglo-Norman world which had created the material fabric of seventeenth century Fassadinin. In the beginning of the century, the 10th Earl of Ormonde was extending his lordship to the Gaelic lands of Idough. By 1700 the second Duke of Ormonde was withdrawing from the barony. The Gaelic and Anglo-Norman interests had little to do with the new Fassadinin that was emerging from the ruins of war. The next chapter is concerned with the stability of the 'Ascendancy' in a constantly changing and evolving landscape.

CHAPTER IV

STABILITY AND CHANGE 1700-1800.

The main focus in this chapter is on the Wandesforde estate. The discovery of new material in the Wandesforde manuscripts makes possible an appraisal of estate development in the eighteenth century. This documentation contains one of the few detailed surviving accounts of estate management from the mid-eighteenth century and provides new information, particularly on the growth of commercial coalmining in the Castlecomer district.

1. Stability
The ownership of land in Fassadinin in the eighteenth century was vested in the Ascendancy. The stability of a proprietorial class suggests the continuity of a way of life and system of land governance. It would be wrong to assume that the descendants of families who owned estates in Fassadinin circa 1700 composed the landed gentry here in 1800. Overemphasis on stability may hide the fact that the composition of the Ascendancy was subject to change. Although the era of the large scale confiscations and forced expulsion was over, a considerable quantity of land changed hands through marriage, inheritance and purchase. Even if a family enjoyed uninterrupted ownership of an estate over a long period, this does not necessarily indicate that policies of estate management remained the same. Knowledge of the eighteenth century Ascendancy in Fassadinin is greatly fragmented and incomplete. Traces left by them on the landscape have been either erased or overlain by the accretions of later periods. Estate records do not exist for the majority of Fassadinin properties. It was not until landowners realised the need for more efficient management that professional surveyors such as Bernard Scalé were employed.[1] Neither, in the context of Fassadinin, is there any evidence to sustain the view that estate rentals were commonly used until the later half of the century. It is the documentation of the early nineteenth century which records the great change which took place during the period from 1700 to 1800.

One of the major problems in writing about eighteenth century Ireland is in determining how many immigrants from the countries of Britain settled here. These newcomers constituted the estate agents, craftsmen, mining engineers and tenantry who collectively implemented landlord policy in Fassadinin. The absence of statistical data makes any assessment of total population and the relative proportions of Catholics and Protestants in it highly conjectural. Francis James estimated that for Ireland as a whole the Protestant population 1732-33 constituted approximately twenty-seven per cent (527,000) of the total population of 1,934,000.[2] He arrived at this figure by assuming that all Catholic and Protestant householders enumerated in the hearth tax returns had uniform families of five children. The Canon Leslie Mss. collection in the National Library consists of typescript copies of visitation and other returns in the Diocese of Ossory from 1679 to 1853.[3] Only fragments of ecclesiastical records, such as the visitation books, which were written accounts of the state of Protestantism submitted by parish clergy to their bishop, have survived. The visitation books for 1731 recorded that in Attanagh, in the north-west of Fassadinin, only five of the forty families resident in the parish were Protestant. The parish had no glebe or glebe house. Neither was there a 'Mass house' but a Catholic service was "performed in the fields". In the adjoining parish of Donaghmore to the south, only one Protestant family resided although "fifty children attended the English school". This laconic observation identifies one of the more permanent effects of colonisation. The report also noted the existence of a 'Mass house' in Ballyragget. This portion of the Mountgarret estate situated in Donaghmore parish had passed to a junior branch of the family known as the 'Catholic Butlers' in the beginning of the eighteenth century.

Dunmore, the former Ormonde stronghold, had the neatest church in the parish but no Protestant congregation. The body of the church in Castlecomer was in ruins and a 'Mass house' in the town served the spiritual needs of the 'papists'. Eighty of the hundred families resident in the parish were Protestant. The rector of Castlecomer observed that half of the parish tithe consisted of potatoes, "being the ordinary food of the coal carriers and their families". Another one third was paid "in hay and pasturage and the rest in corn, which was used by them for the horses which draw the coal cars". The visitation report of 1781 noted that the parishes of Attanagh and Kilmenan in the north west of the barony had been united. In 1799 there was not one Protestant family in the Union. The returns record the decay of the physical fabric of Protestantism and the absence of a spiritual community in the south and west of the barony. The rector of Rosconnell parish reported that only the old walls of the church were standing and "the Churchyard is perfectly open while the high road runs close to the church wall". By 1799 the parish had no congregation and the rector had left. In the south of the barony, the parishes of Dunmore, 'Macully' and Killmadum had been united. In 1799 'Macully' had two Protestant families and the remaining two had none, The Protestant population of Mothill parish in the south east of the barony in 1781 consisted of four families. The returns of 1799 present a dismal picture of a church in disrepair and recorded that in 1798 the clerk had been killed by the 'rebels' at Castlecomer. A more significant factor noted in the visitation book was the dramatic increase in the number of Protestant families. In the eighteen years from 1781 to 1799 the Protestant population had grown from four to thirty eight families. By 1800 forty-five Protestant families were living in the parish. Castlecomer was the other parish where Protestants were comparatively numerous. The visitation book of 1799 listed one hundred families in the Union and recorded that the Wexford insurgents had destroyed a great part of the town in 1798.

This rather cursory summary of the Protestant population in Fassadinin in the eighteenth century reveals that they were numerically weak. The total Protestant population cannot have exceeded a thousand people as the Visitation Books return only one hundred and forty-seven families. The majority of these were found on the Castlecomer estate in the north east with a. surprisingly large rural pocket in the parish of Mothill in the south east. Nineteenth century records indicate that Protestants in Mothill were concentrated in the hitherto sparsely settled upland townland of Coolcullen. The distribution and density of the non-Catholic population suggests that confiscation policy did not result in large scale immigration or any appreciable exodus of the native population. If the Wandesforde claim, made in the late seventeenth century, that five hundred Protestant families had settled in Castlecomer by 1690 was substantially correct it would mean that very few new families came into the barony in the eighteenth century. Those that did come were invariably specialist mining personnel or estate administrators.

Fassadinin in 1700 bore the stamp of successive settlements which had characterised its history. The Ascendancy was not a homogeneous group but was divided on ethnic, economic and religious lines. These divisions reveal the diverse origins of the landed gentry in the barony. There is little evidence to suggest that Catholic landowners were any different in their lifestyle and attitudes than their Protestant counterparts. They were, however, less likely to have connections with England and were debarred from participating in the administrative and political life of the country. These restrictions may have kept them at home. Transactions concerning land were numerous in the early eighteenth century. Land was the primary source of wealth and as such it was sold outright, mortgaged, leased, let and sublet. The names of the new purchasers have not been found in earlier lists of landowners in the barony. Much of the trafficking consisted of paper transfers: purchasers were often Dublin-based which may imply that they were in the legal profession or the civil service. Social mobility was a feature of Irish Protestant society in the eighteenth century. Many families of humble origins acquired vast estates and respectability through trafficking in land.

In the early eighteenth century the greater portion of Ormonde property in the barony was alienated. The weakening of the Ormonde connection with Fassadinin indicates the changing political function of the surviving Anglo-Norman families. The tenth Earl, circa 1600, was a powerful regional magnate who diligently supervised and extended his Kilkenny estates.

The centralisation of government in Dublin drew his descendants onto a wider stage where the prize of success and the consequence of faiiure were all the greater. The second Duke of Ormonde was Lord Lieutenant of Ireland in the administration of Queen Anne. In 1715 he was attainted for his 'Jacobite' sympathies and deprived of his estates, offices and commands.[4] A special Act of Parliament in 1721 empowered Charles, Earl of Arran, to sell the lands forfeited by his brother.

The contemporary evidence shows, that the greater portion of Ormonde lands had been sold outright or leased before the attainder. The alienation of these lands led either to the enlargement of existing estates or the creation of new ones. The Wandesforde and Mountgarret Butler estates were increased through the purchase of Ormonde property. In both instances the lands acquired were not extensive, but adjoined the existing estates. In 1709 Ormonde granted the lands of Oldtown (except the use of the rabbits to George Butler esq. of Ballyragget.[5] Figure 1.6 demonstrates that Oldtown separated the Butler estate of Ballyragget from the lands of Knockroe to the south. Its purchase helped to consolidate the Ballyragget estate. In the same way the acquisition by the Wandesfordes of 'Clashduffe and Duntrimane' in 1704 extended their property by 287 acres on the south west.[6] The Colles estate of Lisnefunshin was similarly augmented by the grant of Coolcullenduffe in 1714.[7]

The creation of new estates was a more significant consequence of the break up of the Ormonde property (fig. 4.1). These new property units, together with the estates which had their legal origins in the Restoration land Settlement, constituted the framework of the estate system in Fassadinin in the nineteenth century. The reorganisation of Ormonde's land led to the creation of six new estates which varied greatly in size. The estate acquired at this time by the Catholic Bryan family was to remain in the possession of the family until the reorganisation of landownership by the Irish Land Commission in the early part of the present century. The Bryans were a Gaelic family who obtained lands through marriage in Fassadinin circa 1617.[38] By the late seventeenth century they were important tenants on the Ormonde estate.[9] The Bryans supported the 'Jacobite' cause and took part in the Battle of the Boyne and subsequent military engagements. Inevitably, forfeiture followed defeat but they were restored to their estates under the provisions of the Treaty of Limerick.

It is more difficult to explain their ability in retaining, and even augmenting, their Fassadinin property in the early eighteenth century. In 1702 the Bryans were granted the lands of 'Aughatubrid and Clogh' which contained 1,250 acres and were located in north Idough.[10] By 1704 they had acquired an unspecified amount of land which coincided with the northern portion of Dunmore manor in the south of the barony.[11] The Bryan proprietor in 1709 was identified as James Bryan of Jenkinstown. This implies that the physical centre of the estate was located here. Jenkinstown, as the name implies, was originally an Anglo-Norman settlement and in 1659 had, according to the census of that year, a sizeable population.

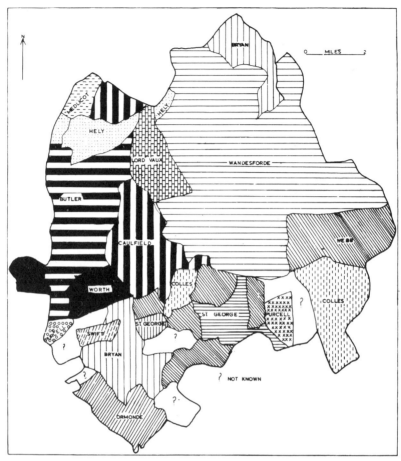

Fig. 4.1 Ownership of land. Fassadinin c.1720.

The Lodge transcripts of the Deeds indicate that Toby Caulfield of Clone, Barony of Galmoy acquired an estate of 3,030 acres in Fassadinin at this period.[12] His lands roughly coincided with the core area of Kilmacar manor and part of the outlying lands of the same manor in the north of the barony (fig. 4.1). Transactions concerning the transfer of these lands to Caulfield indicate that frequent changes in ownership may have been a common feature of the early eighteenth century. This was especially true in the context of small estates. They also suggest that absenteeism was common and that in many instances the new owners functioned as rent receivers only. Not alone was land subject to sale and lease, but the rents and other monies due from land over a period of years were often sold for a bulk sum. The 'lands of Killmocar' contained 2,440 acres and were sold to Henry Gower of Dublin in 1709. The same deed establishes that the money rent and rent in kind was granted for an unspecified term to Michael Worth of Dublin for the sum of £388.

In the same year (1709) Gower and Worth transferred the "benefits of their said contracts" to Toby Caulfield. The Caulfield estate in the barony was augmented by the grant of 'Coolroe and Lewhill' in north Fassadinin in 1713.[13] In some instances the lease of the lands and not the lands was subject to transfer. In 1703, for example, James, Duke of Ormonde, "for the sum of £1,847.12.4 sold in fee farm to the said Michael Worth, the lease for lives renewable for ever made to John Pepper esq. and the fines reserved thereon for renewals, of the Towns and Lands of Coonoghee and Grange McCombe".[14] This type of contract recognised a middle interest in the land. Speculators such as Worth were the precursors of the later middlemen, probably subletting their lands at a profit rent. They also may have sublet the rent over a term of years for a bulk cash sum. The absentee owners in the seventeenth century were the Anglo-Norman merchant families from the city of Kilkenny. It was significant that the parallel group in the early eighteenth century were mainly from the city of Dublin.

The disposal of the Ormonde lands in Fassadinin had commenced prior to 1700. In 1698, land in Co. Kilkenny, including the denominations of Rathgarry and Ballyoskill in north-west Fassadinin, were granted to Sir John Hely.[15] Another deed made in 1698 recorded the transfer of the lands of "Markett Castle alias Castlemarket" which contained 410 acres to Thomas and James Medlicott for "services rendered".[16] Records concerning the Webb estate in the Land Commission files indicate that the Ormonde lands of 'Counfeily and Corfunshun' were demised to Henry Webb of Webbsborough in 1697.[17] This lease was renewed by the Earl of Arran in 1722, to whom "hunting and fishing rights, all mine, minerals and coals and the right of erecting houses for workmen together with power to requisition one acre for each house" were reserved. Although leases, not lands were, in some instances, subject to transfer, subsequent events ensured that this was a permanent alienation. By 1720 the extensive seventeenth century Ormonde estate was reduced to Dunmore in the south of the Barony and the lands adjoining their former countryhouse (fig. 4.1)

Figure 4.2 — a copy of two road maps compiled in 1778 — gives some indication of the number and location of landlord seats in the barony. Although the precincts of Dunmore in the south were thickly wooded, the house was described 'in ruins'. The seat of the O'Briens of Jenkinstown was north of the confluence of the Nore and Dinin. The Big House of the Strangeways was found in the townland of Springhill, which may have been a 'new English' name. Further north the family of Swift were commemorated in the townland name Swiftsheath. This family were not grantees under the Restoration Act of Settlement and may have acquired lands in the north of the forfeited denomination of Foulksrath through purchase. The map shows that the Butlers had removed their residence from the castle to the Big House in the south of the town, overlooking the Nore. To the west of the river in the Barony of Galmoy, lay Ballycondra

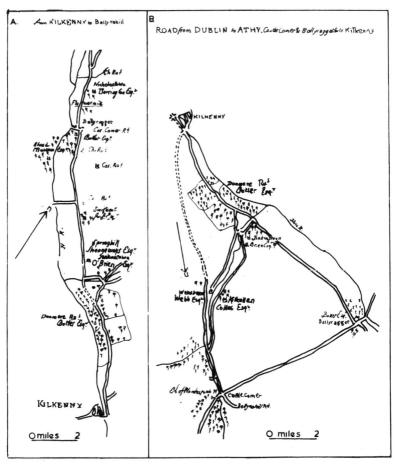

Fig. 4.2 Landlord residences. Fassadinin 1778.

House, seat of the Mountgarrets. The townland of Grange, once farmed by
the monks of the Cistercian Abbey of Jerpoint and then granted to the
Earl of Ormonde, was, in 1778, the location of the family home of the
Mossom family. The residences of the Webb and Colles families were
located on opposite sides of the Dinin river in the central sector of the
barony. Castlecomer was the seat of the Wandesfordes. The outline of the
demesne was clearly visible in Skinner's map, particularly to the north of
the town. Seven of the ten Big Houses in the barony c. 1778 were
located in the district between the Nore and Dinin rivers in west Fassadinin. This area had long been a favoured living place for successive invaders.
The hill country between Castlecomer and Ballyragget and in the north
and south-east of Fassadinin was devoid of the elements of landlordism in
1778.

90

The pattern of ownership was stabilised in the early eighteenth century. By 1800, resident landlords such as, for example, the Wandesfordes of Castlecomer, the Butlers of Ballyragget, the Bryans of Jenkinstown, the Webbs of Webbsborough and the Swifts of Swiftsheath dominated the proprietorial class. Nineteenth century records reveal that estates varied greatly in size. The development of the estate sytem had lessened the efficacy of the manor and civil parish as territorial divisions. Estates were not, however, permanent units and were subject to change through marriage, inheritance and the many transactions concerning property. The employment afforded locally by the Big House has often been overlooked. The reorganisation of ownership in the seventeenth century had led to the growth of comparatively small estates, particularly in the south of the barony. This process was extended to the Ormonde lands in the early eighteenth century. In many instances these estates were too small to support a landlord establishment and were usually administered by an absentee. The break up of the Ormonde estate retarded the growth of the seventeenth century manorial villages of Dunmore and Kilmacar. On the other hand, the consolidation of the Butler and Wandesforde interest led to the development of the comparatively strong urban centres of Ballyragget and Castlecomer.

Some Protestant landowners were involved in church, state and country administration. The absence of data makes it difficult to generalise about their way of life and their impact locally. Perhaps the career of Elland Mossom, who resided at Mount Eland in the townland of Grange to the west of the Nore, typified the general pattern. Mossom graduated from Trinity College, Dublin in 1732 with the degree of M.A.[18] Like many of his compeers he was called to the Bar in 1743. Subsequently he was elected to serve the borough of St. Canices, Kilkenny in the Irish Parliament. The fact that the Wandesforde proprietor, in the early period of the century, served two terms as an M.P. in the British Parliament and was in 1745 Governor of Co. Kilkenny, is a strong pointer to the dual interests of the family.[19] The Wandesfordes did not become permanent residents until the 1750's.

The primary tenet of landlordism was the preservation of the family name and estate. Carefully fostered marriages were primarily responsible for achieving this. By 1800, the principal families in the barony were all connected through marriage. On the death of John Wandesforde, 5th Viscount Castlecomer, without a male heir, the estate passed to his daughter Anne. In 1769, she married John Butler of Garryricken, Co. Kilkenny, to whom the Earldom of Ormonde was restored in 1791. The Ballyragget estate was also linked to the Ormonde family. Robert Butler, who succeeded to the family estate in 1752, had no male issue. He settled his estate on his two surviving brothers, with remainder to Thomas Kavanagh of Borris.[20] The Kavanaghs, who were connected through marriage with the Ormondes, were an old Gaelic family who had transferred their allegiance to Protestantism. By 1850, the related Wandesforde and Kavanagh families held thirty-five per cent (23,961) of the 68,000, acres in the barony. The marriage bonding of Gaelic, 'Old English' and 'New English' families suggested that the passage of time had diluted the ethnic distinction and reinforced the social and economic links between landlord families.

2. Coal and Change

"By the Brenans of Lowan for carriage of 14½ dozen of frame stickes from Ballyroe wood at 2/- doz, £1.9.0.
(From 1717 Account Book of the Wandesforde Collieries).

Boate observed that in the search for iron in Castlecomer the miners "met with sea coale". The coals were sufficient "to furnish a whole country" but were not exploited because of the absence of navigable waterways.[21] J. U. Nef claims that by 1689 a mining company working Castlecomer coal was sending it down the Barrow to be sold at St. Mullins and Ross for transport to the Dublin Market.[22] Thomas Molyneaux provides further evidence of coalmining in Castlecomer when he recorded a visit here in 1707.[23] He noted that the coal and ironworks were located in, "wild, mountainy, sheepwalk country along the Dinin" and referred to "the multitude of exhausted pits along the hills where the old works were". Commercial coalmining may have commenced here in the late seventeenth century. The country was relatively peaceful after the ravages of war. The beginnings of coalmining appear to coincide with the tenure of the estate by Christopher Wandesforde, who was married to Eleanor, daughter of Sir John Lowther of Westmoreland. The Lowthers were amongst the foremost English mining families and controlled the exports of coal from the Cumberland Coalfield after 1680.[24]

A detailed account of mining in Castlecomer in the year 1716-1717 was found amongst the Wandesforde papers. This account is of great significance insofar as it presents evidence of organised mining and describes the methods employed. It also recorded the names of some of the Castlecomer coalminers. It is possible from the report to estimate expenses incurred in provisioning and preparing pits and in the carriage of the coal to the Barrow and downstream. Coalpits were located in the townlands of Moneenroe, Coolbawn, Rossnowle and Clogh. In this basin-shaped depression, north of Castlecomer town, a total of forty pits varying in depth from ten to twelve yards were sunk in the years 1717 and 1718. Payment to estate tenants and specialist hauliers for the transport of the coal to Leighlinbridge and from there downstream to Cusclaty on the Barrow was the largest item of expenditure in the years 1717 and 1718. The cost of transportation amounted to approximately forty four per cent (£478) of the total cost (£1,077) incurred in running the collieries and ironmines in this period.

The disadvantages of inland location were accentuated by the surface topography of the Irish coalfields. According to Nef, coal could be mined almost as cheaply at Kilkenny as at Whitehaven but in Ireland the journey from the pithead to Waterford harbour more than tripled the price. Steep escarpments separate the Castlecomer field from the Barrow to the east and the Nore to the west. The natural outlet from the coal area is through the corridor cut by the waters of the northern Dinin. The evidence reveals that it was not this route to the city of Kilkenny which was followed by the coal carters, but the more arduous journey to Leighlinbridge on the Barrow. The road to Leighlinbridge runs transverse to the surface topography and crosses the escarpment at a height of 950 feet. The slope from the coalfield up to the hill crest was gradual rather than steep and the sharpest incline was on the downhill journey. The greatest 'pull' was out of the deep valley cut through the soft shales by the eastern Dinin. A large proportion of the expenses was incurred in the transportation of materials and coal. Colliery furniture such as, for example, timber for bracing and framing the pits was brought from Gillianstown in the south east of the Wandesforde estate and from 'Ballyroe' (later Swiftsheath) in the south west of the barony. The iron implements used in sinking and boring and in bottoming the water barrels were refined from the ironmine worked by opencast method at Crutt and the 'Hill'

Figure 4.3 shows that the tenants of the estate townlands shared in the carriage of coal. In the period from Michaelmas 1717 to Michaelmas 1718, the tenants of Castlecomer transported 2,434 barrels of coal to Leighlinbridge. The amounts of coal carried varied in relation to the distance of

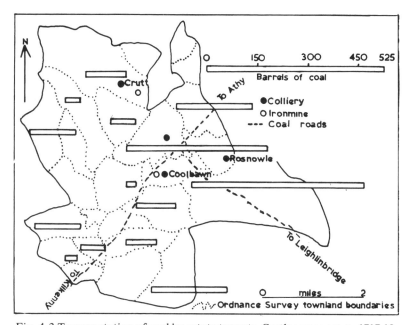

Fig. 4.3 Transportation of coal by estate tenants. Castlecomer estate 1717-18.

the townlands from Leighlinbridge. Figure 4.3 shows that tenants of townlands located on the eastern perimeter of the estate invariably transported more coal than those on the west, south-west and north. Thus, for example, the tenants of Croghtenclogh carried 520 barrels, whereas the occupiers of Moyhora in the north carried 129 barrels. It was significant that the tenants of the townlands of Clogh, Gorteen and Coolbawn, where the working collieries were located, did not participate in the transport of coal. This suggests that a distinction already existed between those who worked the coal and those engaged in ancillary activities. Approximately forty-nine per cent (£234) of the total transport costs was paid to a Mr. Robert Smithwick for "the freight of 6247 barrels of coal sent to Cusclaty by the old boat". Expenditure at the coal terminal in Leighlinbridge included such items as £1-13-6 for "building house, timber, wattles and thatching". Eighteen men were paid nine shillings for "cutting the dock for shipping" and a sum of seven pounds was paid to "180 labourers from time to time from the beginning carrying the coal and helping to load the ships".

Commercial mining was an important agent of change in the Castlecomer district, as the increased traffic of people, commodities and money had important repercussions on society and settlement. The recorded surnames of workers in the industry presents evidence of the presence of a new group of immigrants in north Kilkenny. Names such as, for example, Smithwick, Despard, Sarovy, Wilde, Close, Bradley, Raines and Boothe were not found here in the seventeenth century. Irish families such as the O'Brenans were now coalminers and wood hauliers rather than cattle herders. A distinctive feature of the industry here was the interdependence of coal and land and the dual involvement of estate tenants in mining and agriculture. The account suggests that the cash input from mining was distributed, however unevenly, among the tenantry. There is no evidence that this increased cash inflow had any marked impact on agriculture. Rarely was money acquired through mining expended in the development of farming techniques. The building of a military barracks in Castlecomer town circa 1717 reflects one aspect of mining society. Coal helped to terminate the historical isolation of this part of Kilkenny by giving impetus to road building. Substantial new houses were built to house colliery managers and more ephemeral buildings housed the colliers. The miners brought their cultural baggage with them. It may be assumed that they constituted the majority of the eighty Protestant families listed in the Visitation Book of Castlecomer parish in 1781.

The visible impact of mining was more obvious. The well-defined colliery country was characterised by the untidy landscape of primitive mining. Clusters of working and abandoned pits were scattered over the surface. Technological limitations, such as the inability to cope with excess underground water and the absence of a proper ventilation system, necessitated the sinking of shallow pits in close proximity. Another factor which encouraged the proliferation of pits was the absence of any legislative control on the landlords freedom to mine coal wherever he pleased. Furthermore, in the absence of detailed geological knowledge, mining was still largely a process of trial and error. Each working pit had its hauling apparatus which was probably a hand operated windlass. Pits were highlighted in the landscape by an irregular collection of temporary buildings and distinct heaps of coal and slag. Deserted workings were marked by mounds, newly colonised by scrub and furze. In this place in the seventeenth century, the Anglo-Norman families of Purcell, Archer and Shee were building bawns to house cattle. A hundred years later Yorkshire immigrants such as Booth, Wilde and Close were building bawns to store coal. This was change.

There is little detailed information on mining in Castlecomer in the latter half of the eighteenth century. A colliery official in a letter written to the absentee proprietor in 1742 claimed that colliery employees were engaged in the clandestine sale of coals on the Dublin and Limerick markets to the "detriment of the proprietors profits" and "in an attempt to feather their own nests".[25] He also stated that "the colliers had started to work on February 15th though not with goodwill by reason they are not Entered into Artickle with". This suggests that coalmining was becoming more than a summer occupation and that the colliers had a special contractual agreement with the proprietor. In an agreement signed by the landlord and twenty one colliers in 1755 further evidence of the existence of a contract system is provided.[26] The colliers agreed to go to work "whenever Lord Castlecomer told them". They did not expect any payment more than "the colum and the picking of it for our firing". The landlord for his part guaranteed them security of tenure provided "they worked with him and for him the terms above mentioned". This security of tenure was limited to four acre holdings and a house, and those who held "over and above four acres and a house would hold the portion above four acres during Lord Castlecomer's pleasure". This contract gave the colliers security of tenure for their potato land in lieu of their mining skills. Payment was in kind and this appears to compare unfavourably with the detailed accounting system operating in 1716/17. Culm was the residue from mining and contained much small coal. It was also the principal fuel of the colliers and the surrounding districts. This contractual relationship had important spatial implications. Colliers were now identified with a well defined area, characterised by four acre holdings. The landscape impact of this arrangement was clearly revealed in the estate maps of the early nineteenth century.

Over optimistic estimates of the coal resources of the Leinster coalfield influenced the development of canal and road networks. Many contemporary observers assumed that in terms of quantity and quality, Irish coal compared favourably to deposits in the English fields. The author of the Statistical Survey of the Queen's County typified this attitude when he wrote in 1801 "that from the immense depth and range of this mineral, it is in no way hazardous to assert that it is capable of supplying this island with coal for centuries to come and also to answer every demand that might be for exportation".[27] Canals, it was believed, would overcome the problem of transport from remote inland locations to the urban areas of the east coast. It seems certain that commentators and entrepreneurs had been influenced by the great phase of canal and turnpike road buildings in England.

J. B. Harley has noted that of the 165 canal bills approved in England between 1758 and 1802 over half were primarily concerned with carrying coal.[28] The Newry canal owed its origin to the coal deposits of the Lough Neagh area and the exaggerated prospects held out initially for the Royal Canal were related to the over-optimistic estimate of the mineral wealth of the Arigna coal district in the north Shannon basin. In the same way, the coal resources of the Leinster field influenced the development of the canal network of the Barrow Valley. By 1790, the Barrow Navigation from Athy fifty miles downstream to where the river becomes tidal at St. Mullins was completed. A year later this navigation was linked to the Grand Canal by a feeder from Athy to Lowtown. The Nore never attained the significance of its sister river as an industrial highway. Although many proposals were made to effect a navigable link from Inistiogue, where the river becomes tidal, to Kilkenny city, only four miles of the canal section north of Inistiogue had been completed by 1775. The available evidence suggests that improvements in the canal system did not effect major changes in the traditional market pattern. By 1809, when the canal links had been well established, only 2,476 tons of coal and culm were carried towards Dublin from the Leinster field.[29] Apart from encouraging the outward movement of coal, the canal system enabled importers to distribute cheap English and Welsh coal to the interior. In 1807, coal from the Swansea field was underselling Castlecomer coal in Kilkenny city by as much as fourteen shillings per ton. The steam engines of Thomas Savery and Newcomen and that of James Watt after 1780 had revolutionised the coal industry in Great Britain and the technologically weak Castlecomer field was in no way equipped to meet the challenge of free trade, and the technically superior British mines.

It is possible that the market area for Castlecomer coal had not changed dramatically in the eighteenth century. The traditional outlets to Leighlinbridge on the Barrow, for shipment downstream and to Kilkenny were maintained. Kilkenny in 1798 was an important market centre and was the only inland town in which more than half of the houses paid the hearth tax. The rich agricultural lands within carting radius of the collieries had a comparatively high density of small market towns and landlord establishments. Corn mills and breweries were also found in this prosperous countryside. Small coal and culm were used exclusively for domestic heating and breweries in the collieries. Some of it was used in the lime kilns and the burnt limestone was then applied to the hungry pasturelands of the hill country. The evidence suggests that the Wandesfordes derived a considerable income from the collieries in the second half of the eighteenth century. Thomas Campbell stated that they were drawing £10,000 a year in 1778.[30]

According to William Tighe the profits had decreased to £2,000 in 1799 and in the early years of the nineteenth century expenditure was almost equal to earnings.

3. Land and Change

"However Mr. White and I think your Lordships best and prudential way would be to let the whole lands at a fixed rent to some one solvent tenant who could keep them in subjection and oblige them to pay their respective rents to him and he be obliged to pay your Lordship your rent without dealing with such a lawless clan who are like the highlanders of Scotland that rob and take acres of grass each other at their pleasure without leave or paying for it". (Manuscript survey in Wandesforde papers compiled in 1746 by Lullum Batwell — reference to tenants of Gorteen, north east Fassadinin).

The absence of detailed local studies of rural society in eighteenth century Ireland has resulted in the obscuration of many significant events by the general blanket interpretation. Over-emphasis on the impact of absenteeism and 'penal' legislation has concealed the significance of developments such as accelerated population growth, increased agricultural production and the development of transport networks. These changes, generated by large scale capital investment and changing social attitudes, were to produce the Industrial Revolution in England. The 1717-18 account of mining in Castlecomer revealed the close juxtaposition and interdependence of agrarian and mining industries. This dual economy based primarily on cattle raising and mining also characterised many of the Highland coal areas in Great Britain.[31] The cold, damp and often infertile hill soils of the Irish coalfields were not suitable for large scale arable farming. Large quantities of corn, hay and potatoes were needed to feed the growing population and increasing numbers of animals. This suggests that only small quantities of land were subject to intensive cultivation.

(a) *The Wandesforde estate in 1746*

In 1746, George Wandesforde, absentee proprietor of the Castlecomer property, commissioned Lullum Batwell to survey his Irish estates.[32] The ensuing report is an invaluable addition to the sparse knowledge of rural society in the mid-eighteenth century. Surveys usually followed a change in estate ownership or a marked decline in estate revenue. The latter state of affairs was more likely to occur in the absence of the landlord. The 'discrepancy' noted by the landlord, between colliery returns for Summer and Winter may have led to the Batwell report. The disparity, Batwell explained, arose from the fact that "expenses in Winter greatly exceeded the sums arising from the sales thereof". Whatever about its origin, the survey was mainly concerned with land and the revenue from it. It revealed a haphazard management and accounting system which contrasted sharply with the meticulous book keeping which was such a feature of the 1717-1718 account.

Batwell analysed the existing landlord-tenant relationships and proposed an alternative management system. This, he hoped, would help decrease the rent deficit of £2,300 which was almost equal to the yearly rental of circa £2,700. Batwell presents a picture of a depressed agricultural district characterised by the absence of improvement in land and buildings, the inability or unwillingness of tenants to pay rents, and the existence of semi-independent 'estates' and poor management. It is open to question whether Batwell presented an objective analysis. A reading of the report suggests that he was an ardent champion of long leases. He may accordingly have exaggerated what he assumed to be the results of the shortcomings of the existing tenurial system. His advocacy of the claims of the principal tenants suggests that he was also strongly swayed by what they told him. As many of these were comparatively wealthy, and stood to gain in the short term from leases, Batwell may have received financial inducements to present their case. It was, after all, a long way from Yorkshire!

The survey was primarily concerned with the principal tenants who had a direct financial relationship with the landlord. The holdings of twenty-three of these were enumerated. Their respective rents and arrears were detailed and particulars of the tenurial system under which they held their lands were given. Individual holdings coincided mainly with townland units whose names were found in seventeenth century land inventories. In the majority of cases, tenants held single rather than multiples of town-lands. The townland of 'Lowen' had been subdivided into 'Upper' and 'Lower' divisions, which coincided with the farms of two different tenants. This factor represents another stage in the evolution of the townland as a unit of land ownership rather than settlement. Of the twenty three principal tenants, thirteen had surnames of English origin, seven had Irish names and three Anglo-Norman. Surnames, such as Bradley and Wright, found among the English farmers, occurred in the 1717-1718 colliery accounts. Others such as Anderson, Rosse and Whitehead were not listed previously as either colliers or landholders. This may indicate that a substantial class of 'yeoman' farmers participated in the initial colonisation. One of the Anglo-Norman names, Purcell, was held by prominent Fassadinin land-owners in the first half of the seventeenth century. The Anglo-Norman surname, Denn, was new to the barony. Two of the Gaelic landholders had the surname O'Brenan. The remainder included two Byrnes, a Mulhall and a Fynn.

Batwell did not give the acreage equivalent of 1746 townlands. This omission may mean that they already had well defined boundaries which were known to local farmers. By applying the acreages returned in the 1812 estate survey to the 1746 townlands, it is possible to arrive at a rough estimate of the amount of land held by the various ethnic-historical groupings (fig. 4.4). The estate area was 11,128 acres and the rental came to £2,769. English landholders held forty-one per cent of the estate lands and paid approximately forty-eight per cent (£1,344) of the rental. The Irish tenants paid thirty-six per cent (£997) of the rent. Anglo-Norman

Ordnance Survey townland boundaries

Fig. 4.4 Landholders. Castlecomer estate 1746.

occupiers held only twenty-three per cent of the land and paid sixteen per
cent of the rent. The discrepancy between the percentage of total land
held and rent paid, especially in the context of the Anglo-Norman holdings, is explained by the fact that the Anglo-Normans held infertile land
(fig. 4.4). Five holdings which contained 2,082 acres or eighteen per cent
of the estate area were held by lease and occupiers with Irish surnames held
1,008 acres of these lands.

An examination of the extent of individual holdings showed that William
Denn, a tenant of Anglo-Norman descent, held 1,548 acres. The second
largest farm which contained 1,069 acres was occupied by Owen Brenan.
Surnames are not an infallible guide to religious affiliations but the fact
that these families were Catholic in the early nineteenth century suggests
that the two largest farms in the estate in 1746 were occupied by Catholics.
Discrimination was more evident when Catholic and Protestant tenants
competed for leases. Michael Brophy, for example, tenant of Ballyhimmin
requested a lease for the "mountain part of Donaguile" which adjoined his
farm. Brophy promised that, if given the lease, he would expend "40/-
year in making up the bounds between your Lordship's estate and Captain

99

Johnsons, being at present quite open without any ditch or fence". Thomas Wright offered a rent of £76 for the same area. Batwell recommended that Wright, whom he described as a "fair honest man and a good Protestant tenant", be given the lease, because Brophy was a "Papist".

The report details the varied reasons given by tenants for failing to meet their rental committments. These contained a great variety of information, which contribute to a reconstruction of estate society and affairs at this time. Not all principal tenants were completely dependent on land. A small group either held shops in Castlecomer or were employed as estate or colliery officials in addition to occupying farms. It appears that these individuals were invariably related and may have reached their status through the deployment, in land and commerce, of money earned in the collieries. For example, Mrs. Jane Wright, widow of Thomas Wright, who had been employed as a colliery clerk, held part of the lands of Ardra and Coolbawn. She requested a reduction in rent claiming that her husband in his lifetime was "better enabled to pay said rent by his being concerned in the collieries". It was the families of colliery officials who were likely to benefit from such parental thrift. Their son, Richard Wright, was principal tenant to the lands of Ballycomy, Clashduff and a house and shop in Castlecomer. He claimed that he had agreed to pay a high rent for his house in the town on being promised that "the Courts Leet would be held there and that a turnpike road would be brought by his door". Neither of these promises had been fulfilled and Wright had been obliged to, "leave off selling of drink which was before a great support to his family". He had obviously ingratiated himself with Batwell, who was forced to stay in his house because of the bad condition of the inn. Batwell recommended him as a suitable tenant for the "mountain part of Donaguile" and of "Your Lordships inn in Castlecomer".

Some tenants claimed to have delivered goods to the "castle" of Castlecomer in the years 1738-39. They complained that they had not received payment. This indicates the local importance of the landlord's house as a centre of consumption, especially when the proprietor and his family were resident. The items delivered typified the products of pastoral hill farming and included such items as cheese, butter and butcher's meat. Thomas Denn, tenant of Ballylinnen, claimed that his son, "a man of good circumstance and station in Gibraltar" had sent the landlord a "sum of portwine, two hogsheads of French wine, one hogshead of Madeira, one hogshead of Hermitage". A cash reduction in his rent equivalent to the price of the wines had not been allowed him. Social mobility was a feature of Catholic society in this period. Denn's son and his peers were representatives of a class who, debarred from the professions and political office, sought to acquire status through commerce. It is certain that these emigrant remittances were an important element in maintaining the comparative prosperity of certain sections of the Catholic tenantry in the eighteenth century. The evidence does not suggest that payment in kind was a general feature of estate economy. It appears that one of the earliest

100

achievements of landlordism was to substitute monetary equivalents for all uncertain and ill-defined payments.

Batwell recommended "a certain fixed method, to ascertain the value of damages done to lands by the Collieries". He observed that disruption of agriculture by mining was a "general cause of complaint and cause for stoppage of rents". In a reference to the impact of mining on agriculture in Co. Durham, Hodgson noted that the payment of 'double damage' to royalty owners and tenants for permission to take colliery workings and wayleave through their lands, yielded an annual return that was twice the rental or commercial value of the land.[33] The difference in Castlecomer was that no tenant had a freehold interest in the land. The absence of any proper system to assess damages to land encouraged the tenants to make exaggerated claims. Daniel Fynn, for example, who occupied the colliery townland of Moneenroe was £601 in arrears and claimed a large portion of this for "damages done by colliery roads and large sums of money due for waterpulling". Alexander Bradley, tenant of part of Coolbawn townland, complained that "the said lands have been so greatly damaged by several coalpits that the same is now become useless and unprofitable to him". Extractive industry is wasteful of land and disruptive of agriculture. The system of working in Castlecomer resulted in a large number of shallow pits scattered over a wide area. These pits had an indeterminate but relatively short life span. The surface area of the colliery district was constantly disrupted by the search for and exploitation of the coal seams. In the absence of geological knowledge, exploration was mainly a hit or miss process and bankrupt pits were more than likely to be left in a dangerous state. In an underdeveloped economy, no concessions were likely to be made to agriculture in the quest for coal and money. This conflict between competing claims for land establishes that mining and agriculture were becoming more segregated than in the early period of the century.

Most principal tenants held their lands on a tenancy-at-will basis (fig. 4.4). The duration of these tenancies was subject to landlord discretion. It may have been determined either by the ability of the tenant to remain solvent and fulfil his rent committment, or by landlord failure to find a tenant who would pay more. It was generally believed by agriculturists at the time that long leases were desirable and that their absence was a deterrent to enterprise. The report indicated that a similar view was held by the principal tenants, all of whom were adamant that the possession of a lease was a necessary prerequisite for successful farming. They argued, as did Batwell, that long term leases would give them security and encouragement to improve their lands. Another salient point, which Batwell conveniently omitted, was that leases would give autonomy to principal tenants to impose at will on their undertenants. It would give them the same power over the dependant tenantry as the landlord now had over them. The principal tenants were well aware that a growing population would greatly increase the competition (and renumeration) for land. It is salutory to remember that twenty three principal tenants held approximately twelve thousand acres of estate land.

The tenant's case for long leases was presented in terms of improvements they would undertake if granted them. They asserted that the present decrepit state of their property was the result of insecurity of tenure. George Carpenter of Kilkenny, who held Moyhora, stated that leasehold interest would "encourage him to lay out his money on the said lands, particularly an old house thereon, at present in a ruinous condition". Richard Wright, occupier of the townlands of Ballycomy and Clashduff, requested a lease so that he might improve his lands to "make them dry and fitting, as he had suffered a great loss of cattle and sheep which dyed by the coldness of these lands". Other tenants promised to make ditches and to "manure with lime" all ploughed land. William Denn of Crutt was being honest when he told Batwell that "if he had a lease, he might rely on not being turned out of said lands for want of a lease or have his rents raised".

It seems probable that a great part of the estate was still unenclosed. It may have been that townlands which coincided with individual farms were bounded by clay ditches. Arable portions, especially in the colliery district, were protected by some form of fence. Batwell was more than anxious to devise a system which would ensure a steady income for the landlord, and less than concerned with academic questions concerning improvement. He recommended that proper leases with maps affixed be made so as to prevent disputes in the future. He advised the landlord to maintain a regular rent roll which would list the certain yearly income of the estate. Batwell pointed out that the attempt to extract exorbitant rents from the tenants had failed and created even greater problems. He suggested that the landlord should compromise between high rents and a steady income by letting the lands at a moderate rent to solvent tenants.

Contemporary evidence suggests that the leasehold system was neither producing steady financial returns nor leading to the improvement of estate land. The report shows that only one of the five tenants who held their land by lease was up-to-date in his payments. The other four had combined arrears of £1,304 which was approximately fifty-seven per cent of the total estate arrears of £2,300. It is well to bear in mind that lands held by lease amounted to only eighteen per cent of the estate area (fig. 4.4). The argument proposed by the tenants that improvement was a corollary of leasehold interest appears to have been slightly fallacious. Only one of the five lessors had improved his holding. It is difficult to understand how Batwell recommended the lease system when his own report indicated that it had intensified the abuses it sought to terminate. The insistence upon long leases may have been influenced by the history of landlord-tenant relations on the estate. Money derived from colliery enterprises enabled individuals to ascend the social ladder, and because of this mobility, changes in the tenants-at-will may have been frequent. The recent history of excessive rent demands was probably the major reason why tenants sought the safeguard of leases.

(b) *The origins of the middleman system*

The Batwell report indicated how the system of tenure which characterised the estate in the early nineteenth century originated. Middlemen as a group have been much maligned and little researched and have had a genrally bad press. They were found in all colonial societies and acted as intermediaries between the indigenous occupier and the colonial owner. In Gaelic literature of the early eighteenth century, the middleman, tithe-proctor and hearth-money collector were reviled and castigated for aiding and abetting the conquest. Middlemen in Ireland have been primarily associated with the estate system of landownership introduced in the second half of the seventeenth century. It is certain, however, that individuals who performed similar functions existed in the manorial system of the Anglo-Normans and perhaps also in Gaelic society.

The middleman system in the Castlecomer estate developed under an absentee landlord anxious to secure a steady income but unwilling to establish an accounting or management system which would comprehend all the estate tenants. In Batwell's account of the townland of Gorteen, one can identify some of the circumstances which encouraged absentee landlords to let parts of their estates on long term leases. Batwell found that the tenants of Gorteen were greatly in arrears and observed that: "few if any of them pay any rent at all". He noted that they had a general character of being a "rebellious and ungovernable sort of people". This hill townland is located on the eastern perimeter of the estate and has a long association with coalmining. The tenants of Gorteen, who were named as "Mark Wilson, Thomas Boot and several others", combined cattle raising with coalmining. Attempts to distrain their cattle had failed. When their livestock was impounded, they "used to rise in rebellion and come in a body to Castlecomer to break open the pound".

The rehabilitation of such a group of rebellious tenants would have been a difficult, costly and time consuming job. Batwell recommended an alternative solution. Gorteen should be set to some solvent tenant who would keep them in subjection and oblige them to pay "their respective rents to him and he be obliged to pay your Lordship". This would save the landlord or his agent the task of dealing with such a lawless clan, whom Batwell compared to the "highlanders of Scotland". A postscript to the report indicated that Mr. Emerson, a colliery official, proposed to take a lease of Gorteen provided he had "peacable possession" given to him and that all the "troublesome tenants be got rid off".

The elevation of Mr. Emerson to the rank of middleman was a pragmatic decision. There is also evidence to suggest that principal tenants attained the status of middlemen because of mismanagement. Daniel Fynn, tenant of the colliery townland of Moneenroe, had not paid rent

103

since 1743 and was £746 in arrears. When the landlord's agent attempted to take his cattle, Fynn "filed his Bill for an Injunction to stop your Lordship proceeding at law against him under pretence of many injuries done his lands by the colliery roads and for large sums of money due for waterpulling". Fynn succeeded in his objective "for want of a full answer thereto and your Lordship being out of the Kingdom in which I think there must have been some mismanagement". Because of his success, Fynn "passed for a sort of Lord Chancellor among the tenants and was their principal advisor". He abrogated complete jurisdiction over his lands, "assigned tenancies and collected rents". Fynn was the prototype hybrid figure. "He had", according to Batwell, "been bred up as a sort of law clerk under Mr. Best" and was therefore familiar with the Common Law concerning land. The lawyer in Irish society was accorded high status and Fynn's defiance of the landlord gained him the loyalty which had formerly been accorded to sept leaders. This limited diffusion of the English legal system foreshadowed the momentous development of the nineteenth century when the great majority of the Irish people adopted the language and laws of the new order. Change was not solely the result of coercion but was recognised as an essential prerequisite for material progress.

Middlemen on the Castlecomer estate were either hybrid figures such as Fynn or colliery and estate officials such as Mr. Emerson. Others combined their duties as rent collectors with the role of town shopkeepers or tavern proprietors. Batwell's report suggests that middlemen may not have been as unpopular as has been commonly assumed. The dependent tenantry may, in some instances, have regarded them as defenders of their interests. It was the middleman and tenants-at-will on the Castlecomer property who were instigators of landscape change. They were sensitive to market demand; they enclosed townlands; they built substantial houses. The documentation of the early nineteenth century provides more detailed information on the influence of middlemen on the landscape and estate society.

CHAPTER V

THE WANDESFORDE ESTATE 1800-1840

1. Introduction
   This chapter examines aspects of the ownership and the occupation of
land in the Wandesforde property from the period 1800 to 1831. Background material in the form of detailed estate maps and rentals, which
are absent from the remainder of the barony, have survived for this property. The Wandesforde lands form an ideal unit for observing and measur-
ing change. Ownership throughout this period was retained by the Wandesfordes. The Countess of Ormonde, who held the property as tenant-for-
life in 1800, had succeeded her father, John Wandesforde, in 1789. On her
death in 1830, the estate reverted to the male line and passed to her
youngest son, Charles Harward Butler-Clarke-Southwell-Wandesforde.
Continuous ownership of an estate over a long period does not necessarily
indicate continuity in the policy of estate management. In this chapter,
the impact of change in ownership is assessed. The period under consideration was characterised by change on a national and local basis. The
rapid population growth experienced in the years from 1770 to 1840
was due to a combination of factors − dietary, medical, social and economic. The existence of areas of unoccupied land may also have encouraged population growth. In Fassadinin, the development of commercial
mining led to population growth and the expansion of settlement. The
estate maps reveal the dramatic impact of these factors. This chapter
assesses the nature of that change and attempts to identify those responsible
for it.
   Change was reflected not only in the material fabric of the estate, but
also in the conflict of interests between the diverse classes who constituted
estate society. These groups were more clearly delineated in this period.
The struggle for survival was intensified by the decline in agriculture and
the depression in the coal trade in the 1820's. Each group identified those
immediately superior to them as their oppressors. Contemporary observers
such as Inglis and De Tocqueville described the great poverty which prevailed among the inferior tenantry and the landless labourers.[1] Economic
divisions were accentuated by ethnic and religious differences. The Director
General of the newly formed National School system identified the causes
of conflict in the following terms: "Here" he said, "we have all the evils of
an aristocracy and none of its advantages. There is no moral tie between

105

rich and poor; the difference of political opinion and of religious belief and the actual distance that they lived apart, make them strangers one to the other, one could almost say enemies. The rich landlords extract from their land all it can yield; they profit from the competition caused by poverty; and when they have amassed immense sums of money, they go and spend them abroad". Divisions between economic classes were even more likely to be intensified in times of work and food scarcity. North east Fassadinin in this period was a complex, seething melting pot, characterised especially by poverty and class conflicts.

The uninterrupted possession of an estate over a comparatively long period should be expected to provide an invaluable unbroken sequence of data concerning estate affairs. This is true of the Wandesforde property in the nineteenth century. An important development in estate management of this period was that improving landlords were beginning to employ cartographers to compile estate surveys. In 1812, such a series of maps were drawn up for the Countess of Ormonde by James Healy. This 'atlas' formed part of the Wandesforde papers purchased by the National Library of Ireland circa 1962.[2] The area surveyed included the town of Castlecomer and twenty six townlands totalling 13,488 acres. All of the territorial divisions, apart from 'Tularea', were returned as townlands in the first edition of the Ordnance Survey six inch to the mile maps compiled circa 1838. Individual townland maps were constructed by Healy on the scale of ten inches to the mile. Reference tables accompanying the atlas gave the names of the principal tenants of townlands, and listed all the occupiers in the colliery townlands. The purpose of the survey was to identify rent paying tenants. Rarely were landlords interested in undertenants or sub-tenants who paid rents to middlemen, not to them. The occupiers of land in the colliery townlands had a special relationship with the landlord which gave them the status of freeholders. Individual maps of colliery townlands apart from Cloneen, have details of farm boundaries, settlement and roads and are of immense value in assessing the landscape impact of coalmining. Outline boundaries, internal settlement and roads are depicted on all townland maps. Townland boundaries rarely coincided with roads, which suggests, as earlier asserted, that their extent and limits were well known in the late seventeenth century. In the eight townlands, coinciding with individual farms, holdings of subtenants are not depicted.

These maps and accompanying rentals help greatly in reconstructing the pattern of land occupation in the period before the great surveys of the mid-nineteenth century. By contrasting them with the six inch to the mile townland maps of the Ordnance Survey, it is possible to isolate the features which were produced by the unprecedented expansion of population and settlement in the late eighteenth century. The map of Castlecomer town gives the location of individual houses and the accompanying reference table lists the occupiers. It is possible therefore to evaluate the role of the middleman as the architect of town growth. The estate maps are augmented by a manuscript report compiled circa 1836.[3] This report contains details of 193 leases made by the Countess of Ormonde since the year 1794. The information given includes the name of each lessor; the area of each leasehold; the annual rent paid by lessors; whether lessors were absentee, resident or deceased. In some instances, the material state of the holding is described and the amount of land sublet is given. This helps to isolate improving and non-improving middlemen. By utilising this report, a series of maps were constructed which summarise the impact of middlemen on the estate. Other documentation such as for example, estate and colliery accounts enable the reconstruction of a reasonably accurate picture of the transactions and activities which were part and parcel of estate life in the early years of the nineteenth century.

The Statistical Survey of Co. Kilkenny was compiled for the Dublin Society by Sir William Tighe in 1801.[4] It is one of the best researched and most comprehensive of the county surveys. It contains one of the earliest extant descriptions of the mining landscape in north-east Fassadinin. In 1814, Richard Griffith, energetic surveyor and land valuator, completed his report on mining in the Leinster coalfield.[5] Griffith devised a table of strata for the entire coalfield down to the limestone and added greatly to geological knowledge of the coal district. His survey also detailed the defects in colliery management. In 1832 a Government Commission was established to determine the causes of the violence and disorder which had character-ised the colliery district in the latter half of the previous decade.[6] The enquiry was carried out with the solid thoroughness which typified such endeavours in the nineteenth century. The local witnesses consisted of Catholic and Protestant clergy, minor landowners, colliery proprietors and resident magistrates. Their description of the area and its inhabitants provides a contemporary and local assessment of this part of the barony.

2. The Wandesforde Estate circa 1812

Figure 5.1 is a copy of the general map of Castlecomer estate compiled by Healy in 1812. On it, the location, areas and boundaries of townlands, major roads and some settlement are shown. All the townland names had been used in the seventeenth century to designate settlement and land units. The average townland size in 1812 was 512 acres. Variations which existed between townland areas reflect variations in land fertility. The largest divisions, such as Crutt (1,548) in the north and Croghtenclogh (2,132) in the south east, were located on the hill fringes of the estate. Figure 2.3 shows that these units in 1630 had a comparatively high prop-ortion of non-arable land. On the other hand smaller territorial divisions were located close to the town of Castlecomer and in the corridor of lowland which extended north-east and south-west of the town. Town-land boundaries rarely coincided with roads but the map shows that they did follow river courses. The northern river Dinin formed townland boundaries for the greater portion of its course through the estate (fig. 5.1). The irregular shapes of townlands suggests that their limits coincided with the alignment of local streams. Streams were numerous in the hill

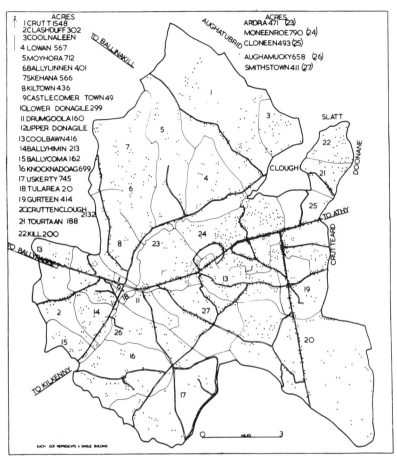

ACRES
1 CRUTT 1548
2 CLASHDUFF 302
3 COOLNALEEN
4 LOWAN 567
5 MOYHORA 712
6 BALLYLINNEN 401
7 SKEHANA 566
8 KILTOWN 436
9 CASTLECOMER TOWN 49
10 LOWER DONAGILE 299
11 DRUMGOOLA 160
12 UPPER DONAGILE
13 COOLBAWN 416
14 BALLYHIMIN 213
15 BALLYCOMA 162
16 KNOCKNADOAG 699
17 USKERTY 745
18 TULAREA 20
19 GURTEEN 414
20 CRUTTENCLOUGH 2132
21 TOURTAAN 188
22 KILL 200

ACRES
ARDRA 471 (23)
MONEENROE 790 (24)
CLONEEN 493 (25)
AUGHAMUCKY 658 (26)
SMITHSTOWN 411 (27)

TO BALLINAKILL
AUGHATUBRID
SLATT
CLOUGH
DOONANE
TO ATHY
CRUTTEARD
TO BALLYRAGGET
TO KILKENNY

EACH DOT REPRESENTS A SINGLE BUILDING

MILES
0   3

Fig. 5.1 Castlecomer estate 1812.

country and the permanence of their courses made them suitable demarcation lines.

A striking feature of the estate in 1812 was the great number of roads which either converged on or terminated in it. Roads were a significant index of economic change and their comparatively high density indicates the commercial nature of the estate economy. The townlands of Moneenroe, Cloneen, Gorteen, and Coolbawn occupied the area "between the small river Dinin and the sides of the hills to the north and east, extending from Castlecomer town to Doonane." In this district which was "three miles in length and two in breadth" the principal coalpits were located. The regular, straight stretches found on the Castlecomer-Athy and Leighlin-bridge-Moneenroe roads suggest that they were of recent origin and may have been laid out by colliery engineers. These individuals may have been influenced by the work of the canal engineers. Richard Griffith noted that the leading roads in the colliery district were generally kept in good repair whereas the bye roads were, in general, execrable. He also observed that the Castlecomer-Kilkenny road was well laid out and that from Castlecomer to Athy was "laid out in a straight line over hill and dale between the two places". Roads were the arteries of the colliery district and the absence of a direct canal link rendered them all the more important. The coal deposits and a comparatively large area of lowlying land were found in conjunction in the river valley of Dinin (Plate 1). The absence of landlord management in the early nineteenth century encouraged the development of lines of collier settlement along the main roads in this district.

Individual townland maps, which are discussed at greater length later, show that the layout of holdings in the colliery district was greatly influenced by the road pattern. This suggests that settlement growth followed the building of roads here. Crossroads provided foci for colliery villages. In the period from 1812 to 1838, the village of Gazebo developed on the site where the Leighlinbridge-Athy road converged in Moneenroe townland. Further south in the townland of Cloneen, the settlement of Railyard was built at the junction of the Leighlinbridge-Carlow road. In the north, north-west and south-east sectors of the estate the road system in 1812 was poorly developed. Coal was not absent from all of this area, but the seams were too deep for exploitation in the early nineteenth century given the limited level of technical expertise. Roads here fulfilled fewer commercial functions than in the collieries and were mainly links between Castlecomer and towns which lay west of the escarpment such as Ballinakill. Minor roads often terminated at the residences of middle tenants.

An examination of individual townland maps for this district suggests that dispersed agricultural settlement had preceded road construction here. It is possible that large scale extension of settlement to the hill lands did not occur on the Castlecomer property. J. H. Andrews has shown elsewhere that the unit of reclamation in this period was the 100 acre holding and not the smaller unit.[7] The complexity of the tenurial system operating on the estate had much to do with the development of this settlement pattern. The next section discusses this tenurial system; the extent or non-extent of proprietorial control and the landscape as depicted in Healy's maps.

Figure 5.2 shows the distribution of farms of 100 acres and over in the estate. It is known from later sources that these holdings were held on long term leases. The map indicates that, apart from the colliery townlands of Moneenroe, Coolbawn and Gurteen and the townlands of Ballyhiminin and Kiltown which adjoined Castlecomer town, these farms were found on all estate townlands. In 1746, complete townlands were the normal letting units but this was not the case in 1812. Where individual farms coincided with townland areas, it implied that leases under which they were held were made previous to 1800. The number of farms of 100 acres and over

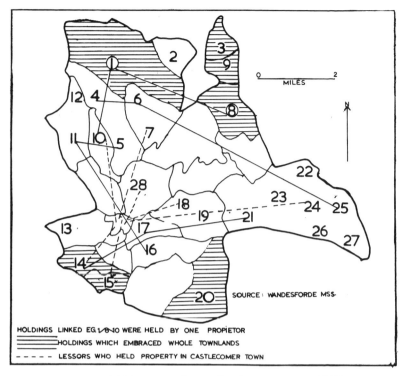

Fig. 5.2 Holdings of 100 acres and over. Castlecomer estate 1812.

on the estate, and the proportion of land they embraced, suggests that this was the prevailing form of tenure in 1812. The resident proprietor of the Castlecomer property in 1812 occupied only 416 acres or approximately three per cent of the total estate area. The lands in her possession extended from the Big House in Tularea north and south along the river Dinin and included the estate demesne and deerpark. This suggests that apart from the portion of the estate contiguous to the Big House the landlord had no extensive impact on landscape modification. Large-scale change was effectively the prerogative of the middle tenants.

An analysis of the reference table accompanying the maps indicated that approximately sixty-six per cent (9,000 acres) of the total estate area was held in leaseholdings of 100 acres and over. A further breakdown of this figure showed that lessors with Irish surnames held forty-six per cent (4,206), Anglo-Norman occupiers had twenty-eight per cent (2,442) and English lessors occupied twenty-six per cent (2,012). A comparison between the percentage proportion of estate lands held by the three ethnic-historical groups in 1746 and 1812 suggests that the Irish share had increased, the Anglo-Norman proportion had remained relatively stable and the English share had declined by almost twenty per cent. This

110

strengthens the thesis that a comparatively wealthy, Gaelic middleclass had evolved in the later half of the eighteenth century, contrary to the prevailing conceptions or misconceptions about the social hierarchy at this time.

Figure 5.2 shows that eleven lessors held more than one property. Four of them held farms which consisted of three detached fragments: seven occupiers held rural farms and buildings in Castlecomer town. The Denn farm, for example, consisted of three fragments which coincided with the townlands of Crutt, Ballylinnen and Cloneen and contained 2,438 acres or approximately one fifth of the estate area. Fragmentation may indicate that leases to the various fragments were acquired at different times. It may also have originated in purchase, inheritance or marriage. The 1746 estate report shows that two separate Denn families held Ballylinnen and Crutt, and that Cloneen was held by Thomas Mulhall. The Denn family were also the dominant occupiers in 1746 and claimed then that their ancestors were "time out of mind tenants to your lordship".[8]

From the English point of view, a major defect in plantation policy, outside of Ulster, had been the inability to entice prosperous English or Scottish farmers to settle in Ireland. In Castlecomer a comparatively large proportion of estate land was held by Gaelic tenants. The O'Brenans, hereditary proprietors of the estate, occupied 1,940 acres. The largest of the Brenan farms consisted of 825 acres and was distributed through the three non-contiguous townlands of Smithstown, Ballylinnen and Moyhora (fig. 5.2). Middletenants in possession of farms in townlands close to the town of Castlecomer invariably held property in the urban area also. Landlord policy and economic forces were together responsible for maintaining the large tenant farmer as the dominant type of occupier. The widely varying expiry dates of existing leases precluded centralised estate planning. It was, in effect, the aspirations and enthusiasm of individual middle tenants which were reflected in the landscape. The next section attempts to identify and analyse the various landscapes depicted on Healy's maps.

The landlord-induced landscape found its fullest expression in the demesne and deerpark which extended along the river, north and south of the Great House. The landlord's residence on the east bank of the Dinin river had been rebuilt after its destruction by the Wexfordmen in the sectarian conflict of 1798. According to estate records in 1822, the Countess of Ormonde paid taxes on 26 fire hearths and 95 window lights (Plate iv). The carefully contrived architecture of the Big House and its environs reflected a set of human values and preferences which had little in common with the world of the colliers and undertenants, living in the shadow of its walls. The mansion house was elegantly set against a background of tall beech trees. The river Dinin curled peacefully by the west side of the house, which was fronted by a small tributary stream over which a 'rustic' bridge had been thrown. Its physical dimensions, isolated and commanding location, lodge house and long symmetrical tree-lined avenue symbol-

Plate IV. The ruins of Castlecomer house, the residence of the Wandesforde family. This house located to the east of Castlecomer town and adjoining the river Dinin was rebuilt c.1800. The original structure on this site dates from c.1692.

ised social dominance and separateness. The demesne adjoining the house contained 346 acres and extended over five townlands (fig. 5.3). The river Dinin formed the focal point and a medley of water and wood were the central elements in this ornate landscape. The estate maps indicate that the demesne was extended at this period by the augmentation of leasehold land in the townland of Smythstown, south of Castlecomer. The construction of a demesne may have been an expensive task in an estate where so much property was held by lease. Interest in the lease had first to be purchased, or lands elsewhere in the estate exchanged for the portion required. Castlecomer town occupied the site on the west bank of the river. The demesne, apart from the deerpark in Moyhora which was located outside the town limits, was concentrated on the east bank of the river Dinin and consisted of a narrow, elongated stretch of land whose shape faithfully reflected the irregular course of the river (fig. 5.3).

The townland of Ardra was characterised by the landlord-induced landscape to a greater degree than other areas of the estate (fig. 5.4). Approximately forty-two per cent of the townland area of 471 acres was in the possession of the Countess of Ormonde in 1812. The remainder was partitioned among fifteen occupiers who were comprised of leaseholders and

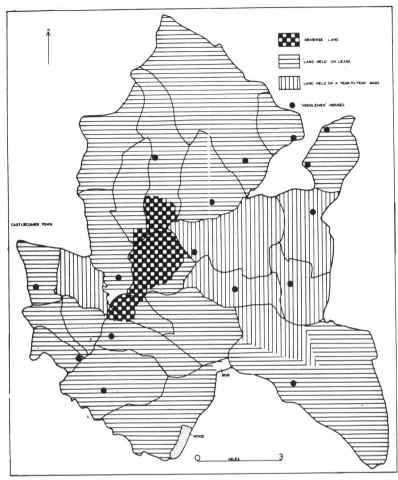

Fig. 5.3 Occupation of land. Castlecomer estate 1812.

undertenants. The demesne lands were separated from the mansion house by the Castlecomer to Leighlinbridge road which crossed the southern sector of the townland. The ornamented area, which occupied the portion of Ardra adjoining the river, was separated from Moneenroe to the north east by a wall which ran close to, and parallel with the townland boundary. Another wall, which extended northwards from the Leighlinbridge-Castlecomer road, formed the demesne boundary to the east. The townland map (fig. 5.4) indicated that eighteen small holdings were found on the west side of this wall in 1812. This encroachment on the demesne may suggest the weakness of proprietorial control in this period. The Protestant church, an adjunct of landlordism, usually found in close proximity to the mansion house, was located in the south of Ardra. The carefully

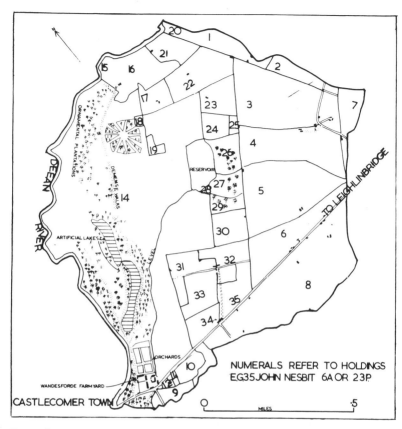

Fig. 5.4 Part of the Wandesforde demesne. Ardra townland 1812.

designed estate farmyard was set back from the road at a discreet distance from the mansion house. Contiguous to it, the estate gardens and orchards were laid out in small, rectangular plots (fig. 5.4). In the demesne lands proper, the elements of wood and water were intermingled to give the effect of elegance, seclusion, tranquillity and grandeur. Two artificial lakes were constructed to enhance the view and more mundanely, for boating in Summer. The reservoir, close to the boundary wall, served a more practical purpose supplying water to the mansion house and part of the town. The demesne, however beautiful, was extremely wasteful of scarce land resources, especially since it was usually the more fertile portions of the estate which were devoted to this non-productive purpose. In a period when land hungry tenants were voraciously extending settlement to the harsh, infertile hill lands, the care lavished on an esoteric demesne illustrates the detachment of the Irish landlord from his dependent tenantry.

114

The rental of the Castlecomer estate amounted to £7,339 in 1821. The arrears which remained after payment of rent came to £3,102.[9] Manuscript evidence indicates that the profits from the colliery enterprises in 1826 had been declining gradually and "instead of producing a profit of £10,000 as it did a few years ago, the net profits last year amounted to £956".[10] It may be assumed that the landlord's annual income in this period was around £8,000. The payment of forty-two per cent of total expenditure (£2,065) in "Tradesman's Bills and other house expenses" indicates that the process of ornamentation was ongoing. The inclusion of items such as "subscription to London for John Bull newspaper and to Scotland for cart wheels" suggests the range of landlord contacts. Approximately twenty-four per cent of outgoings concerned "payment for new buildings and other town Improvements". This relatively minor expenditure allows one to infer the limited contribution of the landlord to urban genesis in Castlecomer. The remaining items cover a great variety of things. Charity was dispensed to the poor of the estate and to the "distressed peasantry of Ireland". The sum of £2-16-5 was spent "on thatching in Chatsworth Row and other assistance to the poor whose houses suffered by storm". The ability of landlords to maintain their lifestyle was related to the availability and low cost of domestic labour. The accounts show that eleven per cent of total disbursements was paid in wages to estate officials and servants. These included a number of employees, such as woodrangers, coachmen, footmen, porters, sportsmen, schoolmasters and domestic servants. The comparatively small sum of £70 was given to George Scott to "buy stock", which suggests that the landlord was not actively engaged in commercial agriculture at this time. The account indicates the limited range of landlord activity in this period. There is little evidence of her involvement in the areas of the estate outside the demesne walls. Instead much time and money was devoted to the ornamentation of the mansion house and its immediate surroundings. A later section of this chapter discusses the reasons for this absence of participation.

Farms of 100 acres and over were the dominant forms of land occupation on the estate in 1812. Figure 5.3 shows the area of the estate characterised by the landscape of the middletenantry. The middletenantry were not a homogeneous group in 1812. Holding sizes varied from the 2,438 acres of the Denn family to the 104 acres hill farm occupied by Patrick McGenis in Croghtenclogh. Some middletenants resided on and farmed their lands but later evidence suggests that the great majority were absentees. All middletenants sublet lands in their possession and, in some instances, they played only a minor role in landscape modification. The Healy 'Atlas' and accompanying reference tables do not give any indication as to how these tenants managed their farms. It does, however, give a contemporary impression of the impact of this tenurial policy on the landscape. Figure 5.3 illustrates the rural landscape of the estate in 1812. The general map of the estate shows that the townland of Moyhora was more than five times as long as it was broad. Altitude in the north of the townland rises sharply to over 900 feet and in the south, the ground slopes gently towards the river Dinin. These two topographical divisions were reflected in farm size and land use patterns. The Castlecomer-Clogh road crossed the south of Moyhora and a new road which eventually linked the Castlecomer-Clough and Clough-Ballinakill road was under construction (fig. 5.5). The townland map indicates that the new road paid little attention to existing farm boundaries whereas the old road did. The walled deerpark and the inches along the Dinin river formed an

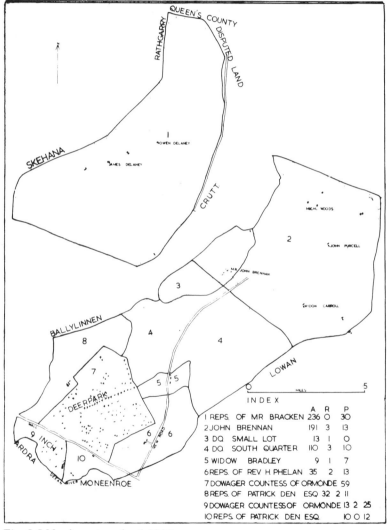

INDEX

		A	R	P
I REPS. OF MR BRACKEN	236	O	30
2 JOHN BRENNAN	191	3	13
3 DQ. SMALL LOT	13	I	O
4 DQ. SOUTH QUARTER	IIO	3	IO
5 WIDOW BRADLEY	9	I	7
6 REPS. OF REV H PHELAN	35	2	13
7 DOWAGER COUNTESS OF ORMONDE	59		
8 REPS OF PATRICK DEN ESQ	32	2	II
9 DOWAGER COUNTESS OF ORMONDE	13	2	25
IO REPS. OF PATRICK DEN ESQ.	IO	O	12

Fig. 5.5 Moyhora townland 1812.

extension of the aesthetic landscape into Moyhora. As altitude increased and quality of the environment deteriorated, leaseholdings became larger in size and more irregular in shape. Farm boundaries consisted of straight lines drawn transverse to the contours.

The division of John Brenan's holding into three separate farms suggests that he held his lands by three separate leases. The dates of these leases may record the chronology of John Brenan's rise in status from smallholder to substantial middletenant. The townland map shows that John Brenan resided on his central farm in Moyhora. The thatched two-storey house was set back from the new road and was approached by an avenue from which trees were conspicuously absent (Plate V). Resident middletenants were beginning to imitate the example of landlord houses in the layout and ornamentation of their own dwellings. John Bracken who held the remaining portion of north Moyhora, occupied two more large farms in the adjoining townland of Loan and the south east of the estate in Croghtenclogh (fig. 5.2). He had three under tenants on his Moyhora farm. Bracken resided in Loan townland and his house, well secluded by trees, was set back from the Castlecomer-Clough road. His Croghtenclogh holding contained 216 acres of infertile, unenclosed hill land which consisted

Plate V. Moyhora house. This house, in which the O'Brenan family who were middlemen on the Wandesforde estate resided, dates from c.1750.

mainly of unreclaimed bog. Bracken and Brenan were representative of middletenants who resided on and farmed the house quarters of their holdings and sublet outlying farms. In the same way the middletenant of Smythstown farmed 69 acres of his leaseholding and partitioned the remaining 316 acres among thirteen undertenants in portions ranging from fifty four to eleven acres. Because of the absence of uniformity in the cartographic treatment of individual townlands, it is not advisable to estimate the frequency of this practice.

From the general map of the estate, it was possible to plot the distribution of comparatively substantial dwelling houses in 1812 (fig. 5.3). These may have been the residences of middletenants. The map indicates that these houses were found in all estate townlands apart from Uskerty, Aughamucky, Ardra, Skehana, Ballylinnen and Clashduff. The density of substantial houses in 1812 indicates that middletenants in the late eighteenth century were usually resident. Their correlation with townlands illustrates that this territorial division was the primary leasing unit. The landscape of resident middlemen was characterised by large houses, situated at a distance from the road and usually secluded by trees. Uniformity in the layout and design of these houses and their embellishments implies the influence of landlordism. Resident middletenants may not have occupied more than 100 acres of the more fertile area of their holdings. This may have been the only portion from which undertenants were excluded. It is certain that the amount of land managed by middletenants was greater than the area they actively farmed. It is impossible to estimate the extent of subletting or to assess the landscape impact of the undertenantry at this period. The example available of the practice suggests that the size of sub-divisions was related to the land quality of the leaseholding. The lands held by Robert Kane, for example, in west Croghtenclogh, were subdivided into twelve farms ranging from three to eighty five acres in size. The general map suggests that the hill fringes of the estate were still relatively empty. This is true of the northern sector of Crutt and the east of Croghtenclogh townland (fig. 5.1). Four of the seven farms in east Croghtenclogh were over 200 acres in area. These large, irregular holdings consisted mainly of unreclaimed bogland located at 900 feet above sea level. The harsh quality of the environment here made it an unattractive living place even at a time when a rapidly rising population was exerting unprecedented pressure on existing land resources. The emptiness of the hill lands was related to the attractions of the commercial economy based on coal in the central area of the barony.

Continuous and intensive mining had a dramatic impact on the nature of tenure, the size of holdings and the density of settlement in the colliery townlands of the estate. Cloneen was one of the townlands held by the Denn family and consequently neither the internal arrangement of farms nor the names of tenants were given. The townland of Moneenroe (fig. 5.6) contained 790 acres of relatively low lying land which extended from the Dinin to the hill ridge in the east. The townland boundary did not

Fig. 5.6 Moneenroe townland 1812.

coincide with the river, except where the course of the Dinin was straight.
This may suggest that the meanders developed after the townland boundary was demarcated. Within this well defined physical area, a community
divorced almost completely from agriculture and dependent on coal for
their livelihood had developed since the late eighteenth century. In 1773,
a rental of the townland listed seventy occupiers. The tenements held
by the majority of these were described as "lots let to freeholders who
pay no rent".[11] By 1812 the number of occupiers had doubled. The

119

reference table accompanying the map indicated that 108 of the tenants held farms of under five acres and that only four farms were in excess of twenty acres. The two largest holdings which occupied land areas over fifty acres were located in the extreme northern and southern ends of the townland (fig. 5.6). This further intensified pressure on the land resources of the central sector of the townland. Smallholdings were laid out in long strips of uniform area, which occupied frontages along the roads which criss-crossed the townland. This pattern was the spatial expression of the contract system which elevated the colliers to the status of freeholders in the eighteenth century. The fact that farm boundaries and road fences coincided infers that the holdings were laid-out after the construction of the roads.

Two distinctive, basic networks can be identified within the crowded landscape of Moneenroe in 1812. The older element was the carefully planned arrangement which was reflected in the uniform layout of holdings. The later, superimposed element, which owed its origin to essentially demographic pressures and the attractiveness of mining in an underdeveloped agricultural economy, was the unplanned distribution of settlement. The concentration of settlement on the main link roads implies that a large proportion of townland inhabitants had no land. Alternatively, it may reflect the inability of the proprietor to prevent squatting by landless labourers. Another characteristic of mining was the comparatively high proportion of occupiers with English surnames, and of widows, found in the list of tenants. Fifty four per cent of the 145 tenants in 1812, for example, had surnames of English origin, and twenty-four per cent of the total townland area of 791 acres was in the possession of widow tenants. The townlands of Coolbawn and Gorteen which adjoined Moneenroe shared a common history of coalmining. These townlands in 1812 reflected past and contemporary mining activity in their settlement density, farm size, proportion of English occupiers and in the number of widows who held farms. In Gorteen twenty-three per cent of the townland area of 414 acres was held by widows, and occupiers with English surnames such as Fluellin, Reynard, Bradley, Booth, Wilson and Stone, held eighty-eight per cent of the townland. The other area of the estate where smallholdings were the dominant form of land occupation was located close to the town of Castlecomer. This area included the townlands of Kiltown, Lower Donaguile and the portion of Ardra townland outside the precincts of the demense.

The simplistic division of the Castlecomer estate into three contrasting landscape regions, the landlord, middle tenant, and mining areas suggests the spatial impact of ownership and tenurial systems. The first item of importance was the small proportion of the estate area in the possession of the landlord and the preoccupation of landlordism with ornamentation to the exclusion of worthwhile farming. The landscape of the middletenantry was a faithful, small-scale, replica of the mansion house and demesne of the landlord. Not alone were middletenants influenced by the physical expression of landlordism, but they also imitated the social characteristics of their peers. The landscape of smallholdings was influenced by proximity to the urban area and the development of coalmining. The absence of the undertenant, subtenant and landless labourers from Healy's maps and the accompanying reference table, makes this analysis necessarily incomplete.

3. Middlemen and Land circa 1838.

"When the late Mr. Wandesforde came into possession of the Castlecomer estate, he found that a number of tenants were holding large tracts of land, and in some cases whole townlands under leases granted by Anne, Countess of Ormonde at very low rents; that many of these tenants had never laid out one shilling on the improvement of these lands; that these tenants had let most of the lands held by them under lease to undertenants at exorbitant rents; that these under-tenants had let to sub-tenants. By a rental of 1831, which gives the names of all the tenants on the estate it appears that Mr. Wandesforde had 713 immediate tenants under him, and these had 2,067 sub-tenants under them"
(Carrick, The Earl of, *A Reply to a Narrative of Landlord Oppression and Tenant Wrong,* (Dublin, 1870)4).

On the death of the Countess of Ormonde in 1830, her fourth son succeeded to the Castlecomer estate. Change in ownership was a prelude to estate and colliery reorganisation and the initiation of landlord attempts to break the accumulated power of the middlemen. "Mr. Wandesforde", wrote the Earl of Carrick, "fearing that these undertenants and sub-tenants would be reduced to poverty and the estate entirely ruined, determined to break the leases which his mother, Anne, Countess of Ormonde had granted, for the sole purpose of benefiting the undertenantry by reducing their rents and giving them assistance".[12] Later commentators pointed to the impact of the Great Hunger on the landless of the estate and asserted that hardship and misfortune were greatest in the townlands held by middlemen. On the other hand, evicted middlemen not surprisingly claimed that landlord policy was to break the economic power of Catholic middlemen and to clear the estate of its redundant population.

The 'Rental and Particulars of Leases made by the late Countess of Ormonde on the Castlecomer property' gives details of 193 leases granted in the years 1794, 1796, 1812, and 1824.[13] The leases referred to 8,810 acres of the estate and were concerned with property in both the urban and rural sectors. A breakdown of the leases indicated that fifty four granted before 1800 referred to 6,665 acres, whereas eighty nine leases made after 1800 related to 2,145 acres. The occupation of land in 1838 was based mainly on leases constructed in the late eighteenth century. By utilising this report, a series of maps were constructed which summarise the impact of middlemen on the estate. In 1838, forty three leaseholdings of 50 acres and over were found in the Castlecomer estate. Figure 5.7 shows the distribution by size of these farms. Eight of these holdings were over 300 acres and in some instances individuals, or representatives of

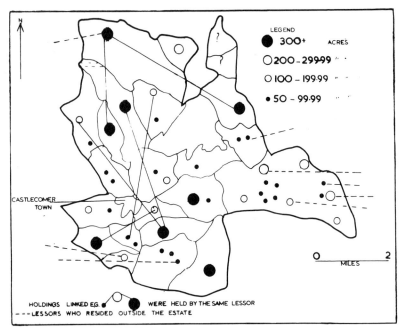

deceased lessors, held considerably more land than this. In Crutt, Cloneen, Ballylinnen, Smithstown, Uskerty and Clashduff, these farms occupied townlands. All but one of these large farms were held on leases granted before 1800. The report indicated that only two of these middlemen resided on, and actively farmed their lands. In the townlands of Crutt, Cloneen, Ballylinnen, Clashduff, Uskerty and Smithstown neither the original lessors nor their representatives resided, and all the lands were sublet to undertenants. Four leaseholdings ranged from 200 to 300 acres in size. Three of these were found in the infertile, hill district of east Croghtenclogh and the other was located in Coolnaleen townland. The occupation of all these farms was based on leases granted before 1800. Three of these four leaseholders were non-resident and had sublet their land.

Nine leaseholdings were between 100 to 200 acres in size. Three of these farms were found in Croghtenclogh and the remaining six were distributed throughout the western section of the estate (fig. 5.7). Occupation was based on leases made before 1800 in five of these farms. As the size of leaseholdings decreased, the number of occupiers who resided and farmed their holdings increased and four of these tenants were resident farmers. Approximately seventeen per cent of lands leased were held in twenty-two farms between 50 to 100 acres. Eleven of these leases were made previous to 1800. Of these twenty two occupiers, five were non-resident and had sublet all their lands; two were occupiers, farming portion and subletting the remainder of their farms; three lessors occupied but were not resident; and twelve lessors resided and farmed. The report indicated that tenants who occupied and were non-resident had other farms outside the estate. John Brenan, for example, held 80 acres in Knockannadogue townland by lease granted in 1829. He resided at Eden Hall, Ballyragget on a farm he held on the Kavanagh estate, employing a herd to supervise his Knockanna-dogue farm. The survey suggests that sub-letting was not a common practice on holdings of 50 to 100 acres. Twenty-three of the forty-three leasehold-ers did not reside on their farms. However, four of these non-residents occupied their farms and did not sublet. Absenteeism was more common on holdings held under leases granted previous to 1800.

Figure 5.8 shows the percentage of lands leased between 1784 and 1838 which were not in the possession of the original lessor in 1838. An examina-tion of the leases establishes that by 1838 a total of 4,348 acres had passed from the hands of the original lessors. The small amount of 631 acres had been transferred by the original lessor selling his interest. In the great majority of cases, interest in the lease had been retained by the kinsfolk of the original occupier. Absence of change through sale suggests the stab-ility of land occupation patterns on the estate in this period. It also implies that income from profit rents levied according to the market value of land

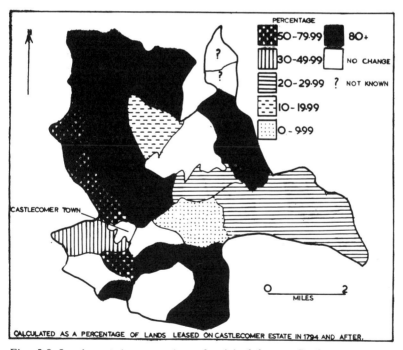

Fig. 5.8 Lands not in possession of original lessor. Castlecomer estate c.1836.

123

in 1838 far exceeded the original rents which were paid by the middle-tenant to the proprietor. In the townlands of Crutt, Cloneen, Ballylinnen, Moyhora, Ardra, Uskerty, Gorteen, Smithstown and Ballycomy all lands leased since 1794 had passed out of the possession of the original lessors. Three of these townlands, Crutt, Ballylinnen and Cloneen, were originally held by the Denn family while Uskerty, Moyhora and Smithstown were occupied since 1794 by members of the O'Brenan family. Townlands where the original lessors were in occupation, such as Moneenroe, Drumgoole, Clashduff and Knockannadogue, were held on leases granted after 1820. The death of the original lessor did not necessarily entail that his successors abandoned the property to undertenants but the weight of evidence from the estate points to this conclusion.

Figure 5.9 shows the average rent per acre paid by principal tenants in 1838. It has been seen that the greater portion of the estate area was held on leases granted previous to 1800. Consequently, their rents would relate to pre-1800 values and should be less than rents assessed after 1800. This was precisely the situation. Variations in average rent per acre was not an indication of variations in land quality. Rather, it was related to the age of leases. Even if all the townland rents had been decided in 1799, it may not have accurately reflected land quality. In the survey it was observed, for example, that Ballylinnen leased at six shillings per acre in 1794, "was one of the townlands which Mr. Denn by his influence with

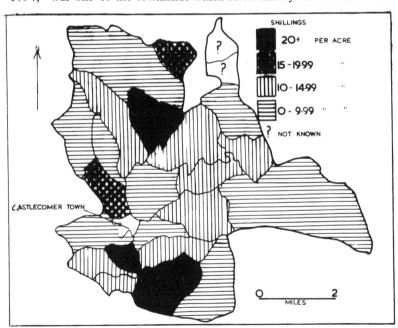

Fig. 5.9 Average rent per acre on a townland basis. Castlecomer estate c.1836.

the family obtained at the extremely low rent of 6/- an acre, at a time when it was worth 26/ ". The assessment of rent was an arbitrary matter influenced by many considerations other than purely economic ones. The lowest average rent per acre was usually found in townlands which had been transferred to representatives of the original lessor. Townlands in which land was held by leases made after 1820 reflect more accurately the quality of land in their rents. Tenants in Loan and Knockannadogue, where twenty-one leases were granted in 1820 in place of earlier ones which had run out, paid twenty shillings per acre. Reorganisation of tenancies in these townlands represent the first landlord onslaught on the primacy of middletenants and reflects the new policy of granting leases for portions of, rather than complete townlands. Average rent was grossly below market value in the Denn townlands of Ballylinnen, Cloneen and Crutt, and the O'Brenan leaseholdings in Moyhora, Skehana, Uskerty and Smithstown. The difference between the average rent paid in the demesne townland of Ardra and the colliery townland of Moneenroe in-dicates the impact of the leasehold system. The middletenant of the lands in Ardra townland adjoining the demesne paid the average rent of nine shillings per acre, whereas the tenants of Moneenroe townland where agricultural land had been damaged by mining, nevertheless paid an average of twelve shillings per acre.

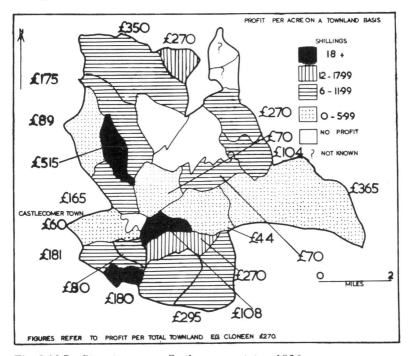

Fig. 5.10 Profit-rent per acre. Castlecomer estate c.1836.

125

This analysis of average rent paid to the estate proprietor revealed great discrepancies between townland rents. Figure 5.10 shows the estimated profit rent accruing to middlemen in 1838 for the rural areas of the estate. The profit rent represented the difference between the rents which the middleman levied on his tenants and the amount which he paid the landlord. It summarises the income which the middleman derived from letting lands at current values, while he paid rents frozen by lease from the late eighteenth century. In the townlands of Loan, Knockannadogue and Moneenroe, no profit rents accrued to middletenants. Significantly, landholding in Loan had been reorganised in 1824 and in Knockannadogue in 1829, and the middleman was never a dominant figure in the colliery townland of Moneenroe. The Report observed that "the lands of Knockannadogue are set at a fair value", and in Moneenroe, "leases were modern, rents fair and the tenants decent and well improved". In Croghtenclogh, Aughamucky, Ardra, Donaguile and Skehana townlands the profit rent varied from 0 to five shillings per acre. In Croghtenclogh, four of the twenty-six leases, by which lands were held, were granted before 1800 and the remainder after 1820. Reorganisation had taken place in the better endowed western portion of the townlands and the infertile bogland in the east was not attractive to undertenants. In 1824, David Ryan had acquired 465 acres in Aughamucky on a lease for three lives at the rent of eleven shillings. He occupied two thirds of this farm and let the remainder. In Skehana, on the hill fringes in the western portion of the estate, the seven lessors granted lands in 1825 were "all decent and improving tenants and all resided on their land". Donaguile, which was "for the most part mountain ground", had been let at full market value. The interest of the lease by which Thomas Earle held Ardra since 1794 was vested in Richard Reecks the estate gardener in 1838. The report observed that "the land is set to 9 or 10 undertenants, and Reecks may have £140 a year profit". The income derived by middlemen from these townlands was not greatly in excess of the rent they themselves paid. This was so because landholding had been subject to reorganisation which gave little scope for subletting. Furthermore, in the areas such as Croghtenclogh and Skehana where leaseholdings were comparatively large, the high proportion of infertile land and the absence of roads discouraged settlement.

Figure 5.10 indicates that in nine townlands on the estate middlemen had on average six to twelve shillings profit rent per acre. It would be wrong to link middleman income solely to profit rents from sublet lands. In many instances, the middletenant resided and farmed his holding, and derived part of his income from the increased market prices he received for his produce while his rent remained at a late eighteenth century level. The representatives of the Denn family held Cloneen at the rent of £230 under a lease made in 1794. In 1838 the Denns were non-resident and the lands were worth "£500 a year, £270 more than at present". Uskerty townland affords a more extreme example. It was held by lease granted in 1794 at the rent of nine shillings. In 1838 the lands were in possession of a representative of the lessor and were divided, "among a great multitude of undertenants who so far from improving are every year making it worse, the land is very bad but it should be worth double the rent". In Clashduff, south west of Castlecomer town, Robert Kane had sublet land leased at thirteen shillings for "about £1-5-0 an acre". The case of Moyhora townland reflects the complexity of operating the leasehold system and the advantages it gave to the middlemen. John Brenan held a total of 314 acres here by three different leases. The first lease concerned a farm of 191 acres let in 1794 at six shillings an acre. In the same year, he acquired another leaseholding at fifteen shillings and his third farm of thirteen acres was held at thirty-two shillings by a lease granted in 1813. The survey stated that "the small lot was held for its full value", but observed that the other two holdings "were worth on an average the sum of 20/- an acre".

Ballyhimmin townland adjoins Castlecomer to the south west and affords an example of the impact of the town on the letting value of land. The townland contained 213 acres of "excellent quality land" which was held in four leaseholdings granted before 1800. In three farms, the original lessor was dead and interest had passed to relatives. The representatives of Ed. Hayes occupied a portion of their 49 acre holding and had let the remainder to "7 or 8 undertenants". The representatives of William Baker had set all their 64-acre farm to undertenants. This holding provides an example of the great number of transactions concerning land in the early nineteenth century. The proprietor of the estate was one of Baker's undertenants. It transpired that Lady Ormonde had taken 13 acres from him and built a bleach mill which had been set to Nathaniel Hayes. The landlord paid £62 rent for this small portion whereas the lessor paid only £50 for his whole farm! Small holdings located close to the town provided a capital return for their occupiers. The widow of Ed. Groom had £15 a year profit rent from a holding of ten acres in Ballyhimmin, which she had let to two undertenants.

In the townlands of Ballylinnen, Drumgoole and Ballycomy, the profit rent in 1838 was estimated at treble the original rent per acre. These townlands were comparatively small in area and were located close to Castlecomer town (fig. 5.1). The primary reason for this relatively high return was that all these divisions were held on pre-1800 leases. The townland of Ballylinnen, for example, was let by lease for two lives in 1794. In 1838, the representatives of the Denn family paid six shillings an acre rent while the land was "all set to undertenants who pay on average about 30/-". Drumgoole townland, in which portion of the demesne was located, provides an example of the immunity of middlemen from landlord interference. Robert Kane's farm of 108 acres was held at six shillings rent and let to "12 undertenants". The Report observed that some of these undertenants "are a great nuisance having cabins either on, or near the demesne wall".

Variations in profit rent are explained, to an extent, by the time differential between the leases. Land quality and location in relation to Castlecomer town were other factors which governed the marketability of land. In east Croghtenclogh, for example, 1,347 acres were held under leases made in 1794. A large portion of this area was sublet, yet the profit rent amounted only to £365. Crutt townland in the north of the estate had a profit rent of approximately £350 and an area of 1,548 acres. This compares with the income of £515 which the middletenant obtained from Ballylinnen townland north of Castlecomer town (fig. 5.1).

Fig. 5.10 shows that in thirteen townlands the profit rent was over £100 per annum and in some instances was greatly in excess of this. Seven middlemen had profits in excess of £100 from their Castlecomer farms. The representatives of the Denn family, for example, derived an annual income of £1,135 from the three townlands they occupied. The Denns were non-resident and sublet all their lands. Of the six other middlemen who obtained this income, only one resided and farmed portion of his holding. Robert Kane resided in Castlecomer town, James Hendricken lived in Ballyragget and the place of residence of the three remaining lessors is not known. Middlemen had about £5,360 profit rent yearly, as contrasted with the rent of £4,574 which the middlemen paid the landlord. This landholding system deprived the landlord of much needed income and weakened greatly his control over the estate. The landlord's view was that excessive subletting would ruin the estate and eventually lead to great hardship for the dependent tenantry. It is certain that these humanitarian motives masked economic considerations. In the Report, the loss of profit rent is emphasised as much as the damage caused through subletting. The leases were legally constituted and were drawn up at a time when solvent tenants were difficult to find and landlords were satisfied with a fixed income rather than an unreliable one.

Changing economic circumstances, caused primarily by the rapid growth in population, led to increased demand and competition for land. The price of agricultural produce rose rapidly during the Napoleonic wars in the early part of the century. Economic historians have shown that the 1820 to 1830 decade was marked by an economic recession. Consequently, rent from land constituted the primary source of income. It was therefore in the landlords interest to reassert his right to all the income from his property. Improving landlords also sought to rearrange the ramshackle landscape which they inherited from an earlier period. It has to be stressed, however, that the management policy in 1838 represented the culmination of the strategy adhered to by their predecessors.

Approximately sixty-two per cent of the 8,810 acres held by lease in 1838 was in the possession of undertenants. Apart from the profit rents derived by middletenants, the report was also concerned with the practise and extent of subletting. Figure 5.11 shows the percentage of leaseholdings which in 1838 were sublet to undertenants. A comparison of this map and fig. 5.7, which shows the distribution of leaseholdings of 50 acres and over demonstrates that subletting was greatest on leaseholdings of 300 acres and over. These were also the holdings in which the original lessor

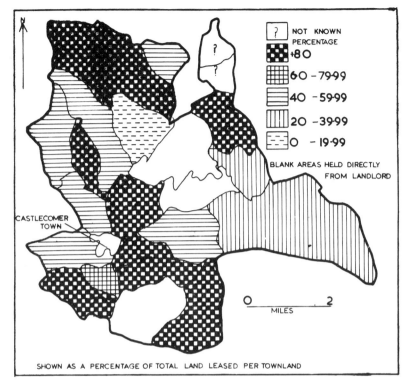

Fig. 5.11 Lands sublet. Castlecomer estate c.1836.

was generally deceased and which in 1838 were held by absentee occupiers. On the other hand, subletting was minimal or non-existent in townlands where leases were modern and where the holdings rarely exceeded 100 acres in size. In the eight townlands of Crutt, Cloneen, Ballylinnen, Ardra, Drumgoole, Uskerty, Smithstown, Ballycomy and Clashduff, one hundred per cent of lands leased were held by undertenants in 1838. The spatial distribution of these territorial divisions suggests that subletting was related more to the tenure under which the principal tenant held rather than to location or quality of land. In all these townlands, the leases were pre-1800 in origin and apart from Ballycomy, Ardra and Drumgoole concerned farms over 300 acres in area.

The survey gives a highly unfavourable impression of the landscape of the undertenantry. On the Denn farm of Ballylinnen, "no buildings or other improvements have been made upon it, except one tolerable farm house built by an undertenant". In Cloneen, the representative of the representative of the original lessor had built "a good dwelling house and brewery concerns", and the Report observed that there were "other slated farmhouses in this townland". The townland of Uskerty in the south of the estate presented a different exterior. "This townland", observed the

129

Report, "is divided amongst a great multitude of undertenants who so far from improving it are every year making it worse nor has there been a decent house built". In the remaining townlands characterised by subletting the report presents a picture of a dishevelled and deteriorating landscape.

In Ballylinnen, undertenants held seventy-nine per cent of the 200 acres leased. Between forty and sixty per cent of the farms held by lease in Coolnaleen, Donaguile and Kiltown was in the possession of undertenants. The occupation of farms by leaseholders reduced the amount of land available for subletting. The Report suggests that the majority of leaseholders who held 50 acres and over sublet to some extent. Subletting by residents led to a greater concentration of undertenants on restricted areas. The lands of Coolnaleen in the north of the estate, for example, were held by a nephew of the original lessor. In 1838, this individual had 63 acres of the farm in his own possession and had "divided the remaining 156 acres amongst no less than 26 undertenants". One of these undertenants had built a good house but according to the Report, "no other improvements whatsoever had been made". Similarly in the townland of Ballyhimmin, south of the town of Castlecomer, eighteen undertenants occupied sixty acres between them. It is not possible to develop this analysis further because the report does not always give the number of undertenants. This reflects the landlord's ignorance of the prevailing conditions in large areas of his property.

In the townlands of Aughamucky, Moyhora, Skehana, Croghtenclogh and Gurteen, undertenants occupied between twenty and forty per cent of farms leased. These townlands, to an extent, reflect the impact of the landlord's rationalising policies. This usually took the form of drastically reducing the area of leaseholdings when the opportunity presented itself on the termination of leases. When this was not done, the landlord was careful to select an industrious, solvent tenant. Examples of both policies are found in the Report. In Skehana townland, 112 acres was held in seven 1825 leaseholdings which were subdivisions of a single leasholding constituted in 1794. The agent of the estate who compiled the report described these lessors as "decent and improving farmers and they all reside on the lands". These tenants paid an annual rent of £60 which represented an average of ten shillings per acre. In the same townland, John Brenan held 125 acres by lease granted in 1794 at six shillings per acre. The Report observed that Brenan "does not occupy one acre himself but has it all set to undertenants". No improvements had been carried out on the farm. A similar pattern had evolved in Croghtenclogh townland. The portion of the townland to the west of the Leighlinbridge road contained 640 acres which had been reorganised into sixteen leaseholdings since 1820. In 1838, all of these tenants occupied the "entire area of their respective holdings" and were "very industrious". To the east of the road in the more hilly land, a different situation existed. Approximately 1,150 acres was held in farms leased mainly before 1801. Four hundred and fifteen acres were farmed by resident tenants but the remainder was either occupied by absentee tenants or completely sublet.

It would be wrong to assume that all middlemen were non-improvers. David Ryan, for example, who succeeded the Garraways as principal tenant of Aughamucky, was a good example of an improving middleman. Ryan who held a farm of 465 acres, "occupied two thirds and the worst of the land". He made "judicious and lasting improvements more than any farmer I know of either upon this or any other estate". He had obviously passed on the principles of good farming and management to his undertenants as they were described as "decent and respectable tenants whose houses are kept clean and comfortable and who receive great encouragement from him in the improvement of their holdings". John Brenan also resided in his leaseholding in Moyhora townland where he built a "very good dwelling house and planted extensively". He held half of this farm of 314 acres in his own hands and the remainder "is held by 6 or 7 undertenants who have improved their respective holdings very considerably by draining and liming". Even in such an impoverished area as east Croghtenclogh Anne Tracy, lessor of 187 acres described as a "mountain farm", had improved the land and "built a good house". The contemporary evidence presented by the report suggests that the great majority of middlemen were content with the income derived from undertenants and were not interested in farming their Castlecomer lands.

The reorganised areas of the estate were favourably commented on in the Report. In these townlands such as, for example, Loan, Knockanna-dogue, west Croghtenclogh and Kiltown, the comparatively small farm was the dominant form of land occupation. It is obvious that the estate agent associated improvement with small farms where the lessors were resident and did not sublet. The uniformity of the estate tenurial system in 1850 is proof of the landlord's success in rationalising landholding. Small holdings had long been the dominant forms of landholding in the colliery townlands of Gorteen, Coolbawn and Moneenroe. Successive landlords had turned a blind eye to the abuses manifest in these townlands. This gives the impression that in the 1830's the landlord was more concerned with eradicating middlemen who were making comparatively large profits. Loan provides a good example of a reorganised townland. In 1812, the townland was held in two large farms of 408 and 105 acres respectively. The occupation of land in 1838 was based on ten leases granted in 1829. The tenant farmers in Knockannadogue derived possession from eleven leases made in 1829 also. "This townland", observed the report, "is set at a fair value, the tenants are industrious and improving and some of them have built good houses and otherwise improved their holdings".

4. The middleman town

"Castlecomer seems at present to be a very poor place for want of some manufacture or public business being carried on there which would increase the town and bring inhabitants to live there especially as there is a very good foot barracks and a river running through the town". (Lullum Batwell Mss. report, 1746).

The Anglo-Normans erected a motte on the east bank of the Dinin in the thirteenth century. By 1300, the site possessed a church which served as a parish centre. There is no evidence to connect the Gaelic overlords of Idough, the O'Brenans, with the development of settlement here. The selection of Castlecomer as the centre of a manorial estate in 1635 provided a further impetus to growth. The conferring of commercial privileges, such as the right to hold a weekly market and three fairs during the year, provided the settlement with a basis for development, and established it as the primary urban centre in the barony. The early town builders perceived the urban area as a cultural and racial island which would advance the church and commonwealth by diffusing true religion and civility of manners. The realisation of these ambitions was twarthed by the continuous political instability of late seventeenth century Ireland. This section is concerned with evaluating the role of the middleman in the growth of Castlecomer in the period from 1796 and 1838.

In 1746, Castlecomer possessed a number of the elementary structures of a landlord town and it served as the administrative centre of the estate, the collieries and the Protestant church. In the absence of the landlord, the principal residents were the estate agent, Protestant clergymen and some prominent middletenants. In some instances, these middlemen held shops in town in addition to their rural farms. The area of Castlecomer town in 1812 suggests considerable development in the period from 1746 to 1812. The Wandesfordes resided here from 1751 and the period was characterised by prosperity in the collieries. The town site occupies a narrow, level area where the waters of the northern Dinin have eroded the upper Carboniferous strata. The ground rises sharply to the east and west of this valley before levelling out at 600 feet. The morphology of the town in 1812 (fig. 5.12) reflected the constraints imposed by the topography and landlord policy. Development westwards was restricted by the sharp rise in altitude. The river placed a barrier to town growth to the east and a more potent obstacle loomed up in the form of the mansion house and demesne. Northwards, the river valley becomes increasingly narrow so that it was only in the south that suitable level land was available for urban expansion. The triangular-shaped town outline reflected the constraints of topography. The 500 feet line formed the base of this triangle and the rivers Clohogue and Dinin comprised the two sides. The town had two major axes which consisted of the Kilkenny-Clogh road in a north south direction and the Ballyragget-Athy thoroughfare running east-west. The streets were aligned along these through routes and the cross, where the four major roads converged, was exactly halfway between the east and west boundaries of the town (Plates VI & VII). The town limits in the east and north were sharply defined by the Dinin and Clohogue rivers and by the town gate and barrack wall in the south and west.

Figure 5.12 is a copy of the 1812 town plan drawn by Healy. In it, the

Fig. 5.12 Castlecomer town 1812.

streets are divided into individual numbered lots. The occupiers of these lots are given on the accompanying reference table. A major deficiency is the absence of the annual rent levied on town houses. Without this evidence, one has to depend on the visible evidence of the manuscript map to indicate variations in the physical morphology of the town. The inventory of occupiers identifies town tenants and makes it possible to assess the number of people who held property in the town and the rural area of the estate. By indicating where a specific group lived within the town, it is possible to make a general appraisal of spatial and social variations in Castlecomer in 1812.

Bridge street (fig. 5.12) occupied the eastern section of the Athy-Ballyragget road. The street extended 260 yards from the crossroads to the bridge over the Dinin, varying in width from 20 to 40 yards. A total of 24 tenements were located here in 1812. Individual buildings had street

133

Plate VI. Castlecomer town. (A) Ruins of Wandesforde mansion house. (B) Wandesforde farmyard. (C) Bridge Street (High Street in 1850). (D) Kilkenny Street. (E) Barrack Street. (F) Chatsworth Row. (G) Bowden's Row. (H) Clohoag Street (Love Lane in 1850). (I) Police Barracks.

Plate VII. Castlecomer town. (A) Robert Kane's house. (B) Market house. (C) Church of Ireland clergyman's residence. (D) Catholic clergyman's residence.

frontages varying from fifteen to seventeen yards. The comparatively low density of houses per acre facilitated the construction of ornamental gardens which extended from the rear of the dwellings to the rivers Clohogue and Dinin. The combination of an unusually spacious street and substantial buildings with mature plantations created a townscape of considerable aesthetic merit. The Protestant church and the Big House lay secluded beyond the Dinin. Of the twelve urban dwellers differentiated from the remainder by the use of the prefix, 'mr.', or the suffix, 'esq.', nine were occupiers in Bridge Street. Five of these were middlemen who held considerable property in the rural part of the estate. For example, Mr. Henry Garraway held over 500 acres in Aughamucky and occupied two buildings in Bridge Street (89, 95). Both dwellings had spacious gardens of over an acre in size attached. It is probable that the majority of residents held rural farms. Those who were landless were invariably involved in estate or church administration.

Kilkenny Street was some 360 yards long and 10 to 15 yards wide. Its elongated form reflected site topography which restricted building to the level land parallel to the river. Kilkenny Street was aligned along the Castlecomer-Kilkenny road (from which it derived its name.) It extended from the central crossroads to the town gate which marked the urban boundary to the south. The Catholic chapel, sited on a ridge of high ground overlooking the town, was located outside the town gate (fig. 5.12). The shabbiness of town architecture contiguous to the Catholic church contrasts with the spacious grandeur of the glebe lands and precincts of the Protestant church in Bridge Street. The location of the churches at opposite ends of the town symbolises the theological and social distance which separated the religious groups and their respective congregations.

The reference table listed fifty-four holdings in Kilkenny Street. Considerable variations in allotment and house sizes within the street is evident from the map. The streetscape was not continuous and gaps of over forty yards between buildings are apparent on the east side. Houses located in the east of the street and particularly those found close to the crossroads were similar in size and layout to those of Bridge Street. To the South of the market house the west side of Kilkenny Street was divided into thirty-two uniformly small allotments. Each holding had a road frontage of from five to ten yards, with gardens laid out in long angular strips, terminating at the ridge of high ground to the west.

In 1812, Bartholomew Brophy was the principal occupier in Kilkenny Street and held three large sites. He held tenement 37 which contained two-thirds of an acre. Opposite to this he occupied holdings 73 and 76 which contained over two acres. His urban holdings had a road frontage of 120 yards, which obviously allowed him considerable scope for urban entrepreneurship. Brophy, in 1812, was returned as lessor of portion of Ballyhimmin townland south of the town. Only two other rural middle-tenants held property in Kilkenny Street. This street in 1812 contained elements of a substantial townscape in the northern sector which corresponded to the core area of the town. The western sector was a more recent creation which had a planned appearance. The many gaps in the streetscape ensured that future growth would be related to the infilling of these open spaces rather than to extension of the town limits. The market house dominated the northern sector of the street and gave it a commercial, as distinct from the residential, personality of Bridge Street.

Chatsworth Row derived its name from the townland of Chatsworth in the Bryan estate to the north. The townland name commemorated Chatsworth in Derbyshire. Local tradition ascribed the origin of the name to the influence of the proprietor of Chatsworth with the Wandesfordes, and his dislike of the original name of the street which led to his estate. The street was a continuation of Kilkenny Street and led to the mining village of Clogh in the north of the estate. It extended from the cross-roads 180 yards north to the river Clohogue. The eastern sector consisted of nine allotments which increased in size towards the town periphery. The western sector was comprised of three holdings which were occupied by Robert Kane, a major middleman on the estate. The map shows that the west side of the street was built up by 1812. Kane's house (144) was one of the most substantial buildings in the town. It occupied a prime site overlooking Bridge Street and the elaborately embellished gardens contained over an acre of ground.

Plate VIII. This house which is located in west Chatsworth Street, Castle-comer, was built by Robert Kane, a wealthy middleman on the Wandesforde estate, c.1820.

Kane typified the role of the property entrepreneur in early nineteenth century Ireland. He held over 800 acres in the rural townlands of Croghtenclogh, Drumgoole and Clashduff and imposing town buildings in Bridge Street. This analysis asserts that it was individuals such as Kane, rather than landlords, who shaped the physical fabric of Castlecomer town. Barrack street derived its name from the foot barracks erected in 1717 on an elevated site to the west of the town. In 1812 no town development had occurred beyond this limit. The east of Barrack Street was the most congested townscape in 1812 (fig. 5.12). The twenty five holdings located here, in a site restricted by the topography, had extremely narrow road frontages and uniformly small gardens. Despite the limitations of site, the houses and allotments presented a planned appearance typical of the town in general. West of Barrack Street the peripheries of the town merged with the rural area of the estate.

Our major source of information on urban growth and occupation of buildings in Castlecomer town is the 'Rental and particulars of Leases made by the Countess of Ormonde on the Castlecomer estate'. This survey does not define the town boundaries but returns the occupiers of the urban area and the built-up fringes of the rural townlands of Ballyhimmin, Donaguile and Kiltown adjoining. A great variety of information concerning seventy three leases granted to town tenants in the 1796 to 1838 period is given. This data includes: the names of individual occupiers; the date on which their lease commenced; the annual rent payable; a short account of their leaseholdings. Changes in occupation through decease of original lessors or purchase of interest were specified in the rental. The identity of the personnel responsible for the construction of individual buildings or sections of the town was recorded. The town area was not divided into its component streets but it is possible to identify locations by comparing occupiers names with those given in 1812. This identification of town builders is of primary importance as it indicates the limited role of the landlord in urban genesis in Castlecomer. It suggests that in the context of Castlecomer the customary description "landlord town" is a misleading misnomer. Parallel research may show that this is also true of other Irish towns which developed at this period. This implies that the middleman made a positive contribution to urban growth and had a developmental role which has been rarely attributed to him.

The rental indicates that the Countess of Ormonde was responsible for building a total of nine houses, or approximately one eight of the total number erected, from 1796 to 1838. The landlord's role in town development was as limited as her participation in rural parts of the property. Six of these houses were described as "small houses built by Lady Ormonde and occupied by the tenants to whom she set them". These single-storey buildings were located in the cul-de-sac, at the rear of the market house, which in Griffiths valuation was named Bowdens Row. The three other dwellings erected by Lady Ormonde in Bridge or Main Street represented a more substantial addition to the townscape. The Rental observed that "she

137

had rented a large lot in the south side of Main Street, at the yearly rent of £27 and built the house in which Mr. Despard lives, and was building the house she agreed to let Mr. McGowan for an inn, when she died". Transactions concerning urban sites were numerous and the single site was sold and re-sold before building commenced. The original lessor of this site, for example, was Robert Power. On his death, the six acres of urban land was vested in his daughter, who assigned it to a "man named Comerford from whom Lady Ormonde took it". The compiler of the survey, Richard Eaton, lived in a substantial house built by Lady Ormonde on a site she had purchased from the representatives of Henry Garraway. Eaton, the estate agent, paid a rent of £78 for the house, and this was the second highest amount paid on leasehold dwellings in 1838.

A major deterrent to landlord participation in urban growth was the existence of long term leases for the greater portion of town land. The landlord could either wait until the lives in the lease had become extinct, or purchase the interest from the existing lessor. The second of these alternatives was the one usually adopted. As in the rural estate, improvements in the town took the form of the rationalisation of landlord-tenant relationships through the eradication of middlemen. An account of 'Town Improvements and other new buildings' in the Wandesforde papers, dated 1838 helps to define improvements in the urban context. A total of £96 was paid as "compensation to tenants removed". In contrast to this, only £54 was expended on the erection of "new houses at the town pound in Chatsworth Row". Embellishment of the townscape in a form of a town fountain at the crossroads and a "New Nursery in Chatsworth Row" cost £109, approximately double the amount expended on new houses.

An examination of the rental suggests that capital derived from rural profit rents was, to an extent, reinvested in town buildings. The exploitation of congestion in rural areas for the ornamentation of Main Street has similarities with the general outward movement of capital from rural Ireland in the nineteenth century. Individual middlemen made varied contributions to town growth, ranging from the cabins on the southern periphery of Kilkenny Street to the dwelling of Robert Kane in Chatsworth Row built at a cost of £3,000. The focal point of 'middlemen' activity was Bridge Street. The streetscape here in 1846 was described as being "edificed with two storey, slated houses each side, shaded with trees and disposed in the manner of small malls".[14] The Rental indicates that a total of twenty dwellings were erected in Bridge Street between 1796 and 1838. Of these the landlord had built four. Sixteen houses were built by lessors on sites held by leases granted mainly before 1800. Thirteen houses were built by the original lessor and seven were constructed by purchasers of the interest from original lessors. This suggests that prime lots in the town were a much more marketable commodity than land in the outlying areas of the estate. The survey noted that, in some instances, smaller buildings were demolished to create a more spacious site. Jonathan Bradley, for example, purchased Richard Buggy's interest in a site and house held by lease since 1795 for £100. He proceeded to build an "excellent house and offices" on the north side of Main Street. The Wandesforde papers recorded that in 1838 Jonathan Bradley was given "£50 to finish a new house". Bradley was a successful colliery proprietor who had acquired a small estate in Firoda Lower, to the west of the town.

All of the thirteen houses built by original lessors were in the possession of their representatives in 1838. Thomas Earle who occupied 170 acres in Ardra had built two "very good houses and made other considerable improvements" on two lots he held in south Main Street. In 1838, these houses were occupied by his sons-in-law, Reecks and McGowan. Captain Wilkinson, tenant of large farms in Croghtenclogh, had erected two dwellings in north Main Street, adjoining the river. David Aher, colliery manager and road engineer, was son-in-law to Wilkinson and occupied one of these houses. The other was held by the medical doctor, Hartford. Morgan Brenan was another lessor who had built two houses in Main Street. Brenan was dead in 1838 and the properties were held by his sons-in-law, Grace and Murphy. The rental observed that Grace resided but Murphy had let the other at "six guineas a year". Kieran Doyle, proprietor of 82 acres in Croghtenclogh and a farm of 27 acres in Knockannadogue, was also involved in speculative ventures in the town. He had bought the present post office from the original lessor and then let it to "John McLoughlin the postmaster for £18".

Within Main Street, small houses were interspersed between the dwellings of estate agent, colliery proprietors, clergymen and wealthy farmers. Two adjoining lots held by Pat Coogan and Daniel Ryan were both held at rents under one pound. The evidence suggests however, that in the period up to 1838 landlord and middleman were concerned with developing a uniform and imposing townscape. It is not possible to determine the profit rent accruing from house property. The great majority of dwellings were not sublet but were occupied by those who built them, or their representatives. Subletting of house property was invariably confined to substantial dwellings erected by the landlord and set to estate, colliery or church administrators. The rental shows that only two other houses were let in Main Street and one of these was the post office. It is equally difficult to estimate the cost of house building. The town house of Robert Kane in Chatsworth Row had reputedly cost £3,000 to construct but this can hardly be used as a guideline. Kane's house was a three-storey building of massive proportions with extensive gardens and was considerably larger than the usual Main Street dwelling.

Thirty-one houses were constructed in Kilkenny Street in the period from 1796 to 1838. It has been noted that the 1812 town map shows a total of fifty-four holdings here. An examination of the Rental suggests that thirteen of the houses built previous to 1812 occupied sites close to or on the opposite side of the street from the market house. By 1838, eight of the original lessors were dead, one had sold his interest, and the remaining four were occupiers. The rental indicated that four of these thirteen properties were sublet. The leaseholdings which commenced after 1812 were described as "small lots in the town upon which houses have been built by the leasees, some of whom occupy themselves, but for the most part they are sublet". These 'lots' as depicted on the 1812 map were carefully laid out and presented a uniform appearance.

The contribution of rural middlemen to the townscape of Kilkenny Street was both limited and varied. Henry Garraway had built the manor mills on his site adjoining the river. Robert Kane held a house on the west side of the street adjoining the Roman Catholic chapel. The absence of Bartholomew Brophy from the reference table is surprising, in view of the fact that he held over five acres of land here in 1812. Brophy's lease was broken by the proprietor in 1833, and this represents the beginning of the landlord policy of rationalisation in the town. Local tradition associated the breaking of the lease with the religious bigotry of the then Wandesforde proprietor. An unenclosed portion of Brophy's leaseholding occupied the east bank of the river and adjoined the demesne. This Inch was used by the local populace on Sundays as a gathering place. The landlord "took exception to people being so near his demesne and especially as he said, desecrating the Sabbath and proceeded to break Brophy's lease at the cost of a hundred thousand pounds".[15]

In 1795, John Hendricken was granted a lease of fifteen acres south of the town gate in Kilkenny Street. In 1838, the Rental observed that "this lot is precisely of the same description and similarly circumstanced with that of Bartholomew Brophy whose title has been lately evicted". A great number of "cabins comprising one side of the suburbs of the town, had been built upon it, and although for the most part built by the tenants themselves, the occupiers pay heavy rents to Mr. Hugh Hendricken, the leasees son". Town development in Kilkenny Street consisted of smaller and less durable houses than those of Main Street. The cabins which straddled both sides of the street at the entrance to the town were common and widely noted features of the morphology of small towns in Ireland. Both Hendricken and Brophy derived high profit rents from this emphemeral townscape element. Brophy, however, survives in local folk memory not as a middleman but as a figurehead who defied landlordism. The Rental indicates that subletting was a much more common feature here than in Main Street. This was obviously associated with the low rental valuation of houses here, which ranged from ten shillings to three pounds. In the social and economic climate of early nineteenth century Ireland, tenants capable of paying over £30 a year for house property were a minority group. This factor explains the high rates of owner occupancy in Main Street. As the rental valuation decreased, a far wider section of the population were potential tenants and middlemen made greater profits on town property which required little capital investment. The law of supply and demand conditioned, to an extent, the character of urban development and the resultant townscape.

Building in Chatsworth Row in the period 1795 to 1838 reflects the

140

role of the middleman in town development. Robert Kane was the principal developer here. He built an imposing town house on a site which had formed part of the open town square. In contrast to this durable building, which still stands, he erected cabins on the west side of the street. By 1838, the gaps in the streetscape evident on the 1812 map had been infilled. Richard Reecks, the estate gardener, had built "two good houses and offices, for one of which he gets between £20 and £30 a year and the other is at present untenanted". Reecks occupied a substantial house in Main Street built by his father-in-law, Thomas Earle. He also had inherited the Earle farm of 170 acres in Ardra townland. Ambrose Williams held a house and 'lot' in Chatsworth Row by lease dated 1821. He had built a "very good house with offices and garden which was let to John Hewetson at £30 yearly". Williams held only eight acres in the rural area. He occupied another urban site where he had "built a very good house and made other improvements" on the western hill ridge overlooking the town.

The durability of these houses is emphasised by the fact that many of them are still standing almost one hundred and fifty years later. Significantly, the last phase of building in Chatsworth Row was carried out in 1838 by the estate proprietor. The town nursery was laid out on a central site on the east side of the street. Further north, the built up area was extended to the town pound. Growth in Barrack Street was limited in the 1821 to 1838 period. Absence of development related to two factors. Firstly, the hilly character of the street restricted suitable building areas. Secondly, the framework of buildings in Barrack Street had been laid out in the mid-eighteenth century or earlier, when the barracks and the Dinin Bridge had defined the east-west town boundaries. Apart from the "nine or ten cabins on a lot adjoining the Barracks wall", the leases contain no reference to any substantial additions to the street.

The survey is not an exhaustive source as it does not relate to all town property. Nevertheless it identified the creators of the urban fabric of early nineteenth century Castlecomer. The evidence suggests that direct landlord participation in town development was limited. Landlord influence was exercised indirectly through the granting of leases on favourable terms as an inducement to building. Rigid adherence to the existing street framework indicates a landlord role of supervision rather than participation. The Rental shows that construction of the more substantial town buildings was carried out by tenants who invariably held large farms. These solid houses, located on both sides of Main Street, on the east of Chatsworth Row close to the junction of Main Street and in the unenclosed town square, were invariably owner occupied. Some middletenants had erected two or more houses. These were Thomas Earle, Richard Reecks, Captain Wilkinson, Henry Garraway, Ambrose Williams and Morgan Brenan. All of these apart from Williams and Brenan held substantial rural properties. The Wandesforde papers indicate that Williams was a general merchant.

Houses built on lots leased in 1796 were generally inhabited by representatives of the original lessor. These were built for prestige rather than for commercial motives. Dwellings erected by middletenants after 1820 were invariably sublet. The third group who fashioned the urban landscape were the leaseholders who held town property only. These had built the greater number of dwellings in Kilkenny Street. The Rental suggests that the majority of these houses were sublet in 1838. The fourth component of town morphology was the cabins which occupied sites on the outskirts of Kilkenny and Barrack Street. These transient structures were built by their occupiers in Kilkenny Street, who then paid heavy ground rent to the lessor. The density of these buildings per unit area was comparatively high. In Barrack Street, ten cabins occupied a site which had an area of 2 roods and 19 perches.

5. Middlemen and Coal

Mining since the early eighteenth century had concentrated on the three foot seam, an excellent anthracite, which lay at shallow depths. Pits on this seam were located in the townlands of Moneenroe, Cloneen, Coolbawn and Gorteen in the Wandesforde property and in the townland of Clogh belonging to the Bryan estate. Borings drilled in 1959-63, as part of a Government Enquiry into the resource potential of the field, cut through old workings on the three foot seam at depths which varied from 64'2" in Clogh, 72'11" in Moneenroe to 20'2" in Cloneen.[16] Previous to 1800, sporadic mining had occurred in Firoda townland west of Castlecomer on the Earl of Carrick's estate and in Crutt townland north of the town. In Firoda, a series of shallow pits worked the outcrop of the no. II seam while the Crutt workings caught the outcrop of the Jarrow. The Jarrow coal seam was named by the Durham miners who worked it in the early nineteenth century. This coal was found at depths from 50 to 80 yards and maintained a thickness of 9 to 12 inches over its restricted extent. The central part of the seam was traversed by an oxbow shaped loop, seven miles long by 200-300 yards wide, known as the Jarrow Channel (fig. 5.13). The seam reached a thickness of four feet here. The channel follows an underground course, roughly parallel to and east of the Dinin, through the townlands of Clogh, Loan, Moneenroe and Coolbawn. The coalmining industry here in the nineteenth century was based mainly on the exploitation of the Jarrow seam. Jarrow pits were either close to or on the outcrop of the higher three foot seam so that extension of mining to the deeper Jarrow seam did not alter the locational pattern of the industry.

The concern here is with the middlemen system in the collieries and the landscape of mining in the early nineteenth century. The sinking of pits was carried out by the proprietor. On completion, it was farmed out to a master collier who undertook to obtain a crew and to work the coal for a share of the profits. The master colliers were primarily concerned with the landing of coals. Contemporary evidence shows that they had other interests. Griffith described them as "a species of middlemen between the

142

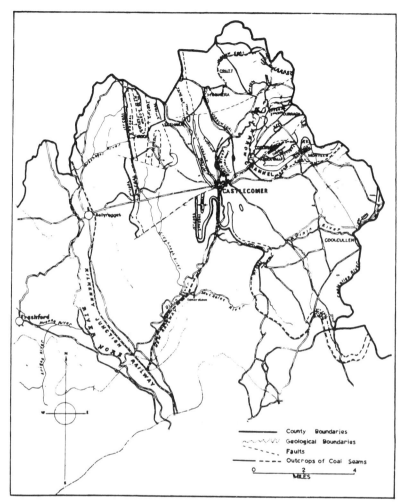

Fig. 5.13 Coal seams Fassadinin.

agent and the colliers". Thomas Bermingham, in evidence before the Commission of Enquiry into outrages in Ireland in 1832, defined them as "people who kept shops, kept long accounts unsettled and got the poor colliers into debt". Tighe had also observed the commercial functions of the master collier and the economic dependence of the colliers on him. He noted that the colliers were paid in notes which were generally passed on at a depreciated rate and that the huxters who were often times master colliers, "impose in their charges for articles of necessity, and the collier is obliged to pay a ½ penny more on the price of a pottle of meal, when he pays in tickets as they are called". Another witness who testified to

143

the Commission on Outrages added a new dimension to the master collier's functions when he described them as "middle sort of persons who had a great deal of influence over the lower class and held from 20 to 40 acres of ground". The status enjoyed by the master colliers was mainly derived from their economic influence. As employers, they provided work in the pits they held under contract: as landholders, they allocated potato land: in their capacity as huxters, they supplied essential provisions. The system had originated in the mid-eighteenth century and was based on contracts made between the colliery proprietors and the colliers. Change in economic circumstances caused by increased competition from the English and Welsh fields and the fact that the coal occurring at shallow depths was exhausted, led to a reappraisal of the management system.

The manuscript evidence suggests that attempts to rationalise colliery procedure began in 1826. David Aher, eminent surveyor and engineer, was suspended by the colliery trustees from his position as manager. A report on colliery affairs, compiled in 1826, observed that "for some years back the produce of the collieries had been declining gradually and instead of producing a profit as it had a few years ago of £10,000, the net profits the last year were £954". A new system was "deemed necessary" and to establish this it was necessary to get rid of, "certain contracts that Mr. Aher had made". The master colliers who held these contracts and others "who claim as assignees and by purchase from the original contractors refused to give them up". Furthermore, the master colliers would not 'allow the pits they held under these contracts to be worked by any other system, or any person than these mentioned in their proposals". The manuscript described both the old and new systems. In the old mode of working, "pits for the purpose of working and making experiments were extended over a surface of upwards of 2,000 acres". This method disrupted agriculture; rendered the soil of "such an extended area unproductive" and greatly increased the claims for damages and working expenses. According to the new plan collieries were to be confined "to a certain space" and "no other pits were to be opened until they are entirely exhausted". This system would have reciprocal beneficial effects on mining and agriculture. Tenants on the parts of the estate unaffected by mining would be allowed to cultivate and improve their lands. The collieries would require "fewer persons to work and superintend the workings and these being better paid, as the profits will then allow a better description of person".

Rationalisation of mining followed a similar chronological sequence to the attempts to eliminate middlemen in land. Both commenced on the death of the Countess of Ormonde. Both policies may be interpreted as an attempt by the incoming proprietor to re-assert his right to the profits from land and coal. The manuscripts indicate that the original contractors who agreed to raise coals at the rate of £3.10.0 per score had subsequently sublet these contracts to others at £5.10.0 a score. This represented a loss to the proprietors of £2,000 a year.

The conflict in the colliery district was symptomatic of the general social and economic unrest in pre-famine Ireland. The depression in the colliery trade was accentuated by the general impoverished state of the country in the decade before the Famine. There is evidence that concentration on beef farming led to contraction in the amount of land available for potato growing. This had important implications for the colliery district where the growing mining population was dependent on smallholders for conacre ground. The rental of 1838, for example, revealed that Richard Wright, who held 6 acres in Coolbawn, resided on his farm and had "4 or 5 cabins occupied by pauper tenants on his land". Observers such as De Tocqueville and Inglis noted the numbers of unemployed, the destitution of the landless labourer and the growing antipathy between the people and their landlords. This antipathy towards the Establishment was manifested in the general opposition towards the payment of Tithe to the clergy of the Established church. It was also reflected in the growth of secret societies such as the Whiteboys and Ribbonmen. In general, these groups sought to regulate land prices and terminate the payment of tithe. They attempted to nullify the policy of eviction by preventing new tenants from taking up possession and destroyed fences and livestock as a protest against the spread of pasture. The social condition of the people and the dilapidated state of the landscape represented the culmination of mismanagement of estate and collieries in the eighteenth century.

In 1826, colliery supervisors were brought from Durham coalfield to effect changes in mining methods of Castlecomer. The extension of working to the deeper Jarrow seams had rendered old methods redundant and obsolete and change in estate ownership encouraged the desire for modification. In evidence before the Commission of Enquiry into Outrages in 1832, Thomas Bermingham, who was one of the colliery personnel brought from Newcastle-on-Tyne, described his attempts to increase profitability. Uneconomic small pits were closed and deep pits with improved ventilation were sunk. The contract system was discontinued and coal was now raised solely to satisfy market demand. Rationalisation affected the old colliers who were unable to work in the deep pits and the numerous watchmen who were previously required to guard the stocks of coal standing on the banks.

Opposition to the new methods took the form of combinations among colliers and carmen who refused either to work or transport the coals. Continuation of the retrenchment policy led to the adoption by the colliers of more extreme methods. Hostility was directed especially towards the visible agents of change, the supervisors brought from England. The clandestine activities of the colliers culminated in the murder of five colliery personnel in 1831. Kilkenny was immediately proclaimed a disturbed county in a state of insurrection and the operation of the ordinary courts was suspended. In 1832 a special Commission was established to ascertain the causes of the outrages. The witnesses who testified to the Commission included resident landlords, land agents, magistrates, clergymen and colliery proprietors. These gave a contemporary impression of the mining landscape and mining operations.

Many of the witnesses were impressed by the dramatic impact of mining on the appearance of the countryside. Robert Stapleton, colliery proprietor and estate owner of Tollerton, Queens County, referred to the "country which up to a few years ago was wild pasture and applied to dairy purposes," and was now a very populous country and almost every road a street." "The population were", he said, "scattered thickly over the area, except in the collieries where the Grand Canal Company had built the village of Newtown in streets with cabins where the working colliers live". Another witness affirmed that the population was "as great if not greater than in any part of Ireland" and described the settlement as consisting of "cabins studded over the entire area". John Edge, proprietor of Doonane colliery, noted that the "population of the three collieries of Newtown, the Lordship and Clough was very great, with the working colliers living in little detached cabins quite close to each other". The manuscript maps of 1812 and the Ordnance Survey six inch to the mile townland maps compiled circa 1839, indicate the accuracy of these verbal descriptions.

The witnesses did not only describe the landscape of mining: they also identified the factors which contributed to the growth in population and the conflict that ensued. The collieries when working extensively brought in a great population, "many of whom built cabins and stopped there". When the collieries declined, the men were obliged to seek work elsewhere, 'leaving their families without subsistence". Landlords were obliged "to get rid of these tenants in consequence of they having no land". The uncertainty which characterised the industry was mirrored in the transitory nature of the buildings which littered the countryside. The year 1831 was a particularly bleak one in the collieries. The combination of colliers and carman had stopped work in the Wandesforde pits. In Tollerton colliery, Queen's County, the "level line which Mr. Stapleton had carried up to his colliery failed, striking a stone fault, the ground became convulsed, the coal was lost and disappeared", and 100 men were out of work. Throughout the coalfield, natural accidents, bankruptcy of operators, combinations of workers and a depressed market had led to decline in mining.

The observations on the character of colliery society, in the Commission of Enquiry were strikingly uniform. The viewpoint that colliers were a drunken set was unanimous. John Edge, a colliery proprietor, who one would presume was familiar with their way of life observed that "they drink whiskey, plenty of it, it being the ruin of them". Addiction to alcohol was common to all social classes and was not confined to the colliers. In 1835, the Poor Inquiry Commission stated: "among the many causes of Irish misery which have been brought to our notice, one of the most prolific, assuredly the most pernicious, and we fear, the most difficult to be reached by any direct legislation, is the inordinate use of ardent spirits, its baneful effects are felt by every class".[17] The comparatively high incidence of drunkeness in colliery society was linked to the fact that their wages were greater than those of the agricultural labourer. They were invariably paid in money, whereas payment in kind was still widespread in respect of other workers. Tighe, whose Statistical Survey of Co. Kilkenny contains an invaluable account of mining society, observed that although colliers had high wages they were "in appearance the most wretched persons in the country". The wages were generally "consumed in the purchase of whiskey, a ruinous habit encouraged by the mode of labour". Tighe's description of the material landscape of mining retained validity for the greater part of the nineteenth century. He observed the "paleness of complexion" which characterised those who worked underground and the disorderly landscape dominated by the flimsy temporary habitations of squatter families. These houses had neither chimneys nor windows. Children were numerous, unhealthy and ill-clad. Rarely did the working colliers survive the rigours of a damp working and living environment beyond fifty years. Alcohol was the only means of enlivening a short and squalid existence replete with sickness and hardship.

The colliers were described as both "improvident and reckless". This improvidence was demonstrated by their failure to 'till' their potato land. "The pecuniary advantages of the coal trade", according to Stapleton, 'appeal to them more than the farming of their land". Their recklessness was demonstrated in their contempt of danger and "utter detestation of authority". Thomas Bermingham observed that life was of little conse- quence to the working collier. They little cared if death came "today or tomorrow". If they held their own lives so cheaply, they were unlikely to set an exaggerated value on that of others. Accordingly, the diffusion of the Whiteboy system among the colliers was explained by their unstable character. Contemporary writers were impressed by the visible evidence of mobility especially among the casual mendicants, evicted tenants and travelling journeymen. Patterns of movement in the colliery were linked to the transportation of coal. Improvement in the road network increased contact with the urban areas of the south-east and east coast and canal construction facilitated the diffusion of radical ideas. Those who had been ostracised from their own communities by landlords or clergy could expect to find a refuge in the collieries.

The Halls visited the collieries of Castlecomer in 1841 and could find "no symptoms of radical improvement in the mining despite the innova- tions, that of late years have been introduced into this country".[18] They concluded that this arose more from "an antipathy on the part of the working collier to the introduction of anything they have not been previ- ously used to and an injudicious selection of colliery agents rather than to a want of spirit and liberality among the proprietors themselves". Colliery middlemen appear to have exercised more influence than their peers in land. They were more visible leaders, insofar as they lived and worked among the colliers.

The contribution of middlemen to the shaping of the Irish landscape in the nineteenth century has not been seriously researched, despite the fact that, as this study shows, they were in effective possession of the resources of this estate from 1800 to 1840. Too much attention has been paid to the middleman as a rent receiver. This chapter has shown that many of them made substantial contributions to the townscape of Castlecomer, and built many of the fine houses which still stand throughout the adjoining country-side.

CHAPTER VI

FASSADININ IN THE MID-NINETEENTH CENTURY

"The whole country figures in my mind like a ragged coat, one huge beggar's gabardine not patched or patchable any longer" (Carlyle, Visit to Ireland in 1849, Quoted in Smith, C. W. *The Great Hunger,* (London, 1964), 376).
"When therefore, it is considered what unexhausted, I might say, unexplored resources remain for the maintenance of any increase of inhabitants that can be expected in any definite period, it must, I think, be evident to every reflecting person, that all fears as to a surplus population are perfectly ideal, and that it is its unequal distribution and not its aggregate amount, which is to be deplored. (Kane, R. *The Industrial Resources of Ireland,* 2nd Edition, (Dublin, 1845) 315).

1. Introduction

This chapter examines the geography of land ownership and occupation in Fassadinin in the mid-nineteenth century. The barony, rather than any specific part of it, is the spatial unit with which it is primarily concerned. For this period there is a comprehensive array of material, including commission reports, census statistics, Ordnance Survey maps and estate papers. The chapter commences with a general assessment of land values, and population distribution, density and change in the decade of hunger from 1841 to 1851. The greater portion of the chapter is concerned with the ownership and occupation of land and buildings in the Barony in 1850. The General Valuation of Rateable property is the main source of information for this section.

2. Land Values in Fassadinin c 1850

Figure 6.1 shows the average value of land per acre in the rural areas of Fassadinin barony in 1850. The valuation map may be regarded as an index to soil fertility. It may be more correct to say that the values given to agricultural land indicated its assumed potential rather than its actual value. In the absence of any detailed soil survey of the kind available for some neighbouring areas, the land valuation map is especially important, not only for what it reveals about the barony in 1850, but also because it may help to explain why groups of people chose to live in specific areas of the barony in the past.

149

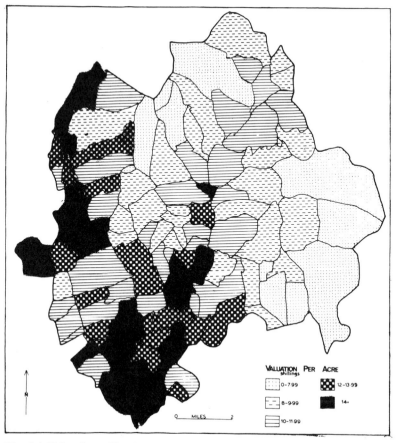

Fig. 6.1 Valuation of land on a townland basis. Fassadinin 1850.

Townlands in which land was valued under eight shillings per acre occupied the hill country north of Castlecomer (fig. 6.1). In this country-side, altitude was generally between 800 and 1,000 feet and poor gley soils, produced by high rainfall on an impermeable parent material of tough sandstones, made commercial agriculture difficult. Location on the fringes of the barony away from the towns of Ballyragget and Castlecomer and from the main roads which crossed Fassadinin through the Nore and Dinin valleys, increased this isolation. Coalmining, which had helped to break the isolation in other parts of the hill lands of Fassadinin, was never carried out on a large scale in these townlands. Townlands in which the average value of land was relatively low were invariably large in area. The average value of land per acre in the townlands of Coolcullen (3,476 statute acres), Croghtenclogh (3,234), and Crutt (2,456) was under eight shillings in 1850. Such poorly-drained, bleak and isolated upland tracts were historically part of the wastelands of Fassadinin. They were outside the former sphere of influence of early Gaelic and Anglo-Norman settlement and there is little evidence to demonstrate that they ever served as refuge areas in the modern period. Neither was there any signs that landlords had remodelled these areas by 1850.

When the distribution of lands described as unprofitable in the mid-seventeenth century is plotted on a map, (fig. 3.2) it is found that there is a marked deterioration in land quality towards the east of the barony and part of its northern fringes. This pattern was repeated in 1850. Measured by almost any standards, physically poor agricultural land was much more common in the townlands located on the hill masses to the east and west of Castlecomer town. Location away from the towns of Ballyragget and Castlecomer increased transport costs and lessened the rent-paying ability and valuation of holdings here. A comparison of figs. 1.3 and 6.1 indicates that lands valued at between eight and ten shillings per acre were typically located where the altitude was between 500 and 800 feet. This association clearly emerges in the east of the barony, where lands of this valuation extend from the southern fringes of Fassadinin to the Dinin valley. Lands of the same valuation to the west of Castlecomer town were invariably found on the ridge of high ground which separated the river valleys of the Nore and Dinin.

Glacial drift is generally absent from areas over 500 feet and soils are derived from the underlying rock formations. The physical, chemical and biological properties of the podzols which form the major soil group in these townlands have been considerably altered by cultivation, drainage and the application of burnt limestone. Evidence in the Wandesforde papers suggests that reclamation was a common feature of land management in the mid-eighteenth century. Land reclamation was both a capital — and labour-intensive activity and must be seen in the context of areas considerably smaller than townlands. Apart from the castle site in Clogharinka townland in the south of the barony, there is no evidence to suggest that settlement in the medieval period was attracted here. One does not find any ancient parochial centre in these territorial divisions. Some substantial houses such as that of Samuel Bradley in Coolbawn townland (valued at £14) were found in these townlands in1850, but no major landlord had settled in them.

Figure 6.1 shows that lands valued at between ten and twelve shillings per acre were distributed widely through the barony. Townlands with these average land values contained 16,354 statute acres and comprised twenty-four per cent of the barony area. In general they occurred on drift covered soils of the shale and lower coal measures series at elevations from 300 to 500 feet. In north-east Fassadinin, these values were found in townlands which occupied the lowlying land on both banks of the Dinin river. This well defined colliery district was typified by high density settlement and relatively good road links with the river Barrow towns of Athy and Carlow. Intensive spade cultivation on the small, regular lots, traditionally associated with the colliers, may have modified soil properties here. Another factor which may have influenced the valuator was the proximity of the district to the town of Castlecomer. The relatively high values found in the townlands of Moneenroe and Cloneen, where mining was continuous and intensive over long periods, may indicate the success of the landlord in terminating the master-collier system and in reclaiming land damaged by mining. Land of this valuation also occupied level, lime-stone-floored areas close to and between the Nore and Dinin rivers in south-west Fassadinin. The names of these territorial divisions such as Clinstown, Lismaine, and Swiftsheath refer to settlement in historical times and commemorate three distinct phases of human settlement in the barony. Some of these places, such as Connahy, Ardaloo and Muckalee, were ancient parochial centres. Six of the fifteen castles listed in the barony surveys of the mid-seventeenth century were located in these townlands. An examination of fig. 3.2 reveals that a relatively high proportion of land

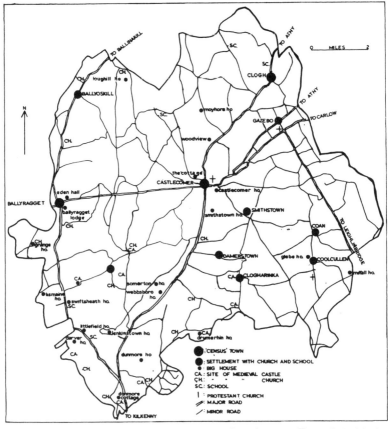

Fig. 6.2 Road network and selected items of settlement. Fassadinin 1850.

described as profitable was also found here. A comparison of the valuation map with fig. 6.2, which shows the distribution of selected settlement items in 1850, indicates that substantial buildings were located in lands of this average value.

The Wandesforde residence in Drumgoole townland south of Castlecomer had a valuation of £70, (Plate IV) and the Swift family, minor landowners in south Fassadinin, lived in the townland of Swiftsheath (Plate IX) which was named after the first settler of this name in Fassadinin. The location of a substantial building in any particular townland may not, in itself, indicate an above average agricultural value of land. The Wandesfordes, for example, owed part of their prosperity to coalmining and occupiers of houses with relatively high valuations in the colliery townlands of Moneenroe and Cloneen were similarly likely to be involved in mining. However, it may be an indication of the aesthetic attractions of a site as the people who lived in these houses were able to select dwelling sites with discrimination.

Approximately twenty-eight per cent (19,000 statute acres) of the barony had land values of twelve shillings and over. Two distinctive blocks of high valuation agricultural land occur in Fassadinin. The most extensive of these consisted of a number of townlands close to and south of the confluence of the Nore and Dinin rivers. Fingers of high valuation land extended from this comparatively level district north along the sheltered valley of the Dinin (fig. 6.1). The second well-defined area was comprised of townlands which adjoined the town of Ballyragget and a belt of land

Plate IX. Swiftsheath house in Swiftsheath townland. The Swift family lived here from the late seventeenth century.

153

which extended from here northwards along the narrow valley of the Ouveg river to the barony boundary. These were the localities where carefully selected settlement centres were sited in the past. Fifteen of the nineteen pre-medieval parochial centres listed in the barony in the thirteenth century, and nine of the fifteen castles recorded by the surveys of the seventeenth century, were found here. It was in these parts of Fassadinin that the manorial organisation had been strongest (fig. 2.4). A high proportion of these territorial divisions was described as arable by the Down Surveyors (fig. 3.2).

Long before 1850, the manorial system of land ownership had been replaced by landlord administered estates. The Kavanaghs, kinsmen of the Mountgarret Butlers, owned almost all of these lands around Ballyragget. The Ormonde family owned considerably less land in 1850 than in 1700, but they still retained portion of the high value lands in the south west fringes of Fassadinin. Overall, there was a greater proportion of resident proprietors here than elsewhere in the barony. Here too there was a number of substantial tenants and elements of a market-oriented economy.

It was not the more favourable physical circumstances alone which influenced land valuations in these districts in 1850. Much of the high value land in the south of the barony was within four miles of the city of Kilkenny. Kilkenny had a population of 19,701 in 1841 and was regarded by many commentators as the most important inland town in Ireland.[1] It was served by an adequate road network and had a rich hinterland, suitable for both tillage and dairy farming. Ballyragget located further north along the Nore valley, had a population of 1,577 in 1841. It was a market centre for grain and butter and had a 'patent' for two fairs annually. Ballyragget had good road links through the Nore corridor with Kilkenny to the south, and with the Grand Canal towns and the Dublin market to the north.

The land valuation map seems to confirm the general accuracy of the Down Survey almost two centuries previously. Territorial divisions which had a comparatively high proportion of their land area described as arable, circa 1654, were generally valued at an average of twelve shillings and over per acre in 1850. Approximately half the land of Fassadinin had an average value of less than ten shillings per acre in 1850. One-third (22,000) was valued between ten and twelve shillings and over. The valuation map shows the impact of altitude on the value and rent paying capacity of agricultural land. The problems of hill-farming such as isolation and poor roads were aggravated by adverse climatic conditions and difficult soils, derived from parent materials of very low base resources. These were the areas least likely to attract landlord investment.

On the other hand lowlying areas of the barony were invariably covered by boulder clay and were well drained and sheltered. There is evidence that in this region there was a greater proportion of resident landlords who, in some instances, had considerably remodelled their estates. Furthermore settlement had been continuous here since at least the early medieval period, whereas the hill country had been relatively empty. The valuation map shows that the early settlers in Fassadinin and their successors, who owned the estates in 1850, were very conscious of land quality and this influenced their choice of settlement sites. The towns of Ballyragget and Castlecomer influenced land values locally and proximity to the city of Kilkenny increased the valuation of agricultural land in south-west Fassadinin.

3. The population of Fassadinin 1841-1851.

(a) *Population distribution in 1841.*

This section examines population distribution, density and change on a parish basis in the decade from 1841 to 1851. The population of Fassadinin barony in 1841 was 30,537 of which 3,867 lived in the three census

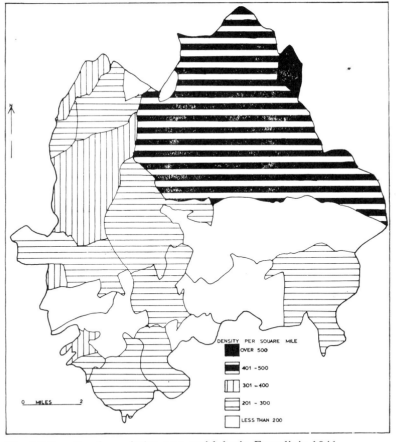

Fig. 6.3 Density of population on a parish basis. Fassadinin 1841.

155

towns of Ballyragget, Castlecomer and Clogh. The average density per
square mile was 287, a figure higher than that for the province of Leinster
as a whole which was 247, but considerably lower than the overall densities
recorded for Munster (332), Connacht (386), and Ulster (406).[2] Parish
areas vary from 21,576 to 354 statute acres and this tends to distort and
inflate densities, when these are plotted on a sketch map, in favour of small
parishes. Figure 6.3 shows that the only parish where population densities
in 1841 were over 500 per square mile was Rathaspick, which borders
Co. Laois in the north east of Fassadinin. Only 639 statute acres of Rathaspick is in Fassadinin and the remainder is in the baronies of Ballyadams
and Slievemargy in Co. Laois. However, an examination of townland
densities indicates that this part of the barony was thickly populated in
1841 (fig. 6.4). Mining was extended here to the relatively deep Jarrow
seam in the 1830's, and in the bordering districts of Doonane and Newtown in Co. Laois coalmining had been continuous and intensive over a
long period. The parish of Castlecomer had a population of 13,535 in
1841 of which 1,765 lived in the town of Castlecomer and 525 in the

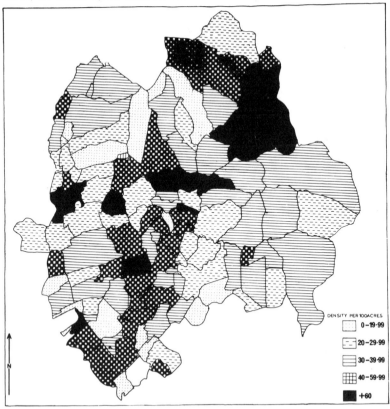

Fig. 6.4 Density of population on a townland basis. Fassadinin 1841.

smaller town of Clogh. T. W. Freeman's map of population density for southeast Ireland (fig. 6.5) shows that Castlecomer was the only parish area, apart from districts close to coastal towns, in which the population density was over 300 per square mile in 1841.

A dense rural population was found in the adjoining townlands of Moneenroe, Cloneen, Coolbawn, and Gorteen, located north-east of

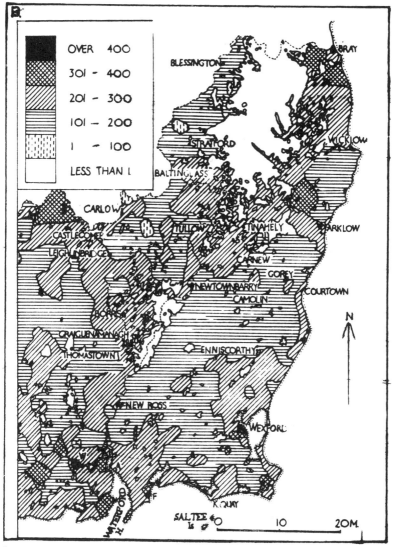

Fig. 6.5 Population density. Southeast Ireland 1841 (After T.W. Freeman).

157

Castlecomer town (fig. 6.4). These territorial divisions have a combined area of 3,468 statute acres and had a population of 4,589 in 1841. The average density per square mile here was 844, a figure not equalled anywhere else in the rural areas of Leinster. Commercial mining exercised an impact on this part of the barony. This district was criss-crossed by roads which afforded settlement sites for the landless colliers who crowded into the area in the 1820's and 1830's. Witnesses, who testified before the Government Commission on Outrages in 1832, gave graphic accounts of the rapid growth in population and settlement which had occurred here during their lifetime. The great majority of people who lived here had little or no stake in the land. Successive proprietors had exercised little control on population movement or on the location of settlement in this district. Indeed, in the 1840's, landlord agents actually encouraged strangers to settle here when local colliers had combined to stop work.[3] Tighe, in his Statistical Survey of Co. Kilkenny published in 1801, noted that collier families were typically large. It is important to remember that in pre-Famine Ireland absence of employment or eviction more frequently resulted in short distance migration than in emigration.[4] This type of movement was a feature of the colliery district, especially in times of comparative prosperity in the coal trade, and accelerated population growth.

The high population densities found in this part of the barony cannot be satisfactorily explained without some reference to the system of landholding. Middlemen, who held townlands on long leases and allowed subdivision to continue unhindered, facilitated population growth. The townland of Cloneen which has an area of 800 statute acres, had a recorded population of 1,196 in 1841. In a pamphlet written in 1870,[5] the Earl of Carrick used Cloneen as an example of a middleman townland in famine times. He wrote that, "In 1796 P. Denn obtained a lease of the townland of Cloneen, 491 acres at £230.15.0. per annum rent; in 1850 the representatives of P. Denn had not a single acre in their own hands, the land being let to 67 tenants; these 67 tenants had 129 sub-tenants under them; of these 129 sub-tenants, 90 lived in cabins, most of them not having a single perch of land". On the other hand it is also true that resident middletenants such as, for example, John Brenan of Moyhora rarely allowed sub-division and in this way restrained population growth locally. Figure 6.4 shows that Moyhora was one of the few townlands in which population density was under 20 per 100 acres in 1841. The contrast between the squalid and overcrowded colliery district and the world of the landlord, especially as manifested and symbolised in the well regulated demesne lands, was strongly apparent in 1841. The expansion of Castlecomer town along the main link roads to the south and the north east was reflected in the relatively high densities found in the adjoining townlands of Donaguile and Drumgoole. In the remainder of the parish, especially on its northern hill fringes, the single, isolated farmstead was the common form of settlement and the high proportion of land devoted to grazing kept population densities comparatively low.

The four Civil parishes of Donaghmore, Odagh, Rathbeagh, and Rosconnell had densities of between 300 and 400 per square mile in 1841. These parochial divisions are located on comparatively high value, level lands in west Fassadinin (fig. 6.1). Only part of the parishes of Odagh (429) statute acres), Rathbeag (354) and Rosconnell (761) were in Fassadinin barony. Figure 6.4 indicates that in the outlying townlands of the parish of Donaghmore densities rarely exceeded 30 per 100 acres and in some instances, such as in the hill lands of Ballymartin, were under 20. These townlands which adjoined the town were generally held by residents of Ballyragget and this explains their low population densities. The towns of pre-Famine Ireland attracted the comparatively wealthy as well as the landless and unemployed. In the seven civil parishes of Kilmenan, Kilmacar, Attanagh, Grangemaccomb, Mothill, Dunmore and Kilmademoge, population densities per square mile were roughly similar to the mean rural density of 254 found in the province of Leinster. The high valuation of land in the parishes of Dunmore, Grangemaccomb, Kilmademoge and Kilmenan in 1880 indicates its agricultural value. In these parishes estates were typically small and the number of substantial tenants was greater than usual in Fassadinin. The townland of Grange in the parish of Grangemaccomb had this type of agrarian structure in 1850. Here, for example, in a townland of 674 statute acres, one of the holdings comprised 223 acres and two others contained 167 and 133 acres respectively. Portion of the parishes of Kilmacar and Mothill consisted of low value hill land over 800 feet. The distribution of population in these parishes in 1841 indicates that despite the high densities found along the Dinin valley and in the colliery district, there was no discernible movement of population to the cold, wet soils of the hill country in pre-Famine Fassadinin.

The western part of Mothill parish, which consists of eight townlands with an area of 2,480 statute acres, had a population density of 305 per square mile in 1841. Townlands here were typically small, land valuations were comparatively high and the area had a long history of human settlement. Resident proprietors such as the Webbs lived in Webbsborough townland. Substantial tenants like John Wood who farmed 87 acres of Lisnafunshin, typified the kind of agrarian society found in this part of Fassadinin. On the other hand, east Mothill consisted of three townland divisions and covered an area of 4,366 statute acres. In this hill country, where the counties of Kilkenny and Carlow adjoin, population density was 200 per square mile in 1841. From medieval times this district had been avoided and initial settlement probably dated from the early eighteenth century. Land values recorded here in 1850 were among the lowest found in the barony area. The six civil parishes of Coolcraheen, Mayne, Abbeyleix, Kilmadum, Dysart and Muckalee had comparatively low densities of between 100 and 200 per square mile. The adjoining parishes of Coolcraheen and Mayne occupied the physically well endowed lands of the Nore valley. A comparatively high proportion of their area was under demesnes or held in farms of 100 acres and over. The townland of Jenkinstown for example, which contained thirty-one per cent of the 1,940 statute acres in Mayne parish, was the demesne of the Bryan family. Figure 6.4 shows that its population density was under 20 per 100 acres. An examination of the land valuation map reveals major variations in land quality between the western and eastern parts of the parishes of Dysart and Muckalee. The comparatively low population densities found here reflected the emphasis on dairying and stock rearing on the heavy boulder clay.

(b) *Summary of the Distributional Evidence*

The spatial distribution of people in Fassadinin barony in 1841 reflects the complexity of the social and economic system which had evolved over a long period. T. W. Freeman observed that in 1841 some of the poorest parts of Ireland had the highest population densities. This was not the case in Fassadinin barony and it is doubtful if it is a valid statement for the country as a whole. If one considers the land valuation of 1850 as a measure of land quality, one finds that townlands with an average valuation under eight shillings per acre were among the most sparsely populated areas in the barony. In some instances, hill townlands, such as Firoda Upper, (where land values were extremely low) had a population density of under 20 per 100 acres. An examination of fig. 6.4 reveals that this low density was also found in the demesne townland of Jenkinstown. A comparison of the valuation map and fig. 6.4 (showing townland densities in 1841) indicates that densities in excess of 40 per 100 acres were generally found in territorial divisions where the land values were on average over ten shillings per acre.

In areas where population densities were comparatively high, landlords did not effectively participate in the management of their estates. The Wandesforde estate, for example, contained some of the most densely populated districts in the barony. In the period from 1800 to 1830, the Countess of Ormonde exercised little or no control in estate affairs outside the precincts of the demesne. The greater part of the estate land and the collieries were administered by a hierarchy of middlemen. Many of these were absentees and merely acted in the capacity of rent receivers. The uncontrolled subdivision of land was a common feature in properties held by absentees and explains, to an extent, the rapid growth of population in these townlands. Where estate proprietors were resident, and in districts which had a high proportion of substantial tenants, settlement was rigidly controlled. This was illustrated in the six inch to the mile townland maps circa 1838 by the arrangement of fields and settlement in parts of Nore Valley and in the district between the Nore and Dinin rivers in south Fassadinin. The reservation of high value land for ornamental purposes had the effect of increasing population pressure locally in the adjoining relatively poorer areas. It is precisely in the lands of intermediate value that the highest population densities in Fassadinin barony occurred in 1841.

The study of local variations in population is a complex issue. Many vital demographic considerations such as variations in birth and death rates on a spatial and social basis have not been examined in the context of Fassadinin. It is almost certain that coal miners married earlier and had larger families than their more prosperous farmer neighbours. There is, according to the economic historian, L. M. Cullen, no evidence of a universal trend towards earlier marriage and definite evidence to suggest that, among the farming community, marriage was entered into cautiously and subdivision restricted in pre-Famine Ireland.[7] It is also important to bear in mind that the social group which constituted the greater proportion of the population could rarely afford to emigrate. In overall terms, the existence of a commercial economy in the rural district of north east Fassadinin was the dominant factor in encouraging population growth.

(c) *Population change, 1841-1851.*

The population of Fassadinin barony fell from 30,537 in 1841 to 20,917 in 1851. The average density per square mile was 196 in 1851 as compared

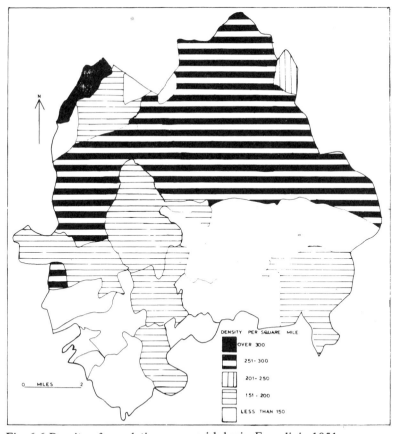

Fig. 6.6 Density of population on a parish basis. Fassadinin 1851.

161

to 257 in 1841. A reduction of population on this scale did not, however, result in any major change in the 1841 pattern: the density was still highest in the colliery district of the north-east and in parts of the Dinin valley. It did reduce the disparity between the least and most densely populated areas. Figure 6.6 shows the population density on a parish basis in 1851 and fig. 6.7 depicts the change in population on a townland basis in the decade from 1841 to 1851. The most densely populated district of Fassadinin was, as in 1841, the northern area in which the three census defined towns of Ballyragget, Castlecomer and Clogh were located. The civil parishes of Castlecomer, Donaghmore, Rosconnell and Rathbeagh were the only divisions with population densities over 250 per square mile (fig. 6.6). Rathaspick in north east Fassadinin was the most densely populated parochial division in 1841. By 1851 its average density had fallen from 500 to 205 per square mile. In general, the parish densities in 1851 indicate that population decline in the 1841 to 1851 decade was especially severe in parishes where the 1841 densities had been comparatively high. Many of the well-endowed divisions in south and south-west Fassadinin

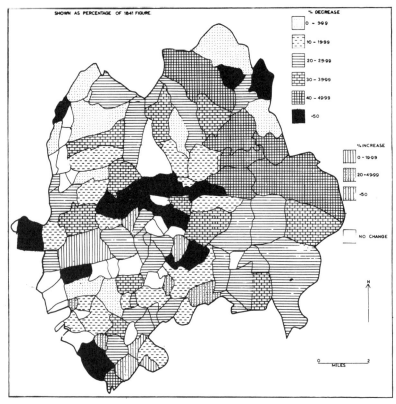

Fig. 6.7 Population change 1841-51. Fassadinin.

such as Mayne and Kilmademoge were hardly affected by the Great Hunger.

The demographic consequences of the Famine were the most important features of the social and economic history of Ireland at any time. Demographers have seen, in the events of these years, the origins of large-scale emigration and rural population decline which later became consistent features of the population history of Ireland. In the 1841 to 1851 decade, 5,333 persons were assisted to emigrate by the proprietor of the Castlecomer estate and over half the recorded population decline in this period can be attributed to emigration. Landlord activity such as planned emigration programmes and the eviction of destitute tenantry influenced local population densities. It is also true that landlord inactivity contributed to maintaining pre-Famine densities in parts of the barony. The population of the mining townland of Cloneen for example, fell only slightly from 1,196 in 1841 to 1,086 in 1851. In the same period, the population of the adjoining townland of Moneenroe suffered a traumatic decline from 2 022 to 947. It is significant that Moneenroe was administered directly by the Wandesforde family and people from here were assisted to emigrate. Cloneen, on the other hand, was occupied by absentee representatives of the Denn family.

The combined population of the three census defined towns of Castlecomer, Clogh and Ballyragget in Fassadinin fell from 3,807 in 1841 to 3,380 in 1851. In 1841, approximately thirteen per cent of the population of the barony lived in these towns. By 1851, the proportion residing in towns had increased to sixteen per cent. This implies that the outmovement of people was not as great from small towns as from rural areas and that town populations remained remarkably stable during the famine decade. The census reveals that the population of Ballyragget fell from 1,577 to 1,170 (thirty-five per cent), Clogh from 525 to 486 (seven per cent) and the population of Castlecomer increased from 1,705 to 1,724 (two per cent). The Wandesforde papers present evidence of emigration from, and the planned clearance of houses in the town of Castlecomer in this period. This leads one to the conclusion that the fall in population must have been greater than that revealed by a comparison of the two censuses. It seems that the census definition of the town excluded the part of Castlecomer which had diffused along the main link roads to the south and north east. One should therefore expect that the decline of population in the townlands immediately adjoining the town would be especially severe. This is true, for example, of Donaguile townland which extended south from the town along the Kilkenny-Castlecomer road. The population of this townland fell from 857 in 1841 to 204 in 1851 and the enumerated houses declined from 146 to 37.

4. The Estate System of Land Ownership in 1850

(a) *Estates of 1,000 acres and over.*

For the purpose of this section, a holding of 100 acres and over held in fee simple or by long-term lease is defined as an estate. Excluded by this definition are farms over 100 acres which were occupied by tenants on a year-to-year basis. Figure 6.8 shows the distribution of estates of 1,000 acres and over and fig. 6.9 the distribution of estates between 500 and 1,000 acres. The estate system was the dominant form of land ownership in the barony circa 1850. It's all-encompassing nature is illustrated by the hierarchical mesh of estates of various sizes which embraced the barony area. Approximately 48,000 of the 68,000 statute acres which comprised the barony were held in estates over 1,000 acres by twelve landowners (Table 6.1). In any comparison between landownership patterns in 1700 and 1850 it is the similarities rather than the differences which are striking. Estate size in 1850 was a function of the past and had been created by the multiple transactions concerning land which were such a feature of the seventeenth and eighteenth century. Changes in land ownership did not lead to any major alterations in estate boundaries. The delimitation of townland boundaries by the Ordnance Survey had given stability to units

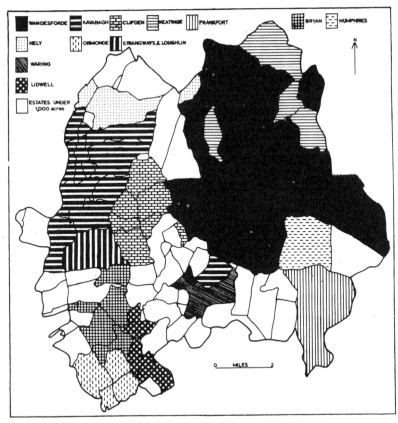

Fig. 6.8 Estates of 1,000 acres and over. Fassadinin 1850

164

of ownership which were not to be disrupted until the great transfers of property in the early part of the twentieth century. This section is concerned with the origins, ownership and spatial organisation of estates in the barony of Fassadinin in 1850.

(i) *Proprietors of English descent.*

If the owners who held 1,000 acres or over in 1850 are classified according to surname origins, it is found that owners descended from emigrants from the counties of Britain in the modern period owned 31,667 acres; proprietors with surnames which may have been of Anglo-Norman origin held 5,201 acres; landowners of Irish origin were in possession of 8,852 acres. This type of classification is but a useful method for facilitating discussion. These groupings have not the same validity as they had in the seventeenth century. The bonds of marriage had diluted the ethnic distinc-

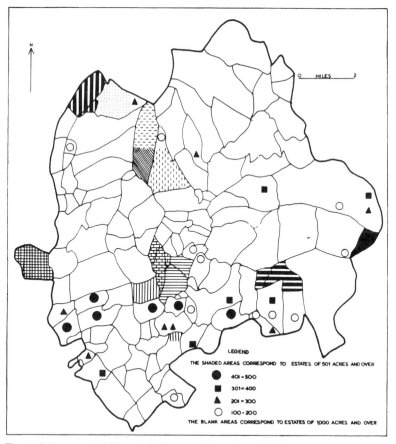

Fig. 6.9 Estates of 100 to 1,000 acres. Fassadinin 1850.

Table 6.1. Proprietors of estates of 1,000 acres and over in Fassadinin barony in 1850.

Estate Owner	Acreage	Total Valuation £	Resident or Absentee
Charles Harward Butler — Clarke — Southwell — Wandesforde	17,522	13,200	Resident
Thomas Kavanagh Esq.	6,439	5,513	Absentee
Viscount Clifden	3,888	2,143	Absentee
Mrs. Gertrude Keating	3,311	1,878	Absentee
Viscount Frankfort	3,132	1,389	Absentee
George Bryan Esq.	2,413	1,996	Resident
Charles Hely Esq.	1,954	1,296	Absentee
Marquis of Ormonde	1,890	1,763	Absentee
Representatives of Connell Loughlin and Joseph Strangways	1,519	1,024	Absentee
William Humpheries Esq.	1,495	989	Absentee
Frederick Lidwell Esq.	1,134	737	Absentee
John Waring Esq.	1,023	700	Absentee

tions and reinforced the social and economic links between landlords. Contemporary accounts indicate that landlords, whatever their background or religious beliefs, did not differ greatly in their treatment of tenants. Alexis de Tocqueville during his tour of Ireland in 1835 was told by a Catholic priest that "Catholics and Protestants oppress the people in about the same way. The moment a Catholic become a great landowner he conceives the same egotistical dislike, which seems natural to the aristocracy, for the interest of the people. Like the others, he eagerly seizes on all means of enriching himself at the expense of the poor".[8] Two of the English proprietors, who held estates of 1,000 acres and over in 1850, could trace their origins in Fassadinin back to the seventeenth century. These were the Wandesfordes whose estate of 17,525 acres included the town of Castlecomer and the Hely family who possessed 1,954 acres in north-west Fassadinin (fig. 6.8). The total valuation of Wandesforde property in 1850 was £13,200 and the average valuation of agricultural land was eleven shillings per acre. This estate was roughly co-extensive with the manor of Castlecomer which was created in 1635. The Hely estate was formerly part of the seventeenth century Ormonde manor of Kilmacar. This property in 1850 had a total valuation of £1,296 and the average value of its agricultural land was twelve shillings. Although this family retained ownership over a two hundred year period, there is no record that they ever resided in Fassadinin.

There is no evidence that any of the other English landed families who held estates of 1,000 acres and over ever settled in Fassadinin. They acted solely in their capacity as rent receivers. Four of the remaining six estates were formerly part of the Ormonde lands in the seventeenth century. These included the properties of Viscount Clifden, William Humphrey, Viscount Frankfort and Joseph Strangways (fig. 6.8). The Clifden lands which contained 3,888 acres occupied eight townlands in the hill country between the Wandesforde and Mountgarret estates. This property was roughly equal to the core area of the seventeenth century Ormonde manor of Kilmacar. The Clifden family, formerly Agars, held prominent political and ecclesiastical positions in late eighteen century Ireland. The first Viscount Clifden was M.P. for the barony of Gowran, Co. Kilkenny and Commissioner of Revenue in Ireland from 1771 to 1785.[9] Another member of this family, who held a smaller estate in Fassadinin, was the Protestant Archbishop of Dublin from 1800 to 1806 and acquired the title Earl of Normanton in 1806.

On the passing of the Act of Union in 1800, many prominent Anglo-Irish families received considerable financial rewards and, in some instances, life peerages to compensate them for the loss of their parliamentary seats. Subsequent evidence indicates that the Clifden family used the money obtained in this manner wisely. By 1883, they had amassed a considerable estate of 49,017 acres. Their Irish properties contained 37,597 acres and were comprised of 35,288 acres in Co. Kilkenny, 821 in Co. Dublin, 978 in Co. Kildare and 500 in Co. Meath. The Clifdens were absentees and maintained two residences at Lanhydrock, Bodmin, Cornwall and Wimpole Hall near Royston in Cambridge.[10] In the six inch to the mile townland map, the manorial centre of Kilmacar is marked by the site of the ancient parochial church and a castle. The same map shows that the small, nucleated settlement of Barrack Village had developed at a crossroad site close to these. It is certain that the continual absence of the landlord retarded the development of the old manorial centre and that Kilmacar in 1850 was a smaller and less important place than it was in 1600.

Viscount Frankfort owned 3,332 acres in the upland townland of Coolcullen in south-east Fassadinin (fig. 6.8). These comparatively low value lands belonged to the Purcells in the early seventeenth century, were expropriated by the Commonwealth Government and regranted to the Butlers of Ormonde at the Restoration. They were subsequently sold at the breakup of the Ormonde property in Fassadinin in the early eighteenth century. The Frankfort interest in Coolcullen derived from the marriage in 1835 of the Viscount to Miss Georgiana Henchy, the female heir to the property.[11] The title of Baron Frankfort was bestowed in 1810 on a member of the Morres family (resident in the barony) of Galmon, Co. Kilkenny.[12] It was obviously a measure of compensation for voting for the Union. In 1816, the Viscountcey was granted and the family were

167

allowed to assume the name of de Montmorency in lieu of Morres. The Frankforts were absentees and had their principal residence at Theydon Bois, near Epping, Essex.

The imprint of landlordism was not evident in the six-inch to the mile townland map of Coolcullen. A small, nucleated settlement had developed around the schoolhouse and the police barracks. Here, surprisingly enough, one finds in 1850 a number of substantial tenant farmers with names such as Shirley, Bradley, Asleford and Willoughby. Settlement in this harsh, bleak place probably predated the erection of the Protestant Church in the 1730's. There is evidence of an increase in the Protestant population here in the 1798 to 1800 period. Possibly they sought refuge from the violence then widespread in the south-east of Ireland. These people have left their trace on this townland. In the landscape, this is illustrated especially by their distinctive two-storied farmhouses with enclosed yards and slated outbuildings.

The Humphries property (fig. 6.8) contained 1,495 acres and occupied the townland of Coan West and part of Coan East. This part of the seventeenth century estate was sold by the O'Brenans to the Butlers of Ormonde. It was subsequently resold to the Webb family of Webbsborough townland in Mothill parish.[13] In 1810 on the death of William Webb, the executors of his will sold the property to William Humphries. The Humphries were absentee proprietors and lived at Ballyhaise House, Co. Cavan. Neither the valuation books nor the Ordnance Survey six-inch to the mile townland maps present any evidence of improvements by either landlord or tenants. The average land valuation of eight shillings adequately reflected the wet, cold soils of this remote upland district and the absence of good roads. The small village of Coan developed on the site of an older settlement centre, which was marked by the location of a castle in 1838. The principal buildings here in 1850 were the Catholic Church, the priest's house and National School. Little is known about the three remaining proprietors who owned estates of 1,000 acres and over in Fassadinin barony, except that all three were absentee. Joseph Strangeways proprietor of 1,159 acres in Connahy townland was probably a representative of the family who lived to the south of here in Springhill townland in the eighteenth century. In this estate, the single, dispersed farmstead was the common form of settlement. The Catholic Church and adjoining National School were surprisingly isolated features and had failed to attract settlement. This may have been related to the fact that Connahy was not given parochial status until 1832. John Waring was returned as lessor of 1,023 acres in Muckalee townland. In this dairying district, holdings were comparatively large and population density was correspondingly low. The estate of Frederick Lidwell comprised part of the seventeenth century manor of the Blanchvildes (Lidwell resided at Drumard in the adjoining county of Tipperary). Large holdings were the dominant form of land occupation in this well-endowed estate. Thus, the townlands of Bullockhill (195 acres) and Kilmademoge (194 acres) were held as single farms.

(ii) *Proprietors of Irish Descent*

Proprietors of estates of 1,000 acres and over, who had surnames which were of Irish origin, owned 8,852 acres in Fassadinin barony in 1850. These were Thomas Kavanagh and George Bryan (fig. 6.8). The Kavanagh estate which contained 6,439 acres and included the landlord town of Ballyragget, had passed to them from the Mountgarret Butlers in the early nineteenth century. It was roughly equal in area to the manor lands of Donaghmore as defined by Inquisition taken at Rosbercon in 1621. Apart from their natural relationship to the Ormonde Butlers, the Kavanaghs were connected through marriage with the Wandesfordes of Castlecomer. In 1850, therefore, approximately thirty eight per cent of the barony was owned by families who were interrelated in some way. It is important to note that the ancestors of these families were also the dominant landowning group in the barony throughout the seventeenth century. The Kavanaghs resided in Borris, Co. Carlow about twenty miles south-east of Ballyragget and administered their estates through a land agent.

The links between the Bryan family and the Butlers of Ormonde in the seventeenth century have already been noted. Not only did the Catholic Bryans manage to survive as landowners but the evidence shows that they succeeded in enlarging their estate. In 1801, George Bryan paid £3,402 for 169 acres of land in Ballyrafton townland to the trustees of the Ormonde property.[14] The lands held in fee by the Bryan family were fragmented. They owned 2,413 acres in the south west of the barony, and here they had their mansion house and demesne (Plate X). Their other property consisted of the two townlands of Aughatubrid and Clogh in the extreme north of the barony of Fassadinin. This detached portion of the estate was occupied by middletenants in 1850. In 1850, the Bryans were completing the building of their new mansion house in Jenkinstown. The unfinished structure was valued at £50. Apart from the mansion house and its detached farmyard, the Bryans failed to establish any permanent nucleated settlement in this part of their property. Clogh, located on their lands in north Fassadinin, was defined as a census town but the Valuation Book suggests that it lacked any substantial buildings and was little more than an agglomeration of collier cabins.

(iii) *Proprietors of Anglo-Norman descent 1850.*

Two proprietors of Anglo-Norman descent owned estates of over 1,000 acres in 1850. The combined acreage of the Keating and Ormonde properties amounted to 5,201 acres or approximately eleven per cent of the land held in estates of this size. The Keating estate was formed by the amalgamation of two middlemen properties. When representatives of the Denn and Keating families, both of whom were of Anglo-Norman descent and Catholics, married in 1814, the lands they held as middletenants were merged. In 1850, the Keating estate consisted of the Wandesforde townlands of Cloneen and Ballylinnen and the Bryan territorial divisions of Aughatubrid and Clogh. Divided property, such as this, was held at a per-

169

Plate X. Jenkinstown house, the residence of the Bryan family. The greater part of the building and the adjoining Roman Catholic Chapel dates from c.1850.

petual rent. The landlord or proprietors in fee simple of the estate were only rent receivers, while the actual rights and functions of the property belonged to the middlemen. The inability of the Wandesfordes to control the subdivision which resulted in the rapid multiplication of smallholdings in the townland of Cloneen in the period from 1830 to 1850 has been demonstrated previously. The comparatively small decline in population in this townland in the decade from 1841 to 1851 indicates that landlord assisted emigration was not extended to here. The Denn-Keating family did not reside on their property in Fassadinin but at Tennypark House in the western suburbs of Kilkenny City. The creation of new estates from the break up of the Ormonde property was the most significant feature in the development of the pattern of landownership which prevailed in Fassadinin in 1850. The portion of their seventeenth century estate which they retained was, in all probability, their first acquisition here in the medieval period. The Ormonde lands consisted of the four townlands of Dunmore, Dunmore East, Dunmore West and Dunmore Park (fig. 6.8). The valuation map reveals the high value of this agricultural land. Here, population was sparse and a high proportion of the land was either untenanted or farmed in units of 100 acres and over.

170

(b) *Estates of 500-1,000 acres in 1850.*

Table 6.2 lists the proprietors and the acreage of estates of 500 to 1,000 acres in Fassadinin barony in 1850.

Table 6.2. Proprietors of estates of 500-1,000 acres in Fassadinin barony in 1850.

Estate Owner	Acreage	Total Valuation	Resident or Absentee
		£	
Lady Carbery and James Saurin	863	403	Absentee
Sir Joshua C. Meredyth	728	466	Absentee
Earl of Normanton	716	577	Absentee
Lord Vaux	677	241	Absentee
Thomas McCartney	660	299	Absentee
Mrs. Catherine Dillon	645	636	Resident
Mrs. Anne Humfrey	628	660	Absentee
Mrs. Eliza Brownrigg	522	178	Absentee
Luke Flood Esq.	512	255	Absentee
Charles Mossom Esq.	510	450	Absentee
Richard Lalor	507	200	Absentee

Figure 6.9 shows that these estates were typically located on the margins of the barony or in districts which marked the former boundary zone between seventeenth century estates. Two of these estates were found in the north-west of the barony where the Ormonde lands bordered on Upper Ossory in the seventeenth century. The townland of Firoda Upper was divided between Lord Vaux and Richard Lalor and another of these estates occupied 863 acres in Firoda Lower. This part of the barony formed the boundary zone between the Wandesforde and Mountgarret properties in the seventeenth century. The pattern of ownership of these estates reveals the complexity and multiplicity of the transactions concerning land and the difficulties inherent in attempting to unravel these transactions over a period of time. Mrs. Catherine Dillon was the only one of the eleven proprietors of estates between 500 and 1,000 acres who resided in Fassadinin. The Valuation of Tenements recorded that she occupied tenement no. 5 in Castlemarket townland, which consisted of twenty three acres of land and a house valued at £10.[15] She was the middletenant of the Earl of Clonmel who inherited this property from his uncle in 1799.[16] Apart from Lord Vaux, who owned 677 acres of the bleak, isolated, upland townland of Firoda Upper, the names of these proprietors

171

are not found in the State ledger books which recorded grants and transactions concerning land in the late seventeenth century. Five of these
estates were formerly part of the Ormonde property in Fassadinin. Landowners such as the Earl of Normanton and Sir Joshua Mereydyth were
direct descendants of the original purchasers of these lands in the 1730's.
This group of proprietors left little imprint on the barony. They were
not commemorated in townland names. Only three of these families built
landlord houses in Fassadinin barony. The Mossom family resided for a
period in Mount Eland House in Grange townland. The Brownrigg family
lived at 'Bellmount' in Coan East up to 1830. Somerton House in Lisnafunshin townland was built in honour of the Earl of Normanton when
he acquired the additional titles of Viscount and Baron Somerton. Many
of these estate owners inherited their Fassadinin properties. They were too
small to support a landlord establishment and consequently formed small
fragments of more extensive property held elsewhere. Furthermore, these
people may not have been attracted to live in Fassadinin barony. They
may have considered it as a remote and isolated place, too far distant from
the urban life to which landlords, as a class, seemed especially attracted.

(c) *Estates of 100 to 500 acres in 1850.*
Thirty one proprietors owned estates of 100 to 500 acres in extent
in 1850. Figure 6.9 shows that the greater number of these properties
were located in the south of Fassadinin barony, between the River Dinin
and the Frankfort estate in Coolcullen. They were also relatively numerous
in the small townlands adjoining the river Nore on the western fringes of
the barony. Throughout the period encompassed by this study the small
estate was the typical form of landownership in this part of Fassadinin.
Eight of these thirty-one proprietors resided in Fassadinin barony but
only three lived on their lands. Four lessors of lands in excess of 100
acres occupied houses in Castlecomer town and one lived in the town of
Ballyragget. One notices from the map that only four lessors of land areas
over 100 and under 500 acres, were recorded in the Wandesforde estate in
1850. This contrasts with the strength and extent of the middleman
system found here in 1812 and 1838 and demonstrates how effectively
the landlord had abolished the middleman system, in the interim period.
It also implies that middlemen were financially ruined by the inability of
their undertenants to meet rental committments in the decade of the
Great Hunger.
Some of these estates were fragments of larger farms granted at the
redistribution of landed property in the barony in the late seventeenth
century. The Webb family, for example, owned 403 statute acres in the
townlands of Webbsborough and Coan East in 1850 (fig. 6.9). They were,
however, recipients of a much greater estate in 1667. The Land Commission Abstract of Title returned Richard Henry Webb as proprietor of 1,167
acres in Fassadinin in 1903. This suggests that the Webb lands were only
temporarily alienated. The Land Commission records also indicate that the

172

Webb estate was heavily encumbranced in this period. By 1903, the sum of £7,000 had been raised by a series of mortgages on these lands. Godwin Swift esq. was returned as lessor of the townland of Swiftsheath. The Swifts who resided in a fine mansion house in this townland, had been in possession here since the late seventeenth century. Esker townland had remained in the hands of the St. George family since 1667 when this and other lands in Fassadinin were granted to them. Roger Matthews owned the lands of Ardaloo north of the confluence of the Nore and Dinin in 1850. The Lodge manuscripts record that in 1668 a Lieutenant Christopher Matthews was granted the lands of "Tullyglasse, Foulkesrath and Suttons-rath" in Fassadinin.

The complex nature of the landowning system in the nineteenth century and the many changes which were brought about through bankruptcy, inheritance, purchase and fragmentation are revealed in the records of the Irish Land Commission concerning the estate of Edmund Bulfin.[17] This estate contained 112 statute acres and was located in the north west of the barony in Loughill townland. The lands of Loughill were in the possession of the Skelton family in 1753. In 1814, the estate was divided by a deed of partition and allocated to four female members of the Skelton family in 1753. On the death of Isabella Fitzpatrick (nee Skelton), her portion was settled on her son William. The Valuation of Tenements lists William Fitzpatrick as holding 93 acres in Loughill in 1850. In 1852, James Lawlor on payment of £530 acquired the lands of William Fitzpatrick under the Encumbered Estates Act. James Lawlor mortgaged this property in 1853, 1858 and 1861. In 1864, an Indenture of Mortgage granted these lands to Patrick Bulfin. On Bulfin's death in 1871 the lands were divided in five equal shares. In 1911, the estate was vested as to 56/70th in Edward Bulfin and the remaining 14/70th in Ignatius Bulfin.

The vast majority of these proprietors had little contact with the barony beyond their function as rent receivers. It is probable that a number of those registered as lessors of property in Fassadinin in 1850 were representatives of insurance companies, commercial banking concerns and solicitors who held property in trust. John Butler, who farmed 357 acres of good agricultural land in Drumerhin townland, resided in a house valued at £10 and had five undertenants (to whom he had sublet a house and garden), typifies the small, resident estate owner of this period. Proprietors of estates of this size in some instances combined the role of middlemen with that of landed proprietor. David Ryan, for example, who held 410 acres in Aghamucky townland by lease from the Wandesfordes, sublet it between eighteen undertenants. The same individual farmed an adjoining holding of 374 acres which he held as tenant from year-to-year.

(d) *Summary of the estate system of landownership.*

The estate system of landownership was grafted onto an older arrangement which did not differ greatly from it. A comparison between figs 2.4 and 6.8 will indicate the similarity between estates in 1639 and 1850.

173

In Fassadinin in 1850, approximately forty per cent of the land area was owned by individuals whose descendants were landed proprietors here in 1640. The legal title to land in Ireland was mainly derived from the grants made under the provisions of the Restoration Acts of Settlement and Explanation and enrolled in the state ledger books. The evidence shows that only a very small number of landowners, who were introduced into the barony as a result of the redistributions of property in the late seventeenth century, had remained. The Webb and St. George families, who between them owned 854 acres in 1850 may have been the only direct descendants of Cromwellians who had received land here in the seventeenth century.

The pattern of landownership had been stabilised by 1800. The Humpherey estate was the only property over 1,000 acres which had been acquired through purchase after this date. In the first half of the nineteenth century, landed property in Fassadinin was rarely for sale. The proprietors of estates in 1850 had mainly derived their title to Fassadinin land either through inheritance or marriage. The estate system in 1850 had been fashioned by private enterprise in the preceding centuries.

Continuity in ownership was not the only feature which reflected past arrangements in Fassadinin barony. The landlord mansion house, as in Castlecomer and Ballyragget for example, often replaced the Anglo-Norman castle which had served a similar function in previous centuries. Estate owners have been credited with many development functions such as the building of market towns. The country house had been described as, "the residential focus of an extensive settlement complex, which included a home farm and frequently, an 'extra-mural' village for demesne workers and servants."[18] This type of landlord establishment was not widespread in Fassadinin. It was only on the Wandesforde, Kavanagh and Bryan estates that these settlements had developed. Estates elsewhere in the barony such as the Webb and Swift properties were too small to provide a nucleus for such development. It is also true that the general prevalence of absenteeism precluded the building by landlords of any residential or administrative buildings on the majority of estates in Fassadinin barony. In these districts, nucleated settlements were grouped around institutions such as the Catholic Church and National School which served the needs of the occupiers (fig. 6.2).

Georgian mansions built by landlords formed a significant new element in the pattern of Fassadinin settlement. The six-inch to the mile townland maps c. 1838 show that the carefully planned gardens and plantations laid out in the late eighteenth century were now reaching maturity. The woodlands enclosed within demesne walls in Castlecomer, Jenkinstown, Ballyragget and Dunmore Park gave a distinctive appearance and added diversity to the countryside. It is significant that the areas under plantations were more widespread in the parts of south Fassadinin which were mainly devoid of trees in the seventeenth century. When proprietors of comparatively small estates, or middlemen such as John Brennan of Moy-

174

hora were resident, they attempted to imitate the layout of the landscape of landlordism. Their residences were usually marked on the Ordnance Survey maps by the suffix 'Ho' combined with the townland or other commemorative names as the prefix. These houses were typically surrounded by mature trees and large, regular fields. In some instances they had gate-lodges and long, tree-lined avenues.

Development functions such as town building have been too readily credited to estate owners. The evidence for Fassadinin leads to the unexpected conclusion that Ballyragget may have been the only true landlord town in the barony. The known facts sustain the view that the physical development of Castlecomer town in the early nineteenth century can be attributed to middleman rather than landlord activity. It was a middleman town. On the other hand an examination of the Rateable Valuation of Tenements suggests that the landlord had a more direct developmental role in the growth of Ballyragget. The fragmentation through sale of the Ormonde property deprived the seventeenth century manorial centres of Kilmacar and Dunmore of their hinterlands and hastened their decline as settlement nuclei. Ballyragget and Castlecomer, which were now associated with the landed families of Kavanagh and Wandesforde, were retained as nodal centres and developed in the eighteenth century as landlord towns. By 1850, both towns had an impressive array of commercial functions and were important local retailing and service centres.

Only eleven of the fifty four landowners who held estates of 100 acres and over in Fassadinin barony in 1880 were resident. Absence from Fassadinin did not necessarily entail residence in Great Britain. It is probable that only two of the ten non-resident proprietors, who held estates of 1,000 acres and over in the barony, lived permanently in England. Those were Viscount Clifden and Viscount Frankfort. Many of the absentees such as the Kavanaghs, Humphries and Lidwells had larger estates elsewhere in Ireland and looked upon their Fassadinin lands as useful subsidiary sources of revenue. Absenteeism by estate owners was not a practice confined to the nineteenth century only. It was the continuation of a tradition of landlord-tenant relationship initiated in Fassadinin in the seventeenth century. Many of the nineteenth century proprietors shunned Fassadinin for the same reasons as their Anglo-Norman counterparts in the early seventeenth century. To many of them, it was a remote and isolated place which contained only a portion of their property. In the absence of landlords, estates were administered by land agents. On the larger estates, such as the Kavanagh property, these individuals were usually barristers-at-law. On the smaller properties, land agents combined management and farming. John Wood, who was agent for the St. George, Clifden and Normanton properties, resided in Somerton House in Lisna-funshin townland and farmed 79 acres here and an additional 120 acres in the townland of Esker.

Estate owners were a self-conscious class who shared a remarkably uniform life style. There was a striking quality of similarity in the physical appearance of the landlord mansion house and demesne throughout Ireland as a whole. The institutional arrangements in rural life reflected the hegemony of the landed gentry. Successive members of the Bryan, Kavanagh and Wandesforde families represented the county of Kilkenny in the House of Commons. They were involved in the local administration of justice and were generally concerned with the maintenance of law and order. External signs of prosperity were evident in Fassadinin in 1850. The Famine had helped to clear estates of a destitute tenantry who had previously hindered improvements. The Bryans of Jenkinstown were in the process of building a new mansion-house and the Wandesfordes had expended £34,000 in "assisting emigrants, in allowing for unrecoverable arrears of rent and as compensation for breaking leases."[19]

There were other signs which intimated that the era of landlord dominance was coming to an end. The Famine had revealed the inadequacy and ineffectiveness of a system which depended primarily on the good will of individual landlords. The state now assumed many of the development functions previously exercised by estate owners. By passing the Encumbered Estates Act in 1848, it hoped to facilitate the sale of debt-ridden estates. During the subsequent fifty years, the State was to become more involved in the massive task of allocating Government funds to facilitate tenant purchase in Ireland. The undoing of the land settlements of the late seventeenth century and the transfer of ownership to the occupiers effected a social revolution without precedent in Ireland and elsewhere in western Europe at the time. The impetus for social innovation came from within Ireland. During the Famine years political activists emerged who clearly understood that the land question could provide the central theme of a new political programme. The rural communities became increasingly better educated and better informed than heretofore. The decline in illiteracy may be attributed to the extension of the National School system of education throughout the whole country. Emigration during the Famine years had established a network of contacts between Ireland and North America and emigrants were to become active supporters of political programmes designed to terminate British Rule and its most obvious manifestation the estate system.

5. The Occupation of Land in Fassadinin Barony in 1850.

The task here is to identify the occupiers of land and to describe the patterns of land occupation in Fassadinin barony in 1850. The occupiers listed in the *General Valuation of Rateable Property* have been classified according to assumed surname origins. A series of maps on the scale of one inch to one mile were then constructed to show the location and the valuation of rateable property held by each of these groupings in the barony. In this way it may be possible to indicate the areas where emigrants from the countries of Britain settled in Fassadinin. It will also assist in the identification of those estates where proprietors were successful in attracting emigrants. By revealing the numerical strength and the acreage of land

176

held by occupiers assumed to be of English, Anglo-Norman and Irish origin, respectively, it will show the impact of the various immigrations through historic time on the composition of the landholding class in Fassadinin in 1850.

(a) *The classification of occupiers by surname on a parish basis.*

Figure 6.10 shows the proportion of the land area of each parish in the barony held by occupiers with surnames which are of English, Irish and Anglo-Norman origin. In 1850, occupiers with surnames of Irish origin held 43,759 statute acres of the 68, 174 statute acres in the barony. Occupiers who may be assumed to have been of English origin held a total of 17,782 statute acres and Anglo-Norman landholders held 6,662 acres. Irish

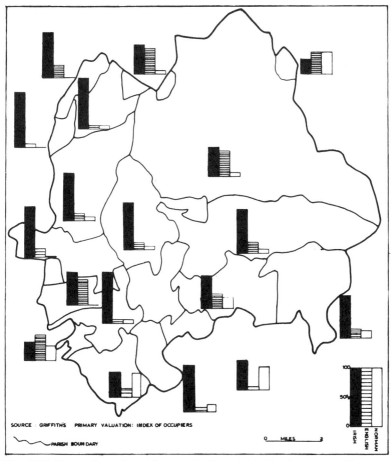

Fig. 6.10 Proportion of parish areas held by Irish, English, Anglo-Norman occupiers. Fassadinin 1850.

177

occupiers held over 80 per cent of the parishes of Attanagh, Donaghmore, Grangemaccomb, Kilmenan, Mayne, Odogh and Rosconnell. Figure 6.1 shows that the values given to agricultural land in these parishes in 1800 were uniformly high. They held between seventy to eighty per cent of the parishes of Kilmacar, Kilmademoge, Mothell and Rathbeag. In Dysart, which formed part of the gaelic territory of Idough in the early seventeenth century, occupiers with surnames of Irish origin held 5,230 of the 7,938 statute acres in the parish. In the civil parishes of Abbeyleix, Castlecomer, Coolcraheen, Kilmadum and Muckalee, Gaelic occupiers held between fifty to sixty per cent of the total area. The proportion of total land area held by Irish occupiers was less than fifty per cent of the total area only in the parishes of Dunmore in the extreme south and Rathaspick in the north east of Fassadinin. The dominance of the Irish occupier in numerical terms and as holders of the greater amount of the barony land suggests that successive confiscations had scarcely affected them. Both the Anglo-Norman landowning class in the early seventeenth century and the Anglo-Irish who succeeded them constituted only a tiny elitist minority of the total population.

Occupiers with surnames which may have been of English origin held forty per cent (256 acres) of the parish of Rathaspick in 1850. It was the only parish in the barony where they were the dominant landholding group. In the Civil Parishes of Abbeyleix and Coolcraheen, English occupiers held between 40 to 50 per cent of the total land area. Occupiers with surnames such as Bradley, Wright and Shirley held twenty six per cent (2,087) of the parish of Dysart. In the parishes of Dunmore, Donaghmore and Grangemaccomb, the proportion of the total area held by English occupiers varied from ten to twenty per cent. The English were less dominant as occupiers in the parishes of Kilmenan, Mayne, Kilmadum and Attanagh where they held less than ten per cent of the total area. The distribution of English occupiers in 1850 reinforces the viewpoint that no large scale immigration followed the redistribution of land in the barony in the late seventeenth century. Apart from the Wandesfordes, who required the technical skill of their Yorkshire emigrants to exploit the iron and coal resources of north-east Fassadinin, estate proprietors, the majority of whom were absentees, had neither the desire nor the financial resources to establish extensive civilian colonies on their lands.

Occupiers with surnames which implied ancestry from medieval Anglo-Norman families such as Butler, Purcell, and Comerford were not a numerous group in Fassadinin in 1850. It was only in the civil parishes of Dunmore and Kilmadum that they held more than forty per cent of the total land area. Even here they were numerically weak and their dominance as landholders was related to the past hegemony of the Ormondes. In Rathaspick, the Anglo-Norman occupiers held thirty-eight per cent (243 acres) of the parish. They held twenty per cent (741 acres) of Muckalee parish and between ten and twenty per cent in the parishes of Rathbeag, Mothell and Kilmademoge. In the parishes of Abbeyleix, Attanagh, Castlecomer,

Coolcraheen, Donaghmore, Dysart, Grangemaccomb, Kilmacar, Mayne and Rosconnell, Anglo-Norman occupiers held less than ten per cent of the total land. There was not a single Anglo-Norman occupier listed in the parishes of Odagh and Kilmenan in 1850. The Anglo-Normans never formed a numerous group in Fassadinin and the confiscations of the seventeenth century further reduced their numbers by removing landowning families such as the Archers, Purcells and Blanchvildes.

(i) *Distribution of the O'Brenans.*

The overwhelming numerical superiority of Irish occupiers was the key factor which led to the eventual termination of landlord power. Irish landholders were found in every territorial division in the barony except in the small townlands of Brackin and Borris Little in the Nore Valley. Our main concern is to examine the distribution of the O'Brenans in Fassadinin in 1850, and to estimate the acreage and rateable valuation of their lands. The O'Brenans were the principal Gaelic landowning family in Fassadinin in the seventeenth century and are the only Gaelic family about whom there is any information in the period preceding 1850. Two hundred and seventy two occupiers with the surname O'Brenan held 5,082 statute acres in the barony in 1850 (fig. 6.11). This amounted to approximately seven per cent of the total area of Fassadinin and contrasted with the estimated one third of the barony which they owned in 1592.

The greater number of occupiers with the surname O'Brenan were found in the Civil Parishes of Castlecomer and Dysart, which roughly corresponded in area to the seventeenth century O'Brenan homeland of Idough. In 1850 one hundred and fifty occupiers held approximately ten per cent (3,030) of the combined area of these two parishes. The O'Brenans were comparatively numerous in the eastern hill portion of Muckalee parish and more especially in the townland of Knockmajor where sixteen O'Brenans held approximately thirty per cent (241 acres) of the townland area. They were not as numerous nor as significant as landholders in the adjoining townland of Clogharinka where, according to tradition, the O'Brenans had built a castle in the late medieval period. The O'Brenans were also found as occupiers in the townlands of Lisnafunshin, Newtown, Esker, Shanganny, Gragara, and Ballyrafton, which are all located on the west bank of the Dinin.

Outside of the parishes of Dysart and Castlecomer, the O'Brenans in 1850 were found mainly in the townlands which were owned by the Purcell family in the early seventeenth century. They were not numerous in the good lands on the western fringes of Fassadinin, which were associated with the Ormonde and Mountgarret families. Neither were they found in the hill district located between the Wandesforde and Mountgarret properties. In the southern portion of the barony the O'Brenans were invariably absent as occupiers in townlands which belonged to the Ormonde, Blanchvilde and Archer families in the early part of the seven-

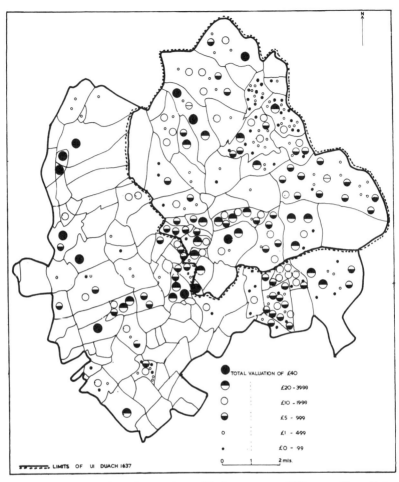

Fig. 6.11 Distribution of occupiers with the surname O'Brenan. Fassadinin 1850.

teenth century. If one compares the distribution of landowners named O'Brenan circa 1635 (fig. 2.3) with occupiers of the same name in 1850 (fig. 6.1) in the parishes of Castlecomer and Dysart, one notes that they were more widely distributed in 1850. They did not occur as occupiers in six of the thirty-two townlands in these parishes. The O'Brenans were absent from the townlands of Firoda Upper and Damerstown East. It is perhaps significant that these were Mountgarret lands in 1635 and were retained by his descendants in 1850. Neither do we encounter the O'Brenans as occupiers in the townland of Coan East, which was among the earliest portions of Idough purchased by the Ormonde family. The absence of the O'Brenans from the townland of Drumgoole, in which the

180

Wandesforde residence was located, and their comparative scarcity in townlands adjoining Castlecomer town suggests that it was landlord policy to exclude them from here in the early period of the colony. The O'Brenans who lived in townlands adjoining and to the north of Ballyragget town were on average considerably wealthier than those who occupied lands in the north-east and south-east of the barony. The average valuation of O'Brenan farms in the parish of Donaghmore was £70 whereas in the parish of Castlecomer it was approximately £2. Even within Castlecomer, substantial variations in the amount of property held by O'Brenans existed. Fifteen occupiers in the townlands of Aughaturbid, Moyhora and Skehana, held land and house property valued at £567. On the other hand forty-three O'Brenan holdings located in the mining townlands of Cloneen, Moneenroe and Gorteen had a combined valuation of £190.

Six of the twelve farms valued over £40 which the O'Brenans occupied in 1850 were held by two individuals. John Brenan resided in a house named Eden Hall, east of Ballyragget town and farmed 466 acres of high value agricultural land scattered throughout the adjoining townlands. This branch of the O'Brenans claimed the right to the title, O'Brenan, which signified descent from the principal medieval family. Members of this family were Justices of the Peace and performed many of the functions usually assigned to minor landlords. John Brenan occupied 371 acres in the townland of Moyhora and was the other major O'Brenan landholder in 1850. The evidence in the Wandesforde papers papers suggests that the O'Brenans were middlemen in this part of the estate as early as 1746. They built a house to which they gave the name 'Moyhora' in this townland in the late eighteenth century. In the 1820's, they moved closer to Castlecomer town and spent, it was claimed, £1,000 in building Woodview House (Plate XI) and a further £600 in the building of out-offices, coach yard, haggard, fruit garden, gate lodge and gate, forming enclosures, avenue, walls, shrubs and laying out the ground. The wealthier members of the O'Brenan family in 1850 consciously imitated the life-style of their landlords. Apart from their surnames and religious affiliations, there was little to differentiate them from the contemporary English landholders who had come to Fassadinin from Yorkshire in the seventeenth century.

(ii) *Distribution of English occupiers*
By plotting on a map the distribution of surnames which are of assumed English origin, it may be possible to determine the influence of the English intrusion to the barony in the late seventeenth and early part of the eighteenth centuries. This method may be more effective than an examination of placename origins (in the context of a small area such as a barony). The available evidence suggests that apart from attempts to find English equivalents for Gaelic names the great majority of townland names remained unchanged over a long period. The names of territorial divisions in modern Fassadinin are mute about the immigration in the seventeenth century. Only two, Webbsborough and Swiftsheath, (of a total of 126 townland

Plate XI. Woodview house in Moyhora townland. The O'Brenan family who held this townland as middletenants of the Wandesfordes, transferred their residence from Moyhora house to Woodview c.1820.

names,) commemorate English families who settled in the barony in this period. Although the Wandesforde family acquired almost one third of the barony *circa* 1636 and retained it for almost three centuries, they did not bestow on it a single territorial name.

The emigrants from the counties of Britain who came to Ireland in the seventeenth century had different religious beliefs from those of the native Irish. Surnames, therefore, may indicate the strength of the non-Catholic religious denominations in Fassadinin in 1850. New English surnames were found in the eighteenth century among the colliers and the substantial tenant farmers on the Wandesforde estate. Apart from landlord names which were invariably English, there is no extant record of the existence of surnames of English origin in the other parts of the barony. The Protestant population in Fassadinin in the late eighteenth century was located in the north-east of the barony in the area which corresponded with the Wandesforde estate and in the south-east on the estate of Viscount Frankfort.

An examination of the Valuation Books reveals that 677 occupiers, who were of assumed English origin, held 17,782 acres of land in Fassadinin in 1850. Of this total number, 411 occupiers in the parishes of Castlecomer and Dysert held 9,695 acres. Figure 6.12 shows that ten of the seventeen townlands, in which the English occupiers held a greater proportion of the land than any other surname group, were located in these parishes. Outside of Castlecomer and Dysart, the English were comparatively numerous as occupiers in the townland of Coolcullen in south-east Fassadinin. In this townland, 44 of the 112 occupiers who were English held 1,538 out ot a total of 3,234 acres. These were the districts in which the majority of the Protestant population in the barony lived circa 1800. Occupiers of English origin may have shared common surnames and religious beliefs but they did not form a homogeneous economic group.

One can distinguish between three types of English occupiers in 1850;

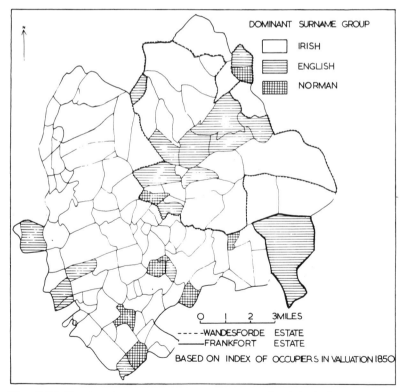

Fig. 6.12 Dominant surname groups on a townland basis i.e. surname groups the net annual value of whose property was greater than that of any other group.

183

those who held little or no property and were typically employed as colliers or as agricultural labourers; occupiers who held between 40 to 100 acres; and a third group farming more substantial holdings which in some instances consisted of whole townlands. The poorer English occupiers were located mainly in the north east mining townlands. These may have been descendants of miners brought from the North East of England in the late seventeenth century or offshoots of the 'yeomen' farm families. The second group were found throughout Fassadinin, but were particularly numerous in the remote hill townlands of Coan East, Coan West and Coolcullen in the east of the barony (fig. 6.13). Neither were the occupiers of substantial holdings of 100 acres and over confined to any particular

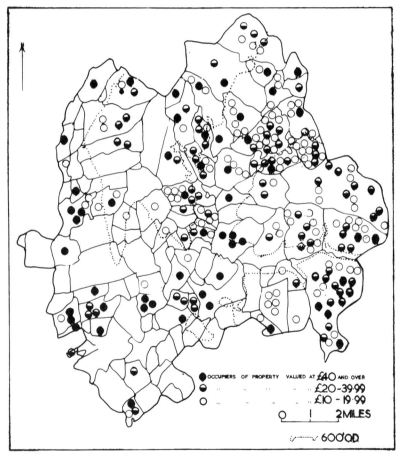

Fig. 6.13 Distribution of occupiers of assumed English origin who held property valued at £10 and over. Fassadinin 1850.

district. They were found in both the colliery townlands on the Castlecomer estate and in the well-endowed area of the Nore valley.

The patterns of land occupation in the townlands of Coolbawn and Foulksrath help to illustrate the distinctions between occupiers of English origin in 1850. Coolbawn townland has an area of 683 acres and is located north east of Castlecomer town. Of the 60 occupiers listed in 1850, 38 with surnames of English origin held 560 acres of the townland. In this territorial division, the relatively prosperous and the propertyless occupiers of English origin are found side by side. Of the 38 holdings, one consisted of a house only, eight were under 1 acre, eight were over 1 and under 5, ten were over 5 and under 15, four were between 15 and 30 and four were over 40 and under 50 acres. Seven of the English occupiers with the surname Bradley held 277 acres in the townland. Samuel Bradley, for example, resided in a substantial house valued at £13.10.0 and farmed 165 acres in Coolbawn. This house still stands on the summit of Coolbawn Hill. The

PLate XII "The Cottage" in Kiltown townland. This house was a colliery manager's residence in the 1850's.

185

longevity of the Bradley connection suggests the durability of the English rural occupation in this part of Fassadinin. Apart from prosperous farmers and less well-to-do small holders and miners, the colliery managerial class was also located in Coolbawn in 1850. Kildare Dobbs held 22 acres of land and a house valued at £8.10.0 Individuals such as Dobbs were invariably recent emigrants from north east England. Their substantial houses dominated the architectural landscape of the colliery townlands and remain today as evidence of their economic power (Plate XII). The 1,538 acres in Coolcullen townland, which was held by occupiers of English origin, was divided into 44 holdings whose average area was thus 34 acres. Fourteen of these farms were over 50 acres and it is the relatively high proportion of farms of this size which differentiated the English settlement in Coolcullen from that in Coolbawn, for example. The presence of such an incongruously large number of English occupiers in this bleak and remote place, the relatively uniform pattern of land occupation and the comparatively high valuations given to dwellings in 1850 implies that this was a consciously planned settlement.

The pattern of land occupation in the townland of Foulksrath, sited on the fertile and attractive lowland between the Nore and Dinin rivers, was very different from that in Coolcullen or Coolbawn. Indeed it may have been quite similar to the type of agrarian structure found here in the medieval period. The whole townland area of 355 acres was held by Thomas Wright Esq. Wright resided in Foulksrath Castle and had four undertenants on his farm.

Two main phases of immigration are represented by the occupiers of English origin in Fassadinin in 1850. The first phase was associated with the foundation of an English colony at Castlecomer in 1636 and more especially with the strengthening of the settlement here in the late seventeenth century. There is no reference to any movement of people in this period in the Wandesforde papers that have survived. The evidence may have been lost or its absence may only suggest that the traffic of people between the Yorkshire and Castlecomer estates was so common that it did not merit special attention. The second phase related to the English settlement in Coolcullen and in the adjacent townlands of Coan East and Coan West to the north. The available evidence suggests that this movement took place in the late eighteenth century. It is possible that this group did not come directly from England but were people of English origin who had first settled elsewhere in Ireland. There was no large scale intrusion of English people to Fassadinin in the nineteenth century. Those that did come were invariably colliery or estate administrators. The two phases seem to be represented in the distinctive English surnames found in Fassadinin in 1850. Names such as Close, Booth, Renor, Flewellin and Copley occur mainly in townlands associated with the Wandesfordes. On the other hand surnames such as Askins, Willoughby, Shirley, Rothwell and Poole were confined to the townlands of Coolcullen, Coan East and Coan West, to which the more recent immigrants had come. Landlord family names such as Wandesforde, Moores and Humpheries do not occur as names of occupiers in 1850. This suggests that landlord-tenant relationships were rarely based on kinship.

(iii) *Distribution of Anglo-Norman occupiers.*
Much of the material fabric which characterised the medieval world in which the Anglo-Normans were dominant had disappeared by 1850. Apart from the few who were commemorated in townland names such as Clinstown, Foulksrath, Ballyragget and Suttonsrath, the majority of the early medieval family names had vanished without trace. The occupiers in 1850 whose surnames denoted their Anglo-Norman ancestry were invariably representative of seventeenth century landowning families such as Purcell and Butler. In 1850, 395 occupiers whose surnames were of Anglo-Norman origin held 6,662 acres of land in Fassadinin barony. The townlands in which the Anglo-Norman occupiers were comparatively numerous in 1850 were outside the areas in which they had formed the dominant landowning class in the early seventeenth century. Even in townlands such as Kilmacar, Dunmore, Muckalee and Kilmademoge, in which the central places of the manorial estates were located, the Anglo-Normans were thin on the ground. Seven of the 22 occupiers listed in the townland of Toortane in the extreme north-west of the barony had the surname Cantwell. These held 172 of the total 308 acres in the townland, in holdings ranging from 2 to 58 acres. In the adjoining townland of Clogh, 25 of a total of 117 occupiers had surnames of Anglo-Norman origin. They held only 52 of the 506 acres in the townland and nineteen of their holdings were under 1 acre. Thirteen of these occupiers had the surname Comerford and the remaining twelve had surnames such as Cody, Purcell and Cantwell. Apart from Purcell, these surnames did not occur among the Anglo-Norman landowning class in Fassadinin in the early seventeenth century. Although Clogh was part of Ormonde's Fassadinin lands the surname Butler is not found here in 1850. Apart from the north-east, pockets of Anglo-Norman occupiers were located in the townlands of Castlemarket and Ballyoskill in north-west Fassadinin, Coolcullen in the south-east and in the townland of Dunmore East in the parish of Dunmore (fig. 6.14).

Figure 6.12 shows that occupiers with surnames of Anglo-Norman origin held the greater proportion of the townlands of Kirwans Inch, Dunmore Park, Bullockhill, Drumerhin, Ballyrafton, Coolcraheen and Toortane. These townlands were located in the area of Fassadinin which represented the most continuous expanse of large scale farming in the barony, with comparatively low population densities and correspondingly high valuation per unit area. Here, appropriately enough, are the remnants of a once more prosperous landowning class. The Butlers occupied the whole townlands of Drumerhin and Dunmore Park, which were both located on the fringes of the barony. The Anglo-Norman occupiers were not numerically dominant in any of these townlands. The complete ab-

187

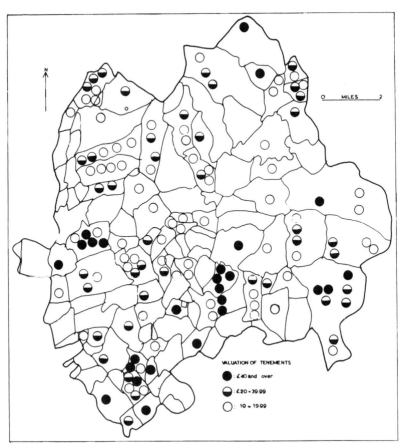

Fig. 6.14 Distribution of occupiers of assumed Angle-Norman origin who held property valued at £10 and over. Fassadinin 1850.

sence from the barony of the surnames Blanchvilde and Archer and the scarcity of occupiers with surnames such as Purcell and Butler adequately reflects the demise of the Anglo-Norman in Fassadinin. The Purcells in 1640 owned approximately one seventh of the barony. In 1850 they were not even landowners and only thirty-eight occupiers with this surname were listed in the General Valuation of Rateable property. These held a combined area of 684 acres, and the largest farm held by a Purcell consisted of 84 acres in the hill townland of Coolcullen. The Purcells circa 1640 were predominantly associated with the fertile and attractive lowlands of Fassadinin. They are not found here in 1850. The Valuation Book returns them as occupiers in the Wandesforde estate, in the bleak hill country in the east of the barony and in the townland of Knockmajor in south-east Fassadinin. They were completely absent from their ancestral

188

townland south of Ballyragget and the sites of long ruined Purcell castles were the only traces of their historical presence here. The distribution of the Butlers, which was the family name of the Ormondes and Mount-garrets, the two most influential landowning families in seventeenth century Fassadinin, reveals a similar pattern.

(b) *Patterns of Land occupation in 1850.*

"The landlord was not, as in England, a partner in agricultural production investing capital in fencing, drainage, farm houses and cottages and bound to the cultivator by social and prescriptive ties, but simply the receiver of a rent charge. From time to time this increased, as the labour of others or the increase of population made occupation of the soil more valuable, but inrespect of it, with few exceptions, no obligations were recognised beyond those of neighbourly feeling, where this might happen to exist. In fact, Irish landlords are to be compared not with English squires, but with the ground landlords of London"

(Bryce, E. (ed.) *Two centuries of Irish history,* (London, 1870) 207).

The ownership of land in Fassadinin in 1850 was vested in a self-conscious minority, the greater number of whom had neither family nor residential links with the barony. Although landlord-tenant relationships as expressed by the tenurial system were surprisingly uniform throughout the barony, this does not imply that occupiers were a homogeneous class. Contemporary observers were well aware of the differences between tenant farmers and landholders as a class, and those who were landless. Richard Eaton differentiated between the large farmers who were "comfortable and respectable", the small farmers who were "of a rather poor description", and the labourers who were "diminished by emigration and whose chances of employment were reduced by "the spread of grazing land".[20] He further observed that the "lower order of tenants had little capital", whereas the better classes were "laying out their capital in buildings and other improvements on their holdings".

The major distinction within the barony was between small holdings which were characterised by subsistence farming and the larger, more substantial holdings which had a market-orientated economy. The pattern of land occupation offers a major insight into rural society in Fassadinin in the mid-nineteenth century. T. Jones Hughes has suggested that agriculture in this part of Ireland was oriented towards either the cultivation of wheat and barley for sale or the fattening of cattle for export or the Dublin markets.[21] T. W. Freeman commented on the wide variety of agricultural commodities produced in the Nore and Barrow river basins.[22] This district had comparatively good road and canal links with both the east and south coast towns and had substantial and long established market towns such as Kilkenny, Carlow and Athy. From his analysis of the 1841 census returns, J. H. Johnson concluded that "the amount of celibacy and the age of marriage for the country as a whole was highest in south-eastern Ireland."[23] In this section an attempt is made to estimate the extent to

189

which rural life in Fassadinin at mid-century was tied into a commercial economy.

Predictably little is known about the pattern of agricultural activity on the scale of the individual holding at this period. The evidence from the Castlecomer estate suggests that because of the termination of the middleman system and the consequent loss of profit rents from sublet land the more substantial farmers now derived a greater part of their income from the sale of farm produce. This conclusion is based on the premise that the economy of holdings in excess of at least 100 acres was market oriented. When the distribution of these holdings is plotted on a sketch map, it should reveal variations in the pattern of land occupation in the barony. A total of 17,017 statute acres was held in 92 holdings of 100 acres and over in 1850 (fig. 6.15). Over forty per cent of the land of the parishes of Coolcraheen (total area, 1,736 acres), Dunmore (2,379), Kilmadum and

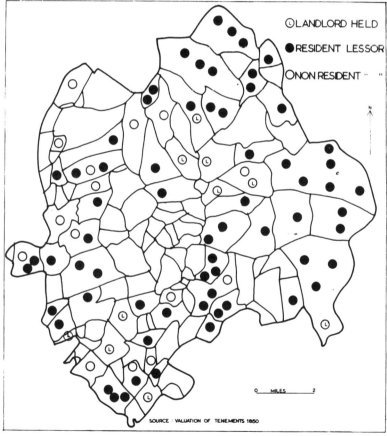

Fig. 6.15 Holdings of 100 acres and over. Fassadinin 1850.

190

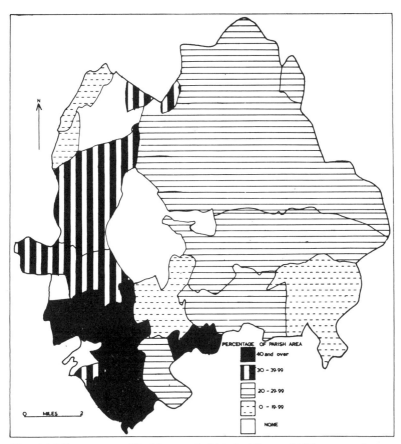

Fig. 6.16 Percentage of Parish areas held in holdings of 100 acres and over.
Fassadinin 1850.

Mayne (1,940) was held in farms of 100 acres and over (fig. 6.16). The
parishes of Donaghmore (5,268), Grangemaccomb (3,483), and Abbeyleix
(680) (which occupied part of the fertile Nore basin) had over thirty per
cent of their total area in farms over 100 acres. Here where the boulder
clay mantled lowlands of North Kilkenny converged on the shale uplands
of the Castlecomer plateau was the core area of commercial farming in
Fassadinin barony. All available indicators such as farm size, the valuation
of agricultural land and the density of townland population in 1851,
suggests that this was a well-endowed district. There are no gaps in the
farming settlement here and the topography gives easy access to the important market town of Kilkenny. Isolated mansion houses such as Jenkinstown House and Swiftsheath House, with their distinctive arrangements of outbuildings and ornamental grounds, and the smaller complexes,
such as Foulksrath Castle, which housed the substantial tenant farmers,

were scattered throughout this area. Here is also found a comparatively high proportion of landlord occupied land which was in some instances the demesne farms of resident proprietors. In the parish of Mayne, 879 acres of the total area of 1,763 was held in two holdings over 100 acres, whereas the remainder of the parish was divided amongst 79 occupiers.

Some of these higher valued lands were surprisingly empty. The Bryans had no undertenants on the 777 acres they held in Mayne parish. They obviously obtained their work force from the small holders in the adjoining townlands. In Coolcraheen parish, estates were typically small and landlords were invariably absentee. Because of this, the substantial tenant farmers formed a significant group and in many instances combined farming with the duties of estate agents. Thomas Wright occupied 205 of a total of 447 acres in Clintstown townland as undertenant to James Lalor, who was the absentee proprietor of the townland. Wright also held the whole townland and the castle of Foulksrath as undertenant to the Earl of Portarlington, another absentee. Nicholas Cahill, who held 291 acres and a house valued at £10, was the principal undertenant of Sydenham Davis Esq., who owned the townland of Lismaine. Approximately one half (851 acres) of the total area of 1,763 acres in Coolcraheen parish was held by two occupiers who were the principal tenants of absentee landlords.

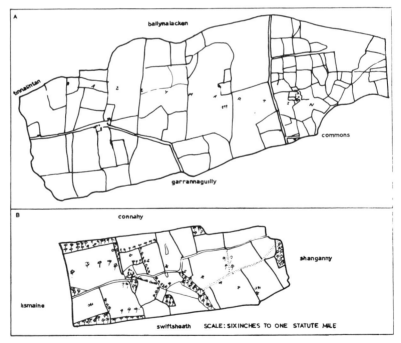

Fig. 6.17 (a) Foulksrath townland c.1843
       (b) Ballymartin townland c.1843

192

Apart from the substantial houses occupied by Wright and Cahill, these farms with their large regular fields had little settlement (fig. 6.17a). Wright who formed 500 acres had only five undertenants, four of whom occupied a house without land.

In Donaghmore parish, 1,781 acres of a total of 5,218 acres was held in holdings of 100 acres and over. The pattern of land occupation in Donaghmore parish was influenced by the location of the central place of Ballyragget which had a population of 1,170 in 1851. Twenty eight tenements, containing 1,709 acres, consisted of land without any buildings. This suggests that a number of occupiers held rural property while residing in the town of Ballyragget. The parish of Donaghmore consists of two distinctive topographical divisions which were also reflected in the patterns of land occupation. East Donaghmore occupies part of the sheltered Nore river basin. The western portion of the parish embraces the outer rim of the Castlecomer plateau. In the hill country, the large farm was the typical landholding unit. Ballymartin townland occupies the rim of the plateau summit and part of the steep escarpment which rises sharply from the Nore valley. The townland area of 875 acres was divided into three holdings (fig. 6.17b). This suggests that the agrarian structure found here in 1850 was similar to that in the better lands of Coolcraheen and Mayne parish to the south. Holdings in the west of the parish were not as large. John Brenan, who occupied but did not reside on his 194 acres farm in Donaghmore townland, who lived in a house valued at thirteen pounds in Ballyragget townland, and who had four undertenants on his Donaghmore lands, probably typified the substantial tenant farmer at this period.

Approximately one third (1,094 acres) of Grangemaccomb parish, which was located in the wide Nore basin to the south of Ballyragget, was held in farms of 100 acres and over in 1850. A comparison of the townlands of Grange and Connahy suggests that the pattern of land occupation varied greatly within the parish. Approximately 520 of a total area of 674 acres in Grange townland was held in three holdings of 100 acres and over. Two of these farms, held by members of the Stannard family, had a combined area of 353 acres and the net annual value of their buildings amounted to £46. On the other hand, only 237 of the total of 1,517 acres in Connahy was held in farms of 100 acres and over. The combined net annual value of buildings, which amounted to only £7 on these farms, does not suggest that they were outstanding features in the landscape. The Catholic church and the police barracks rather than the residences of substantial tenant farmers were the major settlement items in the townland of Connahy.

The difference in landholding patterns in the townland of Connahy and Grange is also revealed by a comparison of the number of holdings under twenty acres. Fifty-seven tenements in Connahy were under twenty acres whereas the corresponding figure in Grange was twenty. These diverse patterns of land occupation may possibly be explained with reference to the system of landownership. Apart from the subdivision of small estates into substantial tenant-farms, the type of agrarian structure found in Grange and in other parts of the Nore basin may have changed little since the late medieval period. The Mossom family who owned Grange townland resided here throughout the eighteenth century. It is probable that the purchasers of Connahy in the early eighteenth century never resided in Fassadinin. The proprietors in 1850 were described in the General Valuation as the "representatives of Joseph Strangways and Connell Loughlin". This suggests that ownership of the townland was vested in a number of people who merely acted in the undemanding capacity of rent receivers. The pattern of land occupation in Connahy townland in 1850 had evolved without direct landlord supervision over a period of one hundred years. It was typical of the communities of smallholders where the dispersed, single-storey, thatched farmstead was the common feature of rural settlement (Plate XII) and where the Catholic church was the major settlement item and a dominant force in rural life.

Between twenty to thirty per cent of the areas of Castlecomer (total area, 21,500 acres), Kilmademoge (1,725), Dysart (7,936), Muckalee, (3,703), and Rathaspick, (639), was held in holdings of 100 acres and over (fig. 6.16). In Castlecomer parish thirty holdings, which contained 6,282 acres, were over 100 acres in extent. Five of these farms were occupied by the estate proprietor and consisted of the demesne farm, plantations and some bogland in the outlying townlands of Crutt and Croghtenclogh. The available evidence (which is later considered in the context of the Wandesforde property) suggests that the landlord farm at Castlecomer was one of the few commercial enterprises in the barony. Detailed accounts of farm transactions such as the profits from the sale of stock and the expenditure on stock purchase, feedstuffs and labour were kept by the estate agent. The pattern of land occupation in this part of the barony was complicated by the existence of commercial mining. In the well-defined district known locally as the collieries, farming was a secondary source of income. Nevertheless, in the townlands of Cloneen, Coolbawn, and Clogh which were congested by any criteria, large commercial holdings were found in 1850. In Coolbawn townland, Samuel Bradley occupied a farm of 165 acres and buildings valued at £13.10.0. In the townland of Cloneen, which had a population of 1,086 in 1851, a farm held by Martha Bradley occupied 114 of the total 875 acres in the townland. In Clogh townland, about sixty per cent (301) of the total area was held in two holdings over 100 acres. The Valuation of Tenements recorded 118 occupiers in this mining townland. Of these, 16 were landless, 65 held under one acre and 16 held over one and under five acres. In a townland with such a degree of overcrowding, it is all the more surprising to find one farm of 193 acres and another of 108 acres. Very few undertenants are found on these holdings despite the extremely high densities of population in this part of Fassadinin. Only four undertenants were recorded on these four farms which had a combined area of 580 acres. This suggests that farms of this size throughout the barony were managed in a similar way.

Population was less dense and occupiers were less numerous in the townlands of Skehana, Moyhora, Loan and Aughamucky which fringed the colliery district. In the mid-eighteenth century these townlands were leasing units: by 1812, the size of leaseholdings had been reduced considerably: in 1850 the average holding size in each of these townlands was under fifty acres. Holdings which were over 100 acres in 1850 may have been the central portions of much larger seventeenth century farms. John Brenan held 371 of a total of 1,172 acres in Moyhora townland in 1850 (fig. 6.18). In 1746, the O'Brenans had occupied the whole townland. One also notes the impact of Castlecomer on the patterns of land occupa-

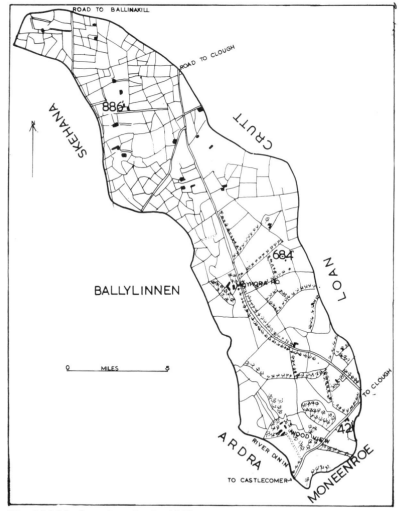

Fig. 6.18 Moyhora townland c.1843.

tion in townlands located close to the town. Isaac Bradley, who held 134 acres in Skehana and David Ryan, who occupied a farm of 374 acres in Aughamucky, resided in Castlecomer town.

The large townlands of Firoda Upper (1,182 acres), Crutt (2,456), Aughatubrid (1,651) and Croghtenclogh, (3,470) occupied the borderlands of Fassadinin barony. The medieval inhabitants of the barony appear to have shunned these remote, infertile places. An examination of the General Valuation of Rateable Property in Fassadinin reveals that only a very small proportion of land in these townlands was described as either untenanted or waste in 1850. Of a total 8,750 acres in Firoda Upper, only 158 (classified as bogland) 9 acres (plantation) and 8 acres ('fox cover'). were untenanted. The average size of holdings was 74 acres in Firoda Upper, 36 in Aughatubrid, 33 in Croghtenclogh and 28 in Crutt. There were still large, empty spaces with little or no settlement items in these townlands in 1850. The net annual value of buildings on the 677 acres farm of Richard Lalor in Firoda Upper, was only £1. It can be assumed that these low value lands were used exclusively as Summer grazing grounds. The differences in the average farm sizes found in these townlands suggests that the extension of settlement took place within estate boundaries in the early part of the century. Both Croghtenclogh and Crutt belonged to the Wandesforde estate and Aughatubrid was part of the equally crowded Denn-Keating property. On the other hand Firoda Upper, in which farm sizes were on average comparatively greater, was the only townland owned by Lord Vaux in Fassadinin barony. Furthermore, coalmining in Crutt and Croghtenclogh led to a greater concentration of settlement and a corresponding reduction of the average size of tenant farms.

The civil parishes of Dysart, Muckalee and Kilmademoge are located in the part of Fassadinin between Castlecomer parish and the barony boundary with Gowran (fig. 1.8). The admixture of old-English and Gaelic elements in the placenames suggests that this district was an zone of contact between these two cultures in medieval times. When the distribution of farms of 100 acres and over was plotted on a sketch map, they were invariably located in townlands which were the centres of either Anglo-Norman manorial estates or Gaelic 'sept' lands in the early part of the seventeenth century (fig. 6.15). In Kilmademoge the townlands of Bullock-hill (total area 196 acres) and Kilmademoge (195) were held as single holdings. Figure 2.4 shows that the central-place of Kilmademoge manor was located in Kilmademoge townland and that here also was the site of the pre-Reformation parish church. In Muckalee parish, seven holdings of 100 acres and over were distributed throughout the townlands of Muckalee, Clogharinka and Gaulstown. Muckalee townland was the site of an early medieval church. The Archer family occupied a castle in Gaulstown and a Purcell castle was sited in Clogharinka townland (fig. 2.4). Six of the twelve farms of 100 acres and over in Dysart parish were found in the adjoining townlands of Knockannadogue and Damerstown East. The principal O'Brenan 'sept' resided in Rathcally, a subdivision of Knockannadogue, in the early seventeenth century. In Damerstown East, which was owned by the Kavanaghs of Borris, the three holdings over 100 acres were occupied by Kavanaghs who were probably kinsfolk of the proprietor. In the remaining townlands in these parishes, such as Coan East and Coan West in Dysart Knockmajor in Muckalee and Knocknew in Kilmademoge, land values were invariably lower and smallholdings which were between thirty to forty acres, on average, predominated. This type of agrarian structure and the circumstances under which it evolved may have been quite similar to that found in Connahy townland in Grangemaccomb parish.

Farms of 100 acres and over were less numerous in the civil parishes of Kilmenan (1,008) and Rosconnell (253) in the north-west and in Mothell (6,844) parish in the south-east of Fassadinin. No farms of this size were found in the parish of Attanagh (1,928) in the north-west nor in Kilmacar (4,815) which occupied part of the hill lands of central Fassadinin (fig. 6.16) The Webb family owned a comparatively small estate in the east of Mothell parish and were the only resident proprietors in all of these parishes. The Agar family who had purchased Kilmacar from the Ormondes in the early part of the eighteenth century, never resided on their Fassadinin property. It was in these densely settled districts that the Catholic churches and National Schools, many of which were built in the period from 1830 to 1845, were most numerous (fig. 6.2). These filled, to an extent, the vacuum left by the absence or disinterest of landlords and be-became the new focal points in rural life.

Although fig. 6.16 shows that in some parishes a greater proportion of land was held in holdings of 100 acres and over than in others, large farms were not exclusively limited to any one district in the barony. Their distributional pattern suggests that they were the remnants of farms which in the eighteenth century corresponded to townland units. An analysis of the Valuation Books suggests that large farms were typically found in areas which had above average land values such as Dunmore Park, and in townlands such as Firoda Upper which consisted of low value, isolated hill land. Dunmore Park was empty because it was reserved for the landlord, whereas settlement was sparse in Firoda Upper because of its remoteness. Smallholdings were the dominant form of land-holding in estates which were owned by absentee landlords. This type of agrarian structure may have developed through a continuous process of subdivision of family farms. In the townland of Connahy, nineteen out of the seventy tenants who had the surname Downey held 491 out of the total townland area of 1,507 acres.

The preoccupation with the role of landlords in rural society in nineteenth century Ireland has resulted in the undervaluation of the significance of the substantial tenant-farmers. In many instances, landlords were no more than figureheads who had little or no contact with the barony of Fassadinin and, consequently, exercised limited influence on the every-day activities of tenant-farmers. Substantial tenant-farmers on the other hand were a much more numerous group and were widely distributed throughout the barony (fig. 6.15). The analysis of the pattern of land occupation on the Wandesforde estate, in the period from 1800 to 1838, indicated that the majority of these substantial tenants were middlemen who derived considerable profit-rents from sublet lands.

The evidence from this period also suggests that well-to-do middlemen participated in the physical growth of Castlecomer town and that they left an enduring imprint on the countryside in the form of two-storied, slated dwellings which were built with stone and had an impressive array of outbuildings. It is also known that many of these occupiers were absentees. The termina- ation of the middleman system deprived these individuals of a substantial part of their incomes and may have forced them to take a more active interest in farming their holdings. Substantial farmers carried out many of the functions which have been commonly ascribed to landlords. They planted trees, laid out gardens and orchards and in general attempted to emulate the arrangement of the demesne. It can also be assumed that this sector of the population was not as mobile as their less prosperous neigh- bours. It was individuals rather than complete families who emigrated from this class. It was from these families that the clergy of the Catholic church were recruited. Some of the them, such as the O'Brenans and Phel- ans of Ballyragget, contributed to the building of Catholic churches in the same way as the landlord endowed Church of Ireland buildings.

CHAPTER SEVEN

THE WANDESFORDE ESTATE c. 1840-1850

"Cloneen, April 24th, 1854.
John Tobin holds one acre of land his father and mother dead no house on the land but a hut. Widow Mick Bradley holds a house and hagert house built by herself. Nickholaus Tobin holds a cabin on William Hayes land and built it himself 14 years ago. The house that was fallen down to send Mick Malone and family to America for there is a woman by the name of Elizabeth Brenan Durick from Doonane got into the old walls of it and has Brigit Mongan in it with her and she is receiving the sum of 1s.4d. outdoor relief".
(copy of letter from a sub-agent of the Wandesforde estate in Wandesforde papers).

1. Introduction

To offer an area like the Wandesforde estate as a suitable venue for a sample study is to invite the criticism that it is atypical of the estates found in Fassadinin barony at this period. The Wandesfordes were resident proprietors whereas the majority of estate owners in the barony were absentees. The Wandesfordes derived a considerable portion of their income from coal-mining whereas income on the other estates consisted mainly of rents paid for agricultural land. In the period under consideration the proprietor of the Castlecomer property was involved in major enterprises such as sending out emigrants to the new world, opening up hitherto untouched coal seams and in planning and implementing a massive programme of estate renewal. The greater number of estates in the barony neither had the finances necessary to embark on such ambitious projects, nor had they inherited problems similar to those found on the Castlecomer property. Although the Castlecomer estate differed greatly from other Fassadinin properties in terms of area and in relation to the range and scale of activities carried on within it, nevertheless, there are compelling reasons for selecting it as a study area. The estate was roughly similar in shape and size to the Territory of Idough purchased by Sir Christopher Wandesforde in 1636. A descendant of the original proprietor was in possession in 1850. The tenurial system, as expressed in the patterns of land occupation, was strikingly uniform throughout the barony in 1850. The Wandesforde estate in many respects serves as a microcosm o the bar-

199

ony area. The existence of the Wandesforde manuscripts is perhaps the major reason for selecting the estate. There is a certain anonymity about small estates in this period. It is difficult if not altogether impossible to unearth records of maps concerning these properties, so that these detailed records are extremely valuable and rare.

2. General description of Estate

The topographical distinction between the lowlands skirting the Dinin and the hill ridges which lay to the east and west is mirrored in the social geography of the estate. Land quality, as defined by the valuations given to agricultural land in 1850, deteriorated away from the central corridor (fig. 6.1). Townland areas were larger, population densities comparatively lower and farms greater towards the hill fringes of the estate. The pre-Famine estate had been shaped by rapid population growth, concurrently with expansion of mining activity and the growing power of the middleman. The reduction of the estate population by about one third and the contraction of mining in the decade from 1841 to 1851 contributed greatly to the moulding of the post-Famine estate. The fact that much of the material legacy of Irish estates was inherited from before the age of improvement was clearly evident in Castlecomer. Untidy accretions of later periods were superimposed on the carefully embellished eighteenth century landscape. This was especially true of the part of the estate where mining was important. The existence of mining complicated the simplistic stratification of the estate into hill and lowland and added to its social diversity. Variations in farm sizes and the number and valuation of buildings gave striking evidence of this. The residences of commercial farmers and colliery managers located in the congested mining townlands contrasted with the dilapidated, transient structures which housed the colliers. Nineteenth century mining has left few material traces on this countryside. Surface items associated with underground mining such as engine houses, windlasses, gin tracks and the once ubiquitous slag heap, have disappeared. The colliers constituted the majority of the people of no property who fled the barony in the decade of Famine.

3. Ownership

The Wandesforde property in 1850 contained 19,920 statute acres. Included in this area was the 3,354 acres of the estate held under lease. The proprietor in 1850 was tenant in-fee-simple of the estate. The importance of the type of legal title by which the landlord held his property has often been overlooked. Contemporary observers such as Richard Eaton, the land agent of the Castlecomer property, stressed the importance of the landlord's title. In evidence before the Devon Commission he asserted that "impediments to improvement" by both tenant and landlord were "diminished" by the fact that the landlord held the estate in fee simple.[1] During the tenure of the Countess of Ormonde, the Castlecomer estate was bound by entail. This meant that she enjoyed the usufruct of the property during her lifetime but did not own it. Consequently, she had no legal power to alienate any portion of the estate by outright sale or long term lease. The Countess of Ormonde did manage to alienate the greater portion of the property by granting long term leases. It is also significant that her period of occupation coincided with the rapid and uncontrolled escalation of population, and the entrenchment of middleman dominance on the estate. This suggests that the ability of a landlord to embark on ambitious programmes of estate improvement such as assisted emigration, was conditioned by factors other than his financial solvency. It also indicates that continuity of ownership by families may conceal important legal aspects of ownership which may have been instrumental in dictating landlord policy.

The landlord in 1850 occupied 1,413 acres of his property which amounted to approximately seven per cent of the estate area. The greater portion of this was under plantations; part of it was untenanted bogland in the hill townlands of Crutt and Croghtenclogh; the remainder was mainly in permanent pasture. Of greater significance was the fact that the proprietor had eighty three per cent (15,677) of the estate area in his possession. The breaking up of the middleman system was one of the primary objectives and major achievements of landlord policy in this period. The manuscripts suggest that the estate proprietor was becoming increasingly involved in the day-to-day administration of the estate. They also indicate that the Castlecomer landlord was engaged in estate stocktaking before the onslaught of the Great Hunger. Landlords such as the Wandesfordes, whose predecessors had facilitated and encouraged the growth of the middlemen system, now found that it drastically reduced the revenue they received in the form of rent. The growth in population and the increase in commercial farming had both intensified the demand for land. Apart from the damaging effect which the uncontrolled subdivision of middlemen lands had on the estate, it is certain that these financial considerations were taken into account in the termination of the system.

In 1850, 3,354 acres amounting to approximately seventeen per cent of the estate area was in the possession of middlemen. Six of the seven leaseholdings were over 200 acres but only two leaseholdings consisted of whole townlands. Since the mid-eighteenth century the land leasing unit had become progressively smaller. Mrs. Gertrude Keating, the representative of the Denn family, was the primary leaseholder in 1850. She held the townlands of Ballylinnen and Cloneen which had a combined area of 1,459 acres. It is significant that two of the remaining middletenants, David Ryan who held 410 acres in Aughamucky and John Brenan who was in possession of 274 acres in Ballylinnen, were described as improving tenants in 1838. Three middletenants held a combined area of 819 acres in the eastern part of Croghtenclogh townland. Their survival as middletenants may be attributed to the fact that neither landlord nor undertenants had much interest in the cold, bleak and impoverished lands they occupied.

The termination of the middleman system helped to standardise the pattern of land occupation within the estate. Richard Eaton, in evidence before the Devon Commission, stated that the majority of the occupiers held their lands as tenants from year-to-year. Tenants in the town and rural tenants who held a small portion of land with a cottage also held from year-to-year. Such tenancies did not have a written contract, but were regarded as tenancies in perpetuity from the payment of annual rent. Tenancy from year-to-year was subject to great abuses. Landlords by serving a notice to quit could compel the tenant either to surrender his holding or more commonly to pay an increased rent. Tenancies-at-will were not common on the estate and were restricted to those holding directly from middlemen. *The Rateable Valuation of Tenements* indicates that farms held in partnership were not numerous on the estate. Only two such holdings were recorded. One farm in Crutt townland had an area of 381 acres and was occupied by ten tenants, five of whom were named Dunphy. The other holding located in Croghtenclogh townland contained 296 acres partitioned in unequal shares amongst fifteen tenants, ten of whom were named Brenan. Subletting was not permitted by the landlord and when lands were sublet without his permission, the offending tenant was served with notice to quit. Nevertheless, the practice of subletting was prevalent on lands held by middlemen over whom the landlord had no control. This summary of tenurial arrangements on the Castlecomer estate shows that the scope and range of estate management had developed considerably since the early part of the century. In contrast to the earlier period when the landlord was rarely concerned with the affairs of the estate outside the demesne walls, the evidence suggests that the proprietor in 1850 exercised an increasing degree of control over all his tenants.

The landlord in this period was concerned with a great variety of estate matters. Improvements of a practical nature such as land drainage, fertiliser application and the renewal and construction of houses, were oriented towards increasing the area of productive land and with regulating the appearance of the countryside. Major improvement schemes, such as land drainage, which affected large areas of the estate were carried out independently by the landlord. Landlord assistance was given either in the form of materials such as timber for the erection of dwellings or fences, or as financial help to defray tenant expenses. The manuscript evidence provides a contemporary insight into the working of the estate system and provides revealing examples of landlord activity. Apart from assisting tenants to improve their holdings, the Wandesfordes attempted to regularise tenant activities through the imposition of a set of rules and regulations. One such list of precepts[2] entitled, 'Regulations to be observed by the Tenants in Castlecomer Estate', was issued in 1850. This stipulated that tenants were not to 'break up' grassland, to erect buildings, to make drains or to cut hedges within one mile of the town of Castlecomer without first receiving permission from the estate office. The greater part of the estate demesne was located within this one-mile zone and it also included the town suburbs in which much uncontrolled adventitious development by middlemen had taken place in the first half of the century. Outside this well-defined area, the rules were less restrictive. Buildings and yards were to be kept in a proper state of repair and cleanliness; hedges, fences and gates were to be kept in order; ditches were to be scoured out; tenants were directed to preserve trees found on their land; they were to root up or cut weeds before they went to seed. The maintenance of estate roads was the responsibility of tenants whose lands adjoined them. There is a striking similarity between this kind of directive and the stipulations concerning buildings, enclosures and plantations, which were generally included in the land leases of the late seventeenth century.

The evidence in the estate papers suggests that failure to comply with these regulations was punishable by an increase in rent, by the loss of undefined privileges and in some instances by eviction. Improvements led to increased productivity which, under favourable market circumstances, led to corresponding increases in tenant income. Historians commonly assert that the visible signs of improvements were one of the ways by which landlords could measure tenant capacity to meet rent increases and that accordingly tenants were discouraged from participating in improvement schemes. This does not appear to have been the situation in the Castlecomer property in this period. The directives issued to the new agent, Richard Cooke, by the estate proprietor in 1859 support this contention. Wandesforde wrote. "Raise the rent of Foley Cloneen for the disgraceful state of his farm, Widow Fogarty committed a fraud, White's land at Smithestowne just as disgraceful as it was in 1830, get him to give it up. Currans at Aughamucky, raise their rent as their land is also in a disgraceful state. Enquire re house Ryan is building in Ward's land, let MacMillans lease with Lady Ormonde be broken, on which land Wards now live and let the undertenants become my tenants."[3] Here was at least one landlord who was penalising tenants for *not* improving their holdings.

The influence of a resident proprietor must not be seen only in terms of prescriptive rules and regulations which attempted to improve the appearance and profitability of estate land. The estate farm was an important centre of innovation which introduced new agricultural techniques into north-east Fassadinin. Although the estate proprietor occupied 1,413 acres in 1850, much of this was under plantations or consisted of non-productive bog land. The estate farm contained approximately 500 acres and was scattered throughout the townlands of Moyhora, Ardra, Kiltown, Drumgoole and Ballyhimmin. Dairying was the major farm enterprise here and the estate papers indicate that the fattening of store cattle was an important subsidiary activity. The development of the cattle trade in this period was greatly facilitated by the expansion of the rail and sea transport networks and the ease of access this gave to the burgeoning Dublin and English markets. The evidence in the Wandesforde papers suggests that it was a common practise to drive cattle on the hoof to Athy from where they were transported by rail to Dublin. Cattle were sometimes shipped to Liverpool and the manuscripts in 1841 record that William Somerville, the farm steward, was paid £27.2.3. for "expenses at Liverpool for sale of cattle." Because the estate of Castlecomer had established a network of contacts with the British market, it may have substantially shaped the pattern of commercial farming within north east Fassadinin.

4. Landlord assisted emigration 1841-1853.

"4,854 individuals have been assisted by me to migrate, all at their own earnest request, at a cost of £14,525. I paid the cost of their passage, and gave them a certain sum per head. In addition to this assistance, they were compensated for any improvements and permitted to sell the materials of their cabins. Nothing can exceed their desire to emigrate and the desire of their friends to induce them to leave this country. Every letter is a letter of encouragement".

(Quoted in A reply to *A Narrative of Landlord Oppression and Tenant Wrong*, Earl of Carrick, (Dublin 1870), 5).

Emigration was seen not as a final solution but as a palliative to the demographic and economic problems which beset pre-Famine Ireland. The Poor Inquiry Commission in 1835 recommended emigration as, "an auxiliary measure, essential to a continuing course of amelioration."[4] Emigration during the first half of the century was both localised and sporadic and was often of a semi-permanent nature. The typical emigrant up to 1835 was the small farmer in whom both the desire to leave and the means to afford his passage coincided. The outward movement which commenced in the 1840's was different in many respects to that which preceded it. The number of emigrants increased dramatically with the onset of the Famine. It has been estimated that in the decade from 1847 to 1857 more Irish went to America than had left the island in all its earlier history.[5] The pre-Famine emigrant came mainly from the ranks of the small tenant-farmers but the majority of those who fled the country in the decade of Famine had little or no stake in the land.

There is no evidence to suggest that emigration was a feature of rural life in Fassadinin in the first half of the nineteenth century. The number of people who came to the colliery district in search of employment far exceeded those who left. Emigration from the Castlecomer estate must be seen as part of a carefully contrived policy of estate renewal. There are many reasons which induced the landlord to accept a project which necessitated considerable financial outlay. Some commentators have observed that the passing of the Irish Poor Law in 1838, which levied rates on property for the upkeep of the destitute poor, encouraged landlords to think in terms of assisted emigration.[6] It is certain that the Poor Rates in an estate such as Castlecomer, where population densities of 800 per square mile were found, would place a considerable financial burden on the proprietor. The more immediate problems on the Castlecomer property centered on the absence of employment. The failure of the attempt to change the system of mining in the 1830's appears to have led to withdrawal of landlord capital and the consequent contraction of employment.[7] The growing importance of the cattle trade resulted in the extension of grazing land and a reduction in employment for agricultural labourers. Furthermore, the breaking of the middlemen system made the landlord more aware of conditions on the estate outside the demesne walls. It was found that in 1831, "although the Wandesforde rental returned only 713 immediate tenants, there was upwards of 2,067 under-tenants on the property, besides a number of occupiers, or what are usually known as cottiers, most of whom were in a most pauperised and miserable condition".[8] The evidence in the estate papers suggests that the landlord feared that the financial burden for the upkeep of a mainly destitute population would result in the bankruptcy and ruination of his property. Emigration was obviously seen as an attractive alternative. It offered a 'permanent' solution insofar as those who left were unlikely to return. In 1845, Richard Eaton told the Devon Commissioners that farms were consolidated "when the small-holdings that some of the Emigrant people possess and for which they are always compensated are added to the adjacent farms". It is of course important to realise that the policy of assisted emigration could not have either commenced or continued without the willingness of those who left to participate. The surviving manuscript evidence supports the view that they were most anxious to leave. Their prospects in Ireland were so negligible

Table 7.1. Landlord assisted emigration from the Castlecomer estate 1840-1855. From Wandesforde mss.

Year	Expenditure	No. of Persons
1840	£353. 5.3	144
1841	£750. 2.0	362
1842	£754.12.3	368
1843	£763.13.6	486
1844	£1,301. 2.4	606
1845	£1,178.11.3	726
1846	£308.18.6	150
1847	£6,361. 0.0	1,957
1848 1849 1850	£1,487.15.0	424
1851	£399. 0.0	115
1852	£394.16.0	116
1853	£705.18.4	189
1854	£406. 0.0	97
1855	£ 68. 0.0	29
Total	£15,432.14.5	5,769

that emigration, which offered the hope of a better if uncertain future was welcomed.

The importance of the policy of assisted emigration from the landlord point of view is evident from the detailed records which were kept concerning expenditure, the number of families who emigrated and the names of the townlands from which they left. Expenditure was recorded for items such as sea transport, the compensation paid to smallholders who surrendered land and the cost of levelling the cabins of those who departed. Assisted emigration from the Castlecomer estate commenced in 1840 when 144 people from 36 families left at a cost of £353 to the landlord.[9]

The destinations of this group of emigrants were recorded. Of the thirty-six families who departed, thirty-one went to America, seven to Australia, two to Wales, one to Scotland and one to England. The remaining five families were re-settled within Ireland. It is probable that America referred to British North America to where much of the subsequent emigration from the estate was directed. These families surrendered twenty-six houses of which seventeen were promptly levelled and the remaining nine set to new tenants. In the following year, the numbers assisted to leave doubled and the estate papers indicate that a further sixty persons emigrated without the assistance of Mr. Wandesforde. It is likely that the greater number left the townlands where present conditions and future prospects were worst. Because of this, the extent of outward movement from individual townlands may serve as a barometer of indigence on the estate. Of the seventy three families who emigrated in 1841, twenty two left Moneenroe, nineteen went from Coolbawn and nine departed from each of the townlands of Gorteen and Croghtenclogh. A further eight families emigrated from Castlecomer and the townlands of Crutt and Coolnaleen each lost a family. Therefore, outward movement was greatest from the townlands which had had comparatively high population densities in 1841, and in which coalmining had been both continuous and intensive over a long period.

This pattern of movement was repeated in 1842 when £754 was expended in assisting 368 people to emigrate. These emigrants surrendered 111 acres of land and the largest holding vacated was of six acres. The majority of them had little or no property and gave up cabins which were promptly demolished. In the same year, it was reported "that 120 persons sent by the Hon. Mr. Wandesforde to Quebec were absolutely destitute."[10] The eighty-eight families who left the estate in 1843 surrendered 33 acres of land, which implies that they were even poorer than previous groups of emigrants. Of the thirty five families who were assisted to leave Moneenroe, only ten gave up small portions of land. Both emigration and expenditure increased in 1844. In this year a greater number of townlands were involved and it is also noticeable that families who emigrated from non-mining townlands such as Loan and Skehana, for example, usually surrendered the greater amount of land. Roughly the same number of people were assisted to emigrate in 1845 as in 1844.

Table 7.1. shows that the numbers assisted to leave declined sharply in 1846. In this year 150 persons, the smallest number since the beginning of the project, were sent out at the cost of £305. The total failure of the potato in 1847 brought starvation and pestilence in its wake. Death, hunger and sickness ravaged the land and provided a powerful stimulus for emigration. The outward movement from the estate reflected the national trend. In 1847, a total of 1,957 persons, which amounted to sixteen per cent of the total estate population in 1841, left the Castlecomer property. The dimensions of this movement are even more striking when examined on the microscale of the townland (fig. 7.1). Eighty-three families left the townland of Moneenroe. Fifty-eight of these surrendered cabins only, twenty-three gave up a cabin and a small portion of land and the remaining two families had neither land nor a cabin. Table 7.1. shows that from 1847 to 1855 the policy of assisted emigration was continued. The cessation of landlord aided emigration in 1855 did not stem the outward flow. Indeed, the later movement was inextricably bound up

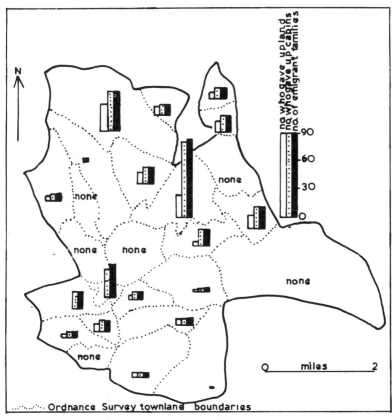

Fig. 7.1 Emigration. Castlecomer estate 1847.

with the fortunes of the Famine emigrants. Those who managed to survive the sea voyage and the desperate period in the fever-ridden quarantine stations were likely to assist in bringing out their relatives to the New World.

The landlord policy of assisted emigration had important results which are worth summarising. The most obvious consequences were demographic. In the period from 1841 to 1851 the population of the estate declined from 12,466 to 6,317. The estate papers indicate that in this decade 5,335 people were given financial assistance to emigrate and that an unknown number left at their own expense. The population of mining townlands was utterly decimated by emigration. In Moneenroe the population fell from 2,022 to 947 in this decade and the number of houses declined by 159. The manuscript evidence shows that Moneenroe townland lost 245 families through emigration. The census statistics indicate that Donaguile townland, which contained part of the southern suburbs of Castlecomer, suffered a particularly heavy population decline. Its population fell from 857 to 204 and the number of houses in the townland declined from 146 to 37. In Moneenroe townland, the decline in population may have resulted in the creation of a pattern of land occupation which was strikingly similar to that which existed in 1812. The reference table accompanying the map of Moneenroe townland in 1812 listed 145 tenants in the townland. In Griffith's Valuation, a total of 113 occupiers and 43 undertenants were returned. Emigration policy was directed towards removing some of the landless labourers who resided in the town and rural areas of the estate.

The landlord justification of emigration policy was that it constituted the only effective check upon a still greater adverse concentration of people, pestilence, unemployment and distress. This viewpoint concurred with the sentiments expressed by some of the Commissions which examined the state of pre-Famine Ireland. The Poor Report Inquiry in 1836 maintained that from one-fourth to nine-tenths of the tenantry would have to be removed in order to secure the remainder steady employment at ten pence a day.[11] Some commentators asserted that the landlord cleared his estate of redundant tenants under the pretext of affording charity to Famine victims. The Catholic clergy accused him of attempting to "extirpate his Catholic tenantry". In 1850 the Kilkenny Journal, a strongly pro-Catholic newspaper, declared "that the Hon. Mr. Wandesforde shipped off 1,855 people from his estate in the year of Our Lord 1847. He has ambitions of exercising almost unlimited despotism over his tenantry and has a strong propensity to thin the population and to level the cabins of the poor, as he levelled the ground and three quarters of the town, which had grown up under Lady Ormonde."[12] The morality of the landlord policy became a contentious issue and was likely to be resurrected in times of landlord-tenant conflict. In 1870 the evicted tenant of the O'Brenan holding in Moyhora bitterly wrote of "the generosity of Mr. Wandesforde in chartering entire ships to transport about 6,000 human beings from Castlecomer, 1,500 of whom lie entombed at Ross Island".[13] This, presumably, should be Grosse Island which was located on the St. Lawrence River, thirty miles downstream from Quebec. The quarantine station for Irish famine emigrants entering Canada was located here and it is estimated that over five thousand fever-stricken emigrants perished in this place. The writer further recalled the grim procession of "the dismal long cars of half-clad, half-starved poor emigrants passing through Castlecomer to the emigrant ships in the depths of winter." Surviving tradition in the Castlecomer district has it that many of the collier emigrants made their way to the coalfields of Pennsylvania. Perhaps their life here was not altogether different from the harsh world, typified by hardwork, early deaths, secret societies, drunkenness and the domination of master-colliers, which they had known so well in Ireland.

5. Ownership in Castlecomer town in 1850.

The *Rateable Valuation of Tenements* is the primary source for this reconstruction of ownership patterns in the town of Castlecomer in 1850. The enumeration of immediate lessors and the valuation of their properties enables one to estimate the amount of urban property owned by individuals and to show if the patterns of ownership of the first half of the century had persisted. By examining the list of immediate lessors and occupiers for the rural parts of the estate, it is possible to indicate whether proprietors of town houses owned or held land.

From 1838 to 1850 landlord policy in Castlecomer town was implemented in two ways. The evidence suggests that the landlord was now adopting an active developmental role as distinct from the passive supervisory role exercised by Lady Ormonde in the early part of the century. Development activity was primarily directed towards removing the flimsy cabins which had been hastily erected on the approach roads to the south and north of the town. Although the records of landlord assisted emigration show that fifty-six families, who each surrendered a cabin, left the town in the period from 1841 to 1851, a comparison of figures returned in respect of population and houses for these years reveals a remarkable stability. In this decade the town population declined from 1,765 to 1,724 and the total number of recorded houses actually increased from 275 in 1841 to 281 in 1851. In his study of the economic history of nineteenth century Ireland, L. M. Cullen noted that: "Apart from a decline in many towns occasioned by a decline in the agriculturally occupied population of the cabin districts on the fringes of the town, town population remained remarkably stable in this period.[14] The area defined as the census town of Castlecomer did not include the town suburbs in Donaguile townland and this explains, to an extent, the apparent population stability. An important result of the change in estate ownership in the early 1830's was the rejection by the new proprietor of the middleman system. In 1838, the estate agent in a letter to a Mr. Cullen, whose interest in the lease of a town house had been terminated, stated that this, "was now the policy which Mr. Wandesforde was adopting in cases where holdings

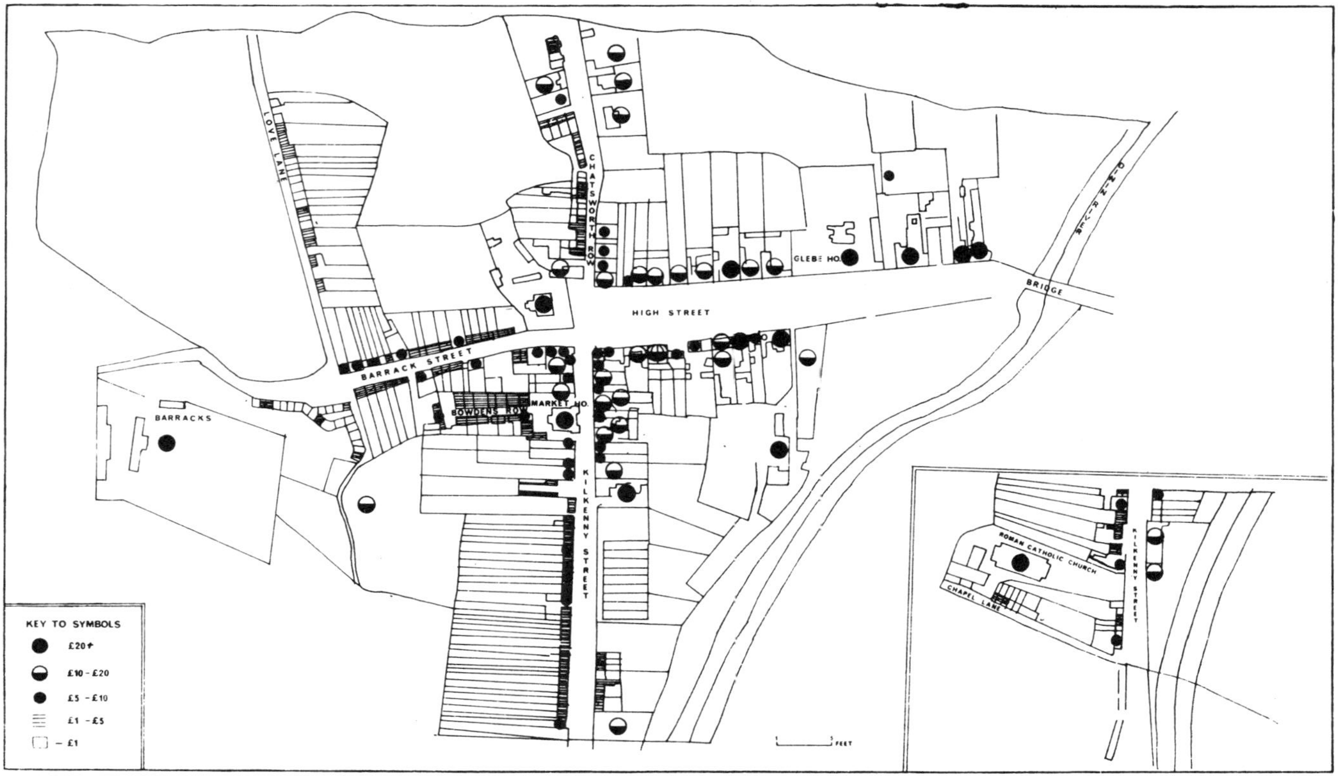

Fig. 7.2 Valuation of buildings. Castlecomer town 1850.

in the town and neighbourhood are not occupied by the persons deriving immediately under himself or when such holdings stand in the way of improvements which he is, and has for some time, been making."[15]

A comparison of fig. 5.12, which depicts the plan of Castlecomer town in 1812, and fig 7.2, which is a copy of the Ordnance Survey map, c. 1838, shows that the overall physical morphology of the town remained unchanged in this period. The more permanent form of development was the infilling of spaces left between buildings of an earlier age. In some instances obsolescent buildings were demolished and replaced by more substantial structures which served similar functions. In 1844 a new Catholic Church was commenced to replace the one which had been erected in 1790.[16] New buildings were erected in the period from 1838 to 1850 to serve the educational needs of the population. In 1834, a Board for the superintendence of a system of national education was established in Ireland. Between 1834 and 1841, the number of schools established increased from 789 to 2,377.[17] The Board recognised the denominational principle in education and the physical separation of the Catholic and Church of Ireland schools in Castlecomer symbolised the social and theological barriers which separated the two communities. The National School for boys was attached to the Catholic Church and that for girls adjoined the Presentation Convent. On the other hand the two Church of Ireland schools were located in west High Street, close to the Protestant Church and the mansion house. The history of buildings and their builders illustrates the contribution of diverse groups and institutions to the physical fabric of the town. The core area was largely the product of landlord activity in the late eighteenth century and development by middlemen in the early part of the nineteenth century. The introduction of the Poor Law system in 1838 provided a basis for local administration and strengthened the service sectors of towns such as Castlecomer. The Poor Law Union of Castlecomer embraced an area of approximately 60,000 statute acres and was divided into seven electoral divisions. The Union Workhouse was located outside the southern boundary of the town in the townland of Donaguile.

Figure 7.2 shows the net annual value of buildings in Castlecomer town, as determined by the *General Valuation of Rateable Property* in Ireland in 1850. Of the 277 buildings listed in the General Valuation, 53 were under £1 in value, 135 were over £1 and under £5, 45 were over £5 and under £10, 31 were over £10 and under £20, and 13 were over £20. There were 92 buildings in Kilkenny Street in 1850. Figure 7.2 shows that three of these, the Market House, the Catholic Church and a private house occupied by Thomas Bradley, were valued at over £20. The majority of buildings in the northern portion of the street, which was part of the old core of the town, had net annual values of £10 and over. The buildings of lowest value were located between the Market House and the Catholic Church on the west side of the street. These artisan dwellings, with their uniform, long-sided plots of ground, were built in the period from 1812

211

to 1838 under leases granted by Lady Ormonde. Barrack Street had 64 buildings in 1850. The general absence of buildings valued at £10 and over suggests that the houses here were smaller than those found in Kilkenny Street. The two buildings valued at over £10 were detached from the street (fig. 7.2). The military barracks valued at £52 marked the western limits of the street and the town. The residence of the Catholic Parish Priest was located on the ridge of high ground, known as 'Mount Williams' to the south of Barrack Street. The name 'Mount Williams', commemorated the middleman who had built this house in the early part of the century.

Chatsworth Row was created by middlemen such as Robert Kane (who had built substantial town houses and more ephermereal cabins here in the 1820's), and the estate proprietor (who was erecting houses in 1838 in the open space which had served formerly as the town pound). A considerable variation in house sizes and quality is suggested by the valuations given to buildings. Houses which had net annual values of £10 and over were located on the east side of Chatsworth Row adjoining High Street. The absence of uniformity was more obvious on the west side of

Plate XIII High Street, Castlecomer.

212

Chatsworth Row where Robert Kane's house valued at £39 adjoined buildings of lesser value. The tree-lined High-Street (named as Bridge Street in 1812 map and as Main Street in the Wandesforde Mss c. 1838) was characterised by slated, two-story buildings which had unusually spacious gardens. Eight of the thirty four buildings located here had net annual values of £20 and over. The residents of High Street included Richard Draper, a substantial farmer, Richard Cooke, estate agent, Kildare Dobbs, colliery manager and Rev. O'Callaghan, Church of Ireland clergyman. Five of the six occupiers in the town who had the suffix esq., attached to their names were resident in High Street. The two streets with the lowest average house values were located on the southern and western fringes of the town. In Chapel Lane, which consisted of a narrow cul-de-sac south of the Catholic Church, nine of the twelve houses were valued under £1. Love Lane (Cloghogue Street in 1812) had no substantial buildings. The average valuation of its nineteen houses was £1.10. Bowden's Row, located at the rear of the Market House, was obviously a planned addition to the town in the period from 1812 to 1838. Its growth may have been associated with the building of the Wesleyan or Methodist meeting house. The nineteen houses in Bowden's Row had an average value of £2.8.0., and they were more substantial than the buildings in either Chapel or Love Lane.

In summary there was little evidence of town growth in the period from 1838 to 1850. The landlord was primarily concerned with the implementation of a policy of small-scale urban renewal which involved the clearance of cabins vacated by emigrants. The houses of highest value had been built by middlemen in the late eighteenth and early nineteenth centuries. Later development such as Bowden's Row and, more especially, Chapel Lane was typified by low value houses. The growth of the educational and administrative functions of the town was an important feature of this period. The new buildings erected such as the Catholic Church, the National Schools and the Workhouse had little to do with the landlord.

Table 7.2. Number and net annual value of houses owned by Landlord and other lessors respectively in Castlecomer town 1850

Street	No. of Dwellings	Total Valuation	Landlord	Other Lessors
Barrack St.	62	£165	(34) £77.17. 0	(28) £87. 3. 0
Bowden's Row	19	£43.17. 0	(12) £20. 8. 0	(7) £22.19. 0
Chapel Lane	12	£10.11. 0	—	(12) £10.11. 0
Chatsworth Row	35	£167. 8. 0	(25)£114. 0. 0	(10) £53. 8. 0
High Street	28	£471.12. 0	(15)£280. 4. 0	(13)£191. 8. 0
Kilkenny St.	87	£440. 0. 0	(37)£221.11. 0	(50)£218. 9. 0
Love Lane	19	£19.14. 0	(15) £17.19. 0	(4) £1.15. 0
Total	262	£1,306.19. 0	(138)£721.19. 0	(124)£585. 0. 0

The purpose of the following section is to identify the individuals who were in possession of urban property valued at £10 and over in 1850. Urban property is defined in this context as buildings which were primarily used as dwelling houses. This definition excludes institutional buildings such as churches, schools and hospitals. Four main patterns of ownership can be identified. The landlord owned and enjoyed the profit rent of the greater number of houses in the town. The urban proprietorial class also consisted of individuals who were resident occupiers of farms in the rural part of the estate. Another group of urban lessors resided in the town but may have derived the greater part of their income from rural occupations. The fourth type of lessors identified in 1850 were the individuals who owned urban property only. The significance of each group is now separately assessed.

In 1838 the greater number of town houses were held under leases granted by the Countess of Ormonde before her death in 1830. Her son who succeeded her endeavoured to regularise the tenurial system in the town and estate by either evicting or purchasing the interest of leases granted by his mother. Table 7.2. indicates that he was partially successful. The landlord was returned as the immediate lessor of 138 houses valued at £721.19. 0, whereas the combined number and net annual value of houses held by all other lessors was 124 and £585 respectively. The landlord owned the greater number of houses in Barrack Street, Bowden's Row, Chatsworth Row, High Street and Love Lane. None of the twelve low-value houses in Chapel Lane were owned by the landlord. This suggests that it had survived the process of town improvement and the associated levelling of cabins on the fringes of the town.

Five individuals who were resident occupiers of farms in the rural part of the estate owned urban property with a combined valuation of £140. Thomas Reecks whose leaseholding of 332 acres was dispersed throughout the townlands of Moyhora, Ardra, Kiltown and Moneenroe, owned six houses valued at £67 in the town. His town property consisted of two houses in Chatsworth Row valued at £23.10.0, a house in Kilkenny Street valued at £7.17. 0 and three houses in Bridge Street which had a combined annual value of £36.15. 0. Evidence in the estate papers proves that Reecks had built the houses in Chatsworth Row and it seems that he had inherited the remaining house property from his father-in-law, Thomas Earle. Reecks appears to have resided on a 58 acres holding in Moyhora townland which he occupied as undertenant to the estate proprietor. His other rural lands were subdivided between nine undertenants. Three of his town houses were described as vacant in 1850.

William Nesbit farmed 105 acres in the adjoining townlands of Knockannadogue and Uskerty and owned six houses in the town which were valued at £21.4.10. His house in Kilkenny Street and one of his five houses in Bowden's Row were uninhabited in 1850. Nesbit was not a rural middleman insofar as he held no land by lease. Kieran White was another urban lessor who sublet his five small houses in Kilkenny Street and farmed a residential holding of 91 acred in the townland of Knockanna-dogue. Both of the two remaining lessors in this group owned a house in High Street which they had sublet. Nathaniel Hayes occupied a holding of 107 acres and the bleach mill in Ballyhimmin townland as undertenant to the landlord. He also held 63 acres by lease in the same townland. All of this was sublet to six undertenants.

Many of the rural middletenants on the estate in the period from 1812 to 1838 lived in substantial town houses, which they themselves had built. Although one can identify such a group in 1850, one finds that they were much weaker numerically than in 1812 and owned far less rural property. Five individuals who owned sixteen houses with a combined value of £99 resided in the town and also held land in the rural part of the estate. Some of these such as, David Ryan were rural middlemen. Ryan farmed 374 acres in Aughamucky townland; sublet a farm of 404 acres which he held by lease in the same townland between eighteen undertenants; sublet his house in Bridge Street, which was valued at £20; resided in the large house in Chatsworth Row which was built by Robert Kane in the 1820's (Plate VIII). This building which was valued at £42 was owned by the estate proprietor in 1850.

The remaining lessors in this category were primarily concerned with urban property and held only small amounts of land. John Sutcliffe, for example, owned five houses in Kilkenny Street valued at £35 and occupied a farm of 31 acres in the townland of Killtown north of Castlecomer. He resided in Kilkenny Street in a house which he held from the landlord. James Jacob owned more houses in the town than Sutcliffe but his urban property had a lower valuation. He was in possession of eight small houses in west Kilkenny Street close to the Catholic Church and his fragmented holding of 46 acres was dispersed throughout the townlands of Donaguile, Ballyhimmin, Ballycomy and Clashduff Lower. Only one of Jacobs eight houses was described as vacant in 1850. Jacob's residence in High Street consisted of a complex of buildings described in the Valuation Book as "house, offices, mill, kiln" and assessed at £65. Another of these lessors, Thomas Bradley, also held urban property in Kilkenny Street. Bradley sublet his three houses valued at £12.8.0 and resided in a house valued at £21.15.0 in east Kilkenny Street. The majority of urban lessors lived in houses which were of higher value than those they sublet. The opposite was true of Miss Bridget Boyle. She had sublet her house in Bridge Street which was valued at £18.16.0 and resided in a premises in the same street which was assigned a value of £14.10.0 in 1850. Thomas Bradley held 16 acres in Ballyhimmin townland and Miss Boyle occupied a small holding of 15 acres in Drumgoole.

The fourth group of urban property owners consisted of individuals who owned town houses only. Eleven such lessors were in possession of 20 houses with a combined value of £164 in Castlecomer town in 1850. Little is known about these people. The place of residence of ten of these lessors is not known, as their names do not occur as occupiers in the town or in the rural parts of the estate. They were, perhaps, a group of absentee landlords who had inherited their property in Castlecomer. Two of these, Edward Giltenan and Thomas Williams, may have been the representatives of middlemen who owned house property in Castlecomer in 1838. Owners of urban property under £10 in value constituted a numerous class in 1850 and were also involved in subletting. Twenty two such lessors who lived in the town owned 42 houses which were all sublet. Sixteen of these lessors owned only one property and this was usually of low value. Jeremiah Curran, for example, occupied a house in Chapel Lane valued at fourteen shillings and was lessor of an adjoining house which had the same valuation. On the other hand, lessors such as Anthony Smith may have derived part of their income from subletting low quality houses in the town. Smith resided in Kilkenny Street and sublet nine houses which he held as lessor. His nine houses, seven of which were located in Chapel Lane and two in Kilkenny Street, had a combined valuation of £8.19.0.

The period 1838-1850 was thus one of transition in patterns of ownership in Castlecomer town. The basic change was related to the declining economic power of the middlemen, many of whom had reverted to the status of tenants. It is probable that the majority of them were peaceably evicted or had the interest in their leases purchased by the landlord. Many of the more substantial town houses were unoccupied at this time. The success of landlord policy had deprived middlemen of their profit rents from agricultural land. It was these monies which had been reinvested in building and maintaining town residences for middlemen in the early nineteenth century.

7. Landlord involvement in mining.

"Formerly the extraction of the coal was very badly managed. The imperfect methods of drainage obliged many shafts to be abandoned when they arrived at a certain depth, a large quantity of coal was left behind, and the amount of labour was excessive".
(Kane, Robert, *The Industrial Resources of Ireland* (Dublin, 1845) 40).

The net annual value of collieries in the Castlecomer estate in 1850 amounted to £779. The collieries were located at Skehana (valuation £230), Moneenroe (£210), Coolbawn (£153), Cloneen (£140), and Gorteen (£46). The workings at Skehana indicate the recent extension of mining to the No. II seam in the north-west of the coalfield. The introduction of the steam engine had facilitated the sinking of deeper pits but it had not altered the locational pattern of coalmining. In some instances, pits marking different technological epochs in mining were on the same site. Apart from the Skehana workings, the majority of pits in 1850 worked the Jarrow or No. IV seam. The mining industry was adversely affected by the general economic depression experienced during the decade of Famine. The fact that the majority of emigrants, assisted to leave the estate in the period

216

from 1840 to 1855, were colliers is but one symptom of the decline. There is evidence from the smaller Slievardagh field, to the west of the River Nore, that the Irish Mining Company were finding it difficult to dispose of coal stocks to farmers.[18] It is important to remember that the major portion of Castlecomer coal was sold within a twenty mile radius of the collieries and that any reduction in farmer incomes would have an adverse effect on the market. The isolation of the Castlecomer field from the lucrative east coast market weakened its ability to compete with British coal. The attempts to provide canal outlets for the coal in the early part of the nineteenth century had been unsuccessful and the coal was still transported by horse and cart in 1850. In 1849, the miners of Castlecomer addressed a memorial to the Board of Ordnance in London requesting that Castlecomer coal be used in the barracks of Kilkenny, Carlow and Castlecomer.[19] The memorialists stated that English and Scottish coal had replaced the domestic fuel in these establishments, despite the fact that home produced coal was cheaper and of equal quality. They further claimed that "owing to the great depression of trade in the country, the memorialists and their families were in the utmost distress."

It would seem that the basic reason for the depressed condition of the collieries in the 1840's was social rather than economic. The landlord attempts to break the master-collier system in the 1830's were not successful, so that he exercised a considerably lesser degree of control over the collieries than over the town and the estate land. According to the Halls, who visited the collieries in 1843, he may have had less interest in mining. They wrote that "the proprietors instead of adopting new measures had abandoned their works; not wishing to risk either their lives or properties in the introduction of new methods which though tending to ameliorate the conditions of the colliers would nevertheless be strenuously opposed by the majority of them as an invasion of their rights." The introduction of new and improved working methods to the tumultuous and turbulent collieries was a formidable task. The opposition to change was not confined to the numerically weak middlemen class. The majority of colliers opposed any innovation which would result in loss of employment. It is also true that the colliers were a much more cohesive group than the occupiers of estate land and were prepared to use the weapon of combinations to achieve their ends.

The upsurge in mining activity in 1849 brought fresh problems. A letter from Thomas Johnson, colliery manager in Castlecomer, to the estate proprietor in 1849 referred to the complaints of the colliers that strangers had been employed to work the Massford and old Jarrow pits to the exclusion of lordshipmen.[20] The colliers claimed that up to sixty of these strangers and their families were in, "full residence on the Castlecomer estate." Johnson admitted that their claim, "is in great measure true, but simply because lordshipmen could not be had, so much so that William Hall and John Lowry had to obtain men from any quarter where they could find them" He further noted that "if they (the colliers) did not give their daughters in marriage to these obnoxious strangers, those settlements could not be made." The terms used here are of interest insofar as they suggest that the estate was more a territorial and social entity to the colliers than to the agricultural occupiers, whose livelihood was seldom threatened by outsiders. Colliers were described, for example, as "Lordshipmen' and individual pits were known as the 'Old Lordship' and the 'New Lordship'. The term 'lordship' was commonly used to denote an estate in the eighteenth century. There was no comparable terms to describe occupiers of estate land. Their associations were with individual townlands rather than with the whole estate. Strangers were defined as those who came from outside the Wandesforde estate and it might be expected that the always considerable animosity towards their employment in the collieries would increase in times of depression. It was also true that management of mining and agricultural activities had not been segregated. The Wandesfordes retained a controlling interest in the collieries and the land agent who was responsible for estate administration was also in charge of mining. The colliers were also estate tenants and they worked in what was still a mainly rural environment. It was this factor above all others which strengthened their association with the estate. It was, in effect, the prolongation of the special contractual relationship which existed between colliers and landlord in the eighteenth century.

The recurrence of similar problems in different epochs was a striking feature of the history of mining in Castlecomer. The topographical character and remoteness of the coalfield always rendered transportation difficult. This problem was even more acute in the mid-nineteenth century because it reduced the competitiveness of Castlecomer coal. As early as 1746, Batwell in his report on the Castlecomer estate referred to the numerous difficulties caused by the absence of a satisfactory method to assess damages to farmland due to colliery work. The situation had not improved in the intervening one hundred years. In 1837 Patrick Purcell landholder in Cloneen townland was forced to write to the estate agent, "after having repeatedly called at the colliery offices for money awarded me for damages done to my land in the Lordship colliery.[21] The difficulties of farming in a colliery townland are adequately demonstrated by Purcell's complaint, "that land which I have had so much trouble and expense in reclaiming again made worse than it was ever before."

218

CHAPTER EIGHT

9 CONCLUSIONS

In the seventeenth century, competing claims to the ownership of the land and the mineral deposits of Fassadinin barony were resolved by a series of legal transactions which were preceded in some instances by the military conquest and displacement of those in possession. The political and military events of the seventeenth century exercised a fundamental impact on the patterns of landownership and land occupation in the barony and led to the rearrangement of existing items and the erection of new structures in the countryside. The Butlers of Ormonde, important and powerful regional magnates, controlled the greater part of south-east Ireland and were actively engaged in extending the authority of the English monarchy to the politically unstable and economically weak Gaelic homelands located on the hill fringes of their great Lordship. The spatial impact of this expansionist policy is clearly revealed in the highly detailed Ormonde documents which record in a systematic way the great variety of transactions concerning the ownership and the occupation of land completed in this period. In 1584, the Anglo-Normans divided Fassadinin barony into two distinct divisions which accorded with diverse social and political systems. This distinction is important insofar as it enables one to measure the extent of Anglo-Norman involvement in the barony and to identify the district which was still Gaelic in character. It also reveals how little was known by contemporaries about the system of landholding and the territorial divisions of the Gaelic lands and suggests that there was little formal contact between the two groups. It is obvious, therefore, that knowledge of Irish society in this period, dependent as it is on documentary evidence compiled by people who confessed their inability to comprehend central aspects of the Gaelic system of landownership, is both fragmentary and distorted.

In the period under review, the transferred homelands of Gaelic families such as the O'Brenans were associated mainly with marginal, isolated hill lands. The lands of Idough located at the ends of the civil county of Kilkenny were remote from the sea, politically unstable, vaguely known and inadequately delimited. On the other hand, the territorial divisions in the greater part of south and west Fassadinin, which corresponded to the zone of durable Anglo-Norman rural occupation, were well known. The Anglo-Norman incursion into Fassadinin barony followed the natural routes provided by the river valleys of the Nore and Dinin rivers and Anglo-Norman soldiers and settlers were strongly attracted to the comparatively level lands of south and west Fassadinin. The participants in the late medieval colonisation of Fassadinin were either kinsfolk of the Butlers of Ormonde, such as the Mountgarrets, or their military followers, such as the Purcells. The comparative recency of this incursion is suggested by the scarcity of placenames which refer to Anglo-Norman settlement in the barony in the medieval period. The number of compound names found among the placenames suggests that Fassadinin in the medieval period was a hybrid area where the two cultures met, intermingled and struggled for supremacy.

The Anglo-Norman imprint in the early seventeenth century is more clearly revealed in the organisation and spatial distribution of manors. One notes the correlation between the layout and distribution of manors in the barony, and the estates which formed the basis of the system of landownership introduced in the second half of the seventeenth century. It also appears that manors may have been superimposed onto an older territorial framework which may not have differed substantially in either form or function. The ability of the newcomers to utilise the existing arrangements in the landscape is also revealed in the continuity of settlement. New buildings may have replaced obsolete structures but similar sites served similar purposes for different groups of people. Very little is known about the economy or way of life in the countryside at this period. The documents which have survived reveal a preoccupation with land and regulations concerning its use and ownership.

The government policy towards the Irish population was implemented locally by the administrators and regional magnates who exercised nominal control over the districts in which the homelands of Irish families were located. In the context of Fassadinin this is demonstrated in the various transactions between the O'Brenans and the Butlers of Ormonde. The Anglo-Normans greatly increased their knowledge of the Gaelic lands of Fassadinin in this period. This changing relationship is revealed in the various ways in which the O'Brenans and their lands were classified in the Ormonde documents. In 1359, the leader of the O'Brenans was described as captain of his own nation. This suggests that the family at this time had political and spatial autonomy. By 1592, the O'Brenans had come within the sphere of influence of government civil servants, who subdivided them into four distinct 'septs' for the purpose of tax assessment. In 1614, the O'Brenans, whose leaders were now referred to as gentlemen and freeholders, accepted the military protection of the Butlers of Ormonde and the English system of landownership. The documentary evidence reveals the spatial contraction of the area held by the O'Brenans and the gradual disintegration of sept homogeneity within this area.

The Inquisition taken in 1635 indicates that by this time a heterogeneous group of landowners, which included Anglo-Norman and New English along with Irish, existed in Idough. Apart from the survival of the family name and a few isolated references in placenames, the O'Brenans who lived in the barony in medieval and early modern times left a surprisingly weak imprint on the landscape. The silent, anonymous nature of their world is a reflection of the thoroughness of their absorption. The Inquisition reveals the close network of permanent land divisions into which the lands of Idough were partitioned. The chief focal points in a landscape that was bleakly deficient in towns and villages were provided by the strongholds of individual septs.

As far as there is ever a new beginning in history, the coming of the New English to Ireland in the seventeenth century was such a beginning. The New English in Fassadinin may be divided into two distinct groups. The first of these to arrive and the most important in the context of the barony, were the individuals such as Wandesforde and Coote who participated in the government presided over by the Earl of Wentworth. These public servants and private entrepreneurs were men of tremendous energy and initiative, who asserted that all their activities were "for the advancement of the King's profit and the civilising of that country". Whatever their motivation, their achievements were impressive. The New English intrusion marks a new phase in the history of the O'Brenans. In 1635, they were described as "mere Irish who had intruded illegally into the lands of Idough". Their exclusion from the ownership of land was to persist until the disintegration of the estate system of landownership at the beginning of the twentieth century.

Changes in ownership led to a reappraisal of resources and resulted in a series of land surveys which delimited boundaries, listed internal divisions and their owners, and recorded the land categories of an area about which so little was known fifty years previously. The spatial implications of military activity and political decisions form the most significant theme in the evolution of patterns of landownership in Fassadinin barony in the second half of the seventeenth century. The redistribution of the lands of the dispossessed was carried out on a sectarian basis and religious affiliations, which previously determined political allegiances, now determined ownership. The disruption of the pattern of living and the deterioration in the quality of the landscape were the more immediate consequences of intermittent warfare. The initiation of a series of surveys, which amounted to a stocktaking of the landscape of the vanquished, was another important effect of these great political and social upheavals. This part of the seventeenth century marks a definite phase in the evolution of the territorial divisions of the countryside, and in the standardisation of the names by which places are known today. The most fundamental impact of war and victory was the introduction of the estate system of landownership. The origins of this colonial form of social organisation are to be found in the land grants enrolled in the state ledger books. The inauguration of this system of land governance influenced both the distribution of people in Fassadinin and their capacity to utilise and organise the local environment, particularly in respect of the ownership and the occupation of land.

A partisan legal system institutionalised access to land and property and ensured the continuity of the proprietorial class established through war.

Because of the absence of documentary evidence in the form of estate rentals or sketch maps, knowledge of the processes which transformed the face of the countryside in the eighteenth century is incomplete. Furthermore, the material imprint of this period on the landscape has either been overlain or obliterated by the accretions of later times. Neither can the general applicability of the findings of this study be tested because comparative surveys of other small rural areas in Ireland in the eighteenth century are non-existent. By 1700, almost every townland in Ireland had been affected by the great land redistributions, which were such a characteristic feature of the seventeenth century. The imprint of the land tenurial system varied from estate to estate and from townland to townland within estates. Variations in the imprint corresponded to differences in the relationships between landlords and tenants as expressed in the legal status of occupiers, and in the final analysis to the attitudes and practices of individual landlords and landholders.

The primary objective of the proprietorial class was to maximise their income from land. Land was sold, mortgaged, leased and further sublet. The cumulative effect of such transactions was the creation of a hierarchy of occupiers who, in the frequent absence of the actual landowners, shaped the local fabric of eighteenth century society. For example, the proprietor of the Wandesforde estate c. 1746 lived in England and was willing to surrender control over portion of his estate in order to secure a guaranteed income. The origins of the distinctive middleman system of landholding are to be found in this practice. It would seem that this tenurial arrangement, which was to persist until the Great Hunger, was first introduced on the estates of landlords who were resident outside Fassadinin barony. Throughout the greater part of eighteenth century, the partisan legislation known as the 'Penal Laws' remained on the statute books. In comparatively isolated districts, such as Fassadinin barony, landlords were more concerned with finding solvent tenants than with applying discriminatory legislation.

The material environments created by landlords, not only in Fassadinin but throughout the whole of Ireland, were remarkably uniform. Many of the propertied class perceived their mission as similar to the 'mission civilisatrice' of the ancient Greek and Roman Empires. In Fassadinin, the administrative centres of seventeenth century manors such as Castlecomer and Ballyragget were selected as town sites and were developed in a planned fashion by landlords. These central places became focal points in rural life and economy and were especially important as strongholds of English influences. The number and size of these settlements was directly related to the number of comparatively large estates in the barony. The smaller estates formed by the disintegration of the Ormonde property were not large enough to sustain similar landlord establishments.

The landlord, in Fassadinin, whether resident or absentee, stood at the apex of estate society in the late eighteenth century. In the absence of the landlord, the agent and colliery manager had considerable status and power. It may have been that these positions were held, as in the nineteenth century, by the same individual. Next to them came a larger and more heterogeneous group whose status was directly related to the amount of land they held. These were the principal tenants who numbered about twenty three people on the Wandesforde estate in 1746. These held varied amounts of land, and consisted of both Catholic and Protestant elements. Some of these combined land management and the running of a shop or public-house. The undertenants and master colliers occupied the next rank. Undertenants were those to whom the principal tenants had let lands on year to year tenancies. Again their status varied in relation to the amount of land they occupied.

The estate undertenants were rarely enumerated in the eighteenth century. They had no direct financial relationship with the landlord and were the concern of the principal tenants to whom they paid their rent. The juxtaposition of coalmining and agriculture adds to the complexity of social divisions in Castlecomer. The master colliers occupied a unique role in estate society. Unlike the undertenants, they had a special contractual relationship with the landlord which guaranteed them security of tenure. They may have been the most homogeneous group in the estate. Cottiers probably made up the bulk of the colliery workers and agricultural labourers. The distinction between this group and the landless labourers is largely an academic one, especially in the context of rural society. In the Castlecomer estate, landless labourers were likely to consist of immigrant or newly arrived mining families, who had been attracted by the existence here of a monetary economy and the absence of strict control on adventitious settlement. All these groups and their landscape impact are more clearly delineated in the early nineteenth century. The population was also divided along religious and ethnic lines. It was not a simplified Protestant/Catholic division but included Baptist, Wesleyan and other non-conformist groups. Protestants were distributed through the whole social spectrum and the poor rural Protestant population found here was perhaps greater than elsewhere in the south of Ireland.

Because of the absence of data, the treatment given to the barony area has been slightly uneven and fragmentary both in a chronological and chorological context. Nevertheless, by using original source materials, it has been shown that many of the widely held assumptions about Irish life and society in this century may be invalid for Fassadinin, at the very least. The manuscripts suggest that a relatively prosperous rural community engaged in the dual economy of mining and agriculture existed here in the early eighteenth century. The development of mining led to a greater immigration here, than was general in other confiscated areas in southern Ireland.

Landlords began to take a greater interest in estate management in the early nineteenth century. Cartographers were commissioned to prepare

223

estate maps and rentals listing the principal tenants on a townland basis were introduced. The social dominance of landlords was reflected in the physical dimensions and the carefully embellished architecture of the Big Houses and in the elegance and beauty of the demesnes. The most striking feature of the landholding system in the Wandesforde estate was the weakness of proprietorial control. The tenurial arrangements in this property were inherited from the late eighteenth century. Because of this situation, a numerically small group of middletenants, whose descendants were in many instances eighteenth century middlemen, emerged as the chief architects of landscape change and the most influential individuals locally. The practice of granting long term leases helped to stabilise the pattern of land occupation and ensured the continuity of landholding families.

Middlemen built Georgian villas and adopted many of the social characteristics of landlords. This had the result of isolating them from their less prosperous neighbours. From a total of forty-three middlemen who held land in the Castlecomer estate in 1836, twenty three were non-resident. Sixty two per cent of the lands leased to middlemen in the late eighteenth century had been sublet by them or their representatives by 1836. The extent of subletting was primarily related to the type of tenure under which lands were held and had little to do with the quality of land. Middlemen built the greater number of the substantial houses in Castlecomer and many of them resided in the town. One of the more positive attributes of the system was that profit rents from rural property were spent locally. Middlemen were also involved in speculative ventures in the town. Some of them sublet building sites and in some instances they built low quality houses which they subsequently sublet. Master-colliers, to whom the working of the collieries was sublet, had many of the characteristics of middlemen. Middlemen, whether they held estate land, town houses or contracts for working coal shared the income from estate resources with the estate owner. The spatial arrangement of farms, fields and settlement, which was systematically revealed in the maps of the Castlecomer property, reflected the great contrasts between the various groups who constituted estate society in the early nineteenth century.

The unequal distribution of people in Fassadinin barony in 1841 reflected both the impact of mining and the estate system of landownership. The reservation of areas where land values were comparatively high for landlord use, and the unattractiveness of infertile, isolated hill lands, had the result of increasing population pressure locally in townlands of intermediate value. In the northern portion of the barony, these townlands were found in the district in which coal mining had been intensive and continuous over a long period of time. The effects of the Great Hunger were confined mainly to the less well off members of the community. This group increased rapidly in population in pre-Famine decades. Population growth was accompanied by a decline in mining and the Famine accelerated the process of accommodating the mining population to its narrowing economic prospects.

224

The large estate characterised the system of land ownership in 1850. The similarity between the spatial pattern of landownership in 1850 and 1700 reflects the continuity of ownership over a long period of time. In 1850 thirty-eight per cent of the barony area was owned by three inter-related families whose descendants were landowners in Fassadinin in 1640. Change in ownership was effected either through marriage or inheritance. The outright sale of land was not a common procedure in Fassadinin at this period. In some instances, estates in the barony were inherited by absentees. The second largest estate in the barony which belonged to the Butlers of Ballyragget, passed to their cousins, the Kavanaghs of Borris, in the early part of the nineteenth century. The great majority of landlords did not reside on their Fassadinin estates in 1850. Only eleven from a total of fifty four landlords who owned estates of 100 acres and over resided in the barony at this time.

Landlord contact with the occupiers of estate lands increased significantly in the second quarter of the nineteenth century. This was marked in Fassadinin and more especially in the Wandesforde estate by the involvement of the landlord in radical programmes of estate renewal. Landlord-tenant relationships were re-arranged by the substitution of long-term leases by year-to-year tenancies. This period marks the end of the middleman system and the extension of the landlord's active involvement to the whole estate. At a time when the landlord was extending his control over estate tenants, his influence in rural life was waning considerably. The unprecedented social disaster experienced in the Famine period exposed the defects of the estate system and led to the greater involvement of central Government in local affairs. In the fifty years which followed the Famine, the pattern of landownership was transformed by a series of political decisions. The termination of the estate system had important repercussions in the landscape and led to the rearrangement of farms and fields.

This work has stressed the importance of the occupier class in the context of rural life. The great majority of occupiers were of Irish origin, because the various immigrations since medieval times did not result in any large scale population movement into the barony. Apart from the Wandesfordes and Viscount Frankfort, there is no evidence to suggest that landlords introduced settlers. Throughout the eighteenth and nineteenth centuries, it is possible to identify a group of substantial tenant-farmers who played a formative role in the development of changing patterns of rural and town life in Fassadinin barony. In 1850, the material imprint of this system of land ownership was impressively visible throughout the countryside.

225

NOTES AND REFERENCES

ABBREVIATIONS
A. Libraries etc.
NLI: National Library of Ireland.
PROI: Public Record Office, Ireland.

B. Journals etc.
Carew Mss: Calendar of the Carew manuscripts.
C.S.P.I.: Calendar of the State Papers Ireland.
Ir. Geogr.: Irish Geography.
Ir. Hist. Stud.: Irish Historical Studies.
J.K.A.S.: Journal of the Kilkenny Archaeological Society.
J.K.S.E.I.A.S.: Journal of the Kilkenny and South East of Ireland Archaeological Society.
J.R.S.A.I.: Journal of the Royal Society of Antiquaries of Ireland.
J.S.S.I.S.I.: Journal of the Statistical and Social Inquiry Society of Ireland.
Ormonde Mss: Calendar of Ormonde Mss ed. Royal Historical Manuscript Commission.
Ormonde Mss N.L.I.: Ormonde manuscripts National Library of Ireland.
P.P.: Parliamentary Papers.
T.I.B.G.: Transactions of the Institute of British Geographers.
T.R.I.A.: Transactions of the Royal Irish Academy.
Wandesforde Mss N.L.I.: Wandesforde Manuscripts National Library of Ireland.

CHAPTER ONE

1. Whittow, J. B. *Geology and Scenery in Ireland*, (Hardmondsworth 1974) 248.
2. Freeman, T. W. *Ireland, A General and Regional Geography*, (London 1950) 321.
3. Petty, W. *New edition of William Petty's Hiberniae Delineatio, 1685*, (Newcastle-upon-Tyne 1968).
4. Petty, W. *New edition of William Petty's tracts relating to Ireland, c. 1680* (Dublin 1769).
5. Dillon, M. and Chadwick, N. *The Celtic Realms*, (London 1967) 92-95.

6. Goblet, Y. M. *Les Noms de lieux Irlandais dans l'oeuvre de Sir W. Petty,* (Paris 1930) 63.

7. Butler, W. F. T. *Gleanings from Irish history,* (London 1925) 298.

8. Graves, J. "Ancient tribes and territories of Ossory", *J.K.A.S.* 1849-51, 1, 230.

9. Carrigan, W. *The History and Antiquities of the Diocese of Ossory,* (Dublin 1905) Appendix C, 1, 387.

10. Curtis, E. (ed.) *Calendar of Ormonde Deeds, 1171-1603,* Six Vols. (Dublin 1932-43) 11, 246.

11. ibid., V, 53.

12. ibid., V, 164.

13. Andrews, J. H. "Geography and government in Elizabethan Ireland" in Stephens, N. and Glasscock, R. G. (eds.) *Irish Geographical Studies in honour of E. Estyn Evans,* (Belfast 1970) 179.

14. Hardiman, J. *Statutes of Kilkenny,* (Dublin 1857) 4.

15. Inquis. Lageniae, Com. Kilkenny 64 Car. 1, 1635 (P.R.O.I.)

16. Lodge Transcripts of the Records of the Rolls (P.R.O.I.) Vol. VI, Charles 1, 408.

17. Collins, J. *Local Government in Ireland,* (Dublin 1963) 17-22.

18. Hughes, K. *The Church in early Irish society,* (London 1966) 270.

19. Carrigan, W. (1905) op. cit. IV, Appendix 1, 369-371.

20. Tithe Composition Applotment Books, c. 1830, (P.R.O.I.).

21. Quoted in Goblet, Y. M. (1930) op. cit., 63.

22. Coghlan, D. *The Ancient land tenures of Ireland,* (Dublin 1933) 31.

23. "Arable and pasture, wood, bog and mountain in Idough"; Wandesforde Mss c. 1630, (N.L.I.).

24. Graves, J. op cit., (1849-51), 230-247.

25. Inquis. Lageniae, Com. Kilkenny 64 Car. 1, 1635 (P.R.O.I.).

26. Lodge Transcripts of the Records of the Rolls (1636), Vol. VI, Charles 1, 300.

27. ibid., 340.

29. Petty, W. (1769 ed.) op. cit., 373.

30. Grants of lands, leases and deeds in the Reign of Queen Anne: Lodge Mss Deed no. 395, (P.R.O.I.).

CHAPTER TWO

1. *Calendar of Ormonde deeds,* (1941) 1, 283.

2. O'Kelly, O. *A history of Co. Kilkenny,* (Donegal 1969) 37.

3. Brooks, E. St. John, *Knight's fees in Cos. Wexford, Carlow and Kilkenny in the 13th and 15th centuries* (Dublin 1950).

4. Jones-Hughes, T. "Town and Baile in Irish place-names", in Stephens, N. and Glasscock, R. G. (eds.) *Irish Geographical Studies in honour of E. Estyn Evans,* (Belfast 1970) 249.

5. Brooks, St. John, (1950) op. cit., 182.

6. *Calendar of Ormonde deeds* (1941) V., 165.

7. ibid., 166.

8. *Calendar of Ormonde deeds,* (1941) II, 241.

9. ibid., V., 175.

10. Curtis, E. (ed.) *Introduction to Calendar of Ormonde deeds*, V, V.
11. *Calendar of Ormonde deeds*, (1941) VI, 72.
12. Quoted in Graves, J. (1849-51) op. cit., 236.
13. Butler, W. F. T. "The policy of Surrender and Regrant", *J.R.S.A.I.*, (1913) III, 100.
14. Graves, J. (1849-51) op. cit.
15. Butler, W. F. T. (1913) op. cit., 101.
16. Lodge transcripts of the Records of the Rolls, (P.R.O.I.) Vol. II, James I, 472.
17. "Proceedings for the Recovery of Castlecomer 1653-4, the rebels had it up to that time since 1641": Wandesforde Mss. (N.L.I.).
18. Inquis. Lageniae, Com. Kilkenny 64 Car. I, (1635) (P.R.O.I.).
19. "Proceedings for the Recovery of Castlecomer . . . etc." (1653-54) op. cit.,.
20. ibid.
21. Lodge transcripts of the Records of the Rolls, (P.R.O.I.) Vol. VI, Charles 1, 406.
22. "Proceedings for the Recovery of Castlecomer . . . etc.," (1653-54) op. cit.,.
23. *C.S.P.I.* 1636, 100.
24. "An estimate what I am to pay of Edough before May next and how I hope to save the monyes towards it": Document dated 29th October 1636 in Wandesforde Mss (N.L.I.).
25. Carrigan, W. (1905) op. cit., 11, Appendix C. 387.
26. Jones-Hughes, T. (1970) op. cit., 246.
27. "Arable and pasture, wood, bog and mountain in Idough C. 1630: Wandesforde Mss (N.L.I.).
28. Carrigan, W. (1905) op. cit., IV, Appendix III, 394.
29. ibid.
30. Quoted in Butler, W. F. T. (1925) op. cit., 1.
31. Jones-Hughes, T. (1970) op. cit., 253.
32. Orpen, G. *Ireland under the Anglo-Normans*, (Dublin, 1920) III, 86.
33. Glasscock, R. E. "Moated sites and deserted boroughs and villages: two neglected aspects of Anglo-Norman settlement in Ireland" in Stephens, N. and Glasscock, R. E. (eds. 1970) op. cit. 172.
34. MacNiocaill, G. *Na buirgéisí*, 2 vols. (Dublin 1965) 1, 135.
35. Brooks, St. John, (1950) op. cit.
36. Ms 2561 (Ormonde Mss) (N.L.I.).
37. *Calendar of Ormonde deeds*, V, 126.
38. ibid., 224.
39. ibid., 265.
40. ibid., 314.
41. Burke, B. and Burke, A. P. *A Genealogical and Heraldic history of the Peerage and Baronetage*, (London, 1907) 1207.
42. Lodge transcripts of the Records of the Rolls (P.R.O.I.) Vol. Vi, Charles 1, 67.
43. Carrigan, W. (1905) op. cit., 111, 162.
44. Inquis. Langeniae quoted in Carrigan, W. (1905) op. cit., 111, 471.
45. Inquis. Lageniae, Com Kilkenny, 50 Car. 1, (1621).
46. Lodge Transcripts, op. cit., Vol. VI, Charles 1, 68.

47. Patent Rolls; Richards II, 1832-3, Quoted in Carrigan, W. (1905) op. cit., III, 174.

48. Hogan, W. *History and Antiquities of Kilkenny County and City,* (Kilkenny 1893) 70.

49. Inquis. Lageniae, Com. Kilkenny, 46 Jac. 1, 1618.

50. *Calendar of Ormonde deeds,* Appendix 1, VI, 120.

51. Lodge Transcripts of the Records of the Rolls (1621) (P.R.O.I.). 2 Charles 1, 65.

52. White, N. B., (ed.) *The Red Book of Ormond* (Dublin 1932) pp. 1-7.

53. Otway-Ruthven, J. *A History of Medieval Ireland* (London 1967) 106-125.

54. Aalen, F. H. A. "The origin of enclosures in eastern Ireland" in Stephens, N. and Glasscock, R. E. (eds. 1970) op. cit., 212.

55. *Calendar of Ormonde deeds,* V, 224.

56. *Calendar of Ormonde deeds* V, 151.

57. ibid., VI, 12.

58. ibid., Appendix 1, VI, 119-147.

59. McNeill, C. (ed.) *Dowdall Deeds,* D. 672 (Dublin 1960) 320.

60. *C.S.P.I.* 1637, 85. Nef, J. U. *The rise of the British coal industry,* (London 1932) 2 Vols.

61. Kearney, H. F. "Richard Boyle, ironmaster: a note on Irish economic history" *J.R.S.A.I.,* (1956) LXXXIII, 156-162.

62. Boate, G. *Ireland's natural history,* (London 1652) 73.

63. "Indenture 31 March 1635, between Elizabeth Blacknell executrix of the Last Will and Testament of Richard Blacknell late of Macroom in the Co. of Cork on the one part and the Right Hon. Christopher Wandesforde Master of the Rolls and George Radcliffe Knight both of his Majesties Privy Councill": Wandesfoge Mss (N.L.I.).

64. "Indenture made the eight day of December in 1622 between Walter Archer of the citie of Kilkenny esq. and Tirlagh Fitzthomas of Kildargan in the countie of Kilkenny gent on the one part and the right honorable Lawrence Lord Desmond Baron of Lymbrick": Wandesforde Mss (N.L.I.).

65. Kearney, H. F. (1950) op. cit., 159.

66. Andrews, J. H. "Note on the historical geography of the Irish iron industry" *Ir. Geogr.* (1956) III, 139-149.

67. Inquis. Lageniae, Com Kilkenny, 46, Jac 1, 1618.

68. "Articles of Agreement 10 August 1637 between Christopher Wandesforde Master of the Rolls and one of his Majesties Council of the Kingdom of Ireland on the one part and John Browne of Spolmaldine in Kent in the realms of England and Captain Richard Steele on the other part . . ." Wandesforde Mss (N.L.I.).

69. O'Sullivan, W. (ed.) "William Molyneaux's Geographical collections for Kerry", *Journal of the Kerry Archaeological Society,* No. 4 (1971) 28.

70. Comber, T. *Life of Christopher Wandesforde,* (London 1778) 70.

CHAPTER THREE

1. Bottigheimer, K. S. *English money and Irish land,* (Oxford 1971) 134.

2. Carrigan, W. (1905) op. cit.,

3. Larcom, T. *History of the Down Survey.* (Dublin 1857) 36.
4. Ms 720 (N.L.I.) Parish maps with terriers showing forfeited lands in Queens County and Co. Kilkenny, commonly known as the "Down Survey". executed under direction of Petty c. 1654, copied O'Brien 1786.
5. *Calendar of Ormonde deeds,* V, 151.
6. Petty, W. (1680), op. cit., 310.
7. "Proceedings for the recovery of Castlecomer 1653-4. The Rebels had it up to that time since 1641": Wandesforde Mss (N.L.I.).
8. ibid.
9. Cooper, J. P. "Wentworth and the Byrne's Country", *Ir. Hist. Stud.,* (1966) XV, 1-22.
10. Carrigan, W. (1905), op, cit., 111, 124.
11. ibid., 150-153.
12. ibid., 128-134.
13. Introduction to Lodge transcripts of the Records of the Rolls (P.R.O.I.) Vols. XI.
14. Beckett, J. C. *The making of modern Ireland,* (London 1966) 120.
15. Petty, W., (1680), op. cit., 305.
16. Simms, J. G. *The Williamite confiscation in Ireland, 1690-1703,* (London 1956) 120.
17. Beckett, J. C. (1966), op. cit., 149; Simms, J. G. (1956) op. cit., 195-196.
18. Down Survey Memoir of the Parish of Mayne in Mss 720. (N.L.I.).
19. Burke, B. and Burke, A. D. (1907) op. cit., 1292.
20. Lodge Transcripts of the Records of the Rolls (P.R.O.I.), Vol. XI, Act of Settlement 1666-67, 20.
21. "Proceedings for the Recovery of Castlecomer . . ." op. cit.,
22. Lodge Transcripts of the Records of the Rolls (P.R.O.I.) Vol. VIII. Charles, II, 33.
23. ibid., Vol. XII, Act of Settlement 1667-69, 33.
24. Simington, R. C. *The Transplantation to Connacht* 1654-58 (Shannon 1970).
25. Quoted in Carrigan, W. (1905) op. cit., Appendix V, Vol. IV; Mss 2515 (N.L.I.).
26. Rental of Ormonde estates, 1648: Ms. 2506 (N.L.I.); Rental dated 1693: Ms 11,053 (N.L.I.); Rental dated 16909-91: Ms 2561 (N.L.I.).
27. Bottigheimer, K. S. (1971) op. cit., 134.
28. Ms 975 (N.L.I.); Lodge Transcripts of the Records of the Rolls (P.R.O.I.) especially vol. XI and XII, Act of Settlement (1666-69).
29. Ms 975.
30. Burtchaell, G. D. *Genealogical memoirs of the Members of Parliament for the county and city of Kilkenny,* (Dublin 1888) 44-49.
31. Lodge Transcripts of the Records of the Rolls (P.R.O.I.) Vol. XII, (1667-69) 33.
32. ibid., 391.
33. Pender, S. (ed.) *Census of Ireland, C. 1659* (Dublin 1939). Hardinage, W. H. "Observations on the earliest known manuscript Census Returns of the people of Ireland", *T.R.I.A.* (XXIV) (1873) 317-329.
34. *Burke, B. A Genealogical and Heraldic Dictionary of the Landed Gentry of Great Britain and Ireland,* (London 1883) 11 1114.

35. Carrigan, W. (1905) op, cit., Appendix V, Vol. IV.

36. Lodge Transcripts of the Records of the Rolls (P.R.O.I.), Vol. IX, Williame III and Anne, 249.

37. Carrigan, W. (1905) op. cit., Appendix V, Vol. IV.

38. Lodge Transcripts op. cit., Vol. XII, Act of Settlement (1667-69) 391.

39. Carrigan, W. op. cit., 11, 84.

40. Lodge Transcripts op. cit., Vol. XII, Act of Settlement (1667-69) 389.

41. Burtchaell, G. D. (1888) op. cit., 48.

42. Thornton, A. *The Wandesfordes of Kirklington and Castlecomer,* (London 1906) 2 Vols. 1, 78.

43. Burtchaell, G. D. (1888) op. cit., 49.

44. ibid.

45. Ms 2561: Ormonde Mss (N.L.I.).

46. Dunton, J. *Conversations in Ireland C. 1698,* (London 1818) 40.

47. Graves, J. (ed.) "A journey to Kilkenny in the year 1709 from the Mss notes of Dr. Thomas Molyneaux", *J.K.S.E.I.A.S.* (1860-61) 298.

CHAPTER FOUR

1. Mss 1568-71: The Ossory Mss, (1776) (N.L.I.).

2. James, F. G. *Ireland in the Empire, 1688-1770* (Cambridge, Mass., 1973) 316.

3. Mss. 2670: Canon Leslie Mss, (N.L.I.).

4. Burke, B. and Burke, A. P. (1907) op. cit., 1 208.

5. Lodge transcripts of grants of lands, leases and deeds in the reign of Queen Anne, (P.R.O.) deed no. 402.

6. ibid., deed no. 395.

7. ibid., deed no. 404.

8. Carrigan, W. (1905) op. cit., 11, 208.

9. Ms 2561: The Ormonde Mss, (N.L.I.).

10. Lodge transcripts of grants of lands etc., op. cit., deed no. 397.

11. Abstract of title of the Bryan estate compiled c. 1903: E.C. 7312, (Archives of the Irish Land Commission, Dublin).

12. Lodge transcripts of grants of lands . . . etc., op. cit., deed no. 396.

13. ibid., deed no. 403.

14. ibid., deed no. 327.

15. ibid., deed no. 128.

16. ibid., deed no. 129.

17. Abstract of title of the Webb estate compiled c. 1903: E.C. 2722. (Archives of the Irish Land Commission, Dublin).

18. Burtchaell, G. D. (1888) op. cit., 144.

19. ibid., 85.

20. Carrigan, W. (1905) op. cit., 11, 96.

21. Boate, G. (1652) op. cit., 84.

22. Nef, J. U. The rise of the British Coal Industry, (London 1932) 1, 75.

23. Graves, J. (1860-61) op. cit., 306.

24. "Nef, J. U. (1932) op. cit., 1, 74.

25. "Letter to George, Viscount Castlecomer from Mr. Emerson of Castlecomer 1742": Wandesforde Mss (N.L.I.).

26. "Agreement between the colliers and Lord Castlecomer 1755; Wandesforde Mss (N.L.I.).

27. Coote, Sir C. *Statistical survey of the Queen's County,* (Dublin 1801) 199.

28. Harley, J. B. "From manpower to steam" in *Man made the land.* ed. by Baker, A. R. H. and Harley, J. B. (Newton Abbot 1973), 172.

29. Cullen, L. M. *An economic history of Ireland since 1660,* (London 1972) 89.

30. Delaney, R. *The canals of the South of Ireland,* (Dublin 1966), 200.

31. Campbell, T. *A philosophical survey of the south of Ireland* (Dublin 1778) 107.

32. Thirsk, J. "Roots of industrial England" in *Man made the land* ed. by Baker, A. R. H. and Harley, J. B. (1973) op. cit., 103.

33. "A report made to the Right Hon. George Viscount Castlecomer by Lullum Batwell upon his inspecting and examining the state and condition of his Lordship's estates and collieries and other affairs at Castlecomer as directed by his Lordship 1746". Wandesforde Mss. N.I.,I.

34. Hodgson, R. J. "Agricultural Improvement and changing regional economies in the eighteenth century" in *Man Made the Land* op. cit., (1973) 151.

CHAPTER FIVE

1. Inglis, H. D. *Ireland in 1834. A journey throughout Ireland during the Spring, Summer and Autumn of 1834 . . .* 2 vols. (London 1834); Tocqueville, A. C. H. de, *Journeys to England and Ireland 1836* ed. by Meyer, J. P. (London 1958).

2. Healy, J. Atlas of 24 coloured maps with names of the tenants of the Lordship of Castlecomer and the townlands of Tomascotha and Julianstown, Co. Kilkenny, 21F139 (1-24) (N.L.I.).

3. "Rental and particulars of leases made by the late Countess of Ormonde on the Castlecomer estate C' 1836": Wanderforde Mss (N.L.I.).

4. Tighe, W. *Statistical observations relative to the county of Kilkenny, made in the years 1880 and 1801,* (Dublin 1802).

5. Griffith, R. *Report on the Leinster Coal District,* (Dublin 1814).

6. *Minutes of evidence before a Select Committee of the House of Commons appointed to examine into the causes of outrages in Ireland,* (Dublin 1832).

7. Andrews, J. H. "Changes in the rural landscape of late eighteenth and early nineteenth century Ireland: an example from county Waterford", unpublished paper read at the conference of Irish geographers, (Belfast 1971).

8. "Report . . . etc. on the Castlecomer estate carried out by Lullum Batwell in 1746": Wandesforde Mss (N.L.I.).

9. "Particulars and Arrears on Irish estates 1821": Wandesforde Mss (N.L.I.).

10. "An account of the Castlecomer collieries 1826" ibid.

11. "Rental of Castlecomer estate, 1773", ibid.

12. Carrick, Earl of. *A reply to a narrative of landlord oppression and tenant wrong*, (Dublin 1870) 4.

13. "Rental and particulars of leases made by the late Countess of Ormonde on the Castlecomer estate c. 1836. Wandesforde Mss (N.L.I.).

14. *Parliamentary Gazateer*, (London 1846) 420.

15. O'Carroll, D. *Historical sketches of the parishes of Castlecomer, Ballyragget, Conahy, Muckalee and Clogh*, (Kilkenny 1906) 20.

16. Geological Survey Office, *Report of the Diamond Drilling Programme in the Leinster Coalfield 1959-63*, (Dublin 1964).

17. p.p., 1836, No. 43, 30.

18. Hall, S. C. and A. M. *Ireland, its scenery, character etc.*, 3 vols (London 1841-3) 39.

CHAPTER SIX

1. Inglis, H. D. (1834) op. cit., 186-87.

2. Freeman, T. W. *Ireland: its Physical, Historical, Social and Economic Geography* (London 1950) 325.

3. Letter to Mr. Wandesforde from Mr. Johnson, manager of the Castlecomer collieries, dated 1849: Wandesforde Mss (N.L.I.).

4. Cousens, S. H. "Regional patterns of emigration during the great Irish Famine 1846-'51", *Trans. Inst. Br. Geogr.* (1960) 28, 128.

5. Freeman, T. W. *Pre-Famine Ireland* (Manchester 1957) 35.

6. Cullen, L. M. (1972), op. cit., 165.

7. De Tocqueville, A. (1958) op. cit., 165.

8. Burtchaell, G.D. (1888) op. cit., 142.

9. Burke, B. and Burke, A. D. (1907) op. cit., 1,400.

10. Abstract of Title of Frankfort estate compiled c. 1903: E. C. 9132, Archives of the Irish Land Commission, Dublin.

11. Burke B. and Burke, A. D. (1907) op. cit., 681.

12. Abstract of Title of the Humphries estate compiled c. 1903: E. C. 3847, Archives of the Irish Land Commission, Dublin.

13. Abstract of Title of the Bryan estate compiled c. 1903: E. C. 1312, Archives of the Irish Land Commission, Dublin.

14. *Valuation of Tenements, Barony of Fassadinin* (Dublin 1850) 8.

15. Abstract of Title of the Earl of Clonmel's estate compiled c. 1903; E. C. 4059, Archives of the Irish Land Commission, Dublin.

16. Abstract of Title of the Bulfin estate compiled c. 1903; E.C. 6736 Archives of the Irish Land Commission, Dublin.

17. Buchanan, R. H. "Rural Settlement in Ireland" in Stephens N. and Glasscock, R. E. (eds.) (1970) op. cit., 155.

18. Carrick, Earl of. (1870) op. cit., 6.

19. Digest of evidence taken before H. M. Commissioners of inquiry into the state of law and practice in respect to the occupation of land in Ireland, (Dublin 1847) 111, 43.

20. Jones-Hughes, T. "Society and Settlement in nineteenth century Ireland". *Ir. Geogr.* 5, No. 2. (1965), 179-96 especially 181-3.
21. Freeman, T. W. (1957), op. cit., 183.
22. Johnson, J. H. "Marriage and Fertility in nineteenth century Londonderry", *J. Stat. and Soc. Inquiry Soc. of Ireland* (1957-8) 21, 112-3.

CHAPTER SEVEN

1. *Minutes of evidence . . . occupation of land in Ireland,* (1847) op. cit., 3, 44.
2. Wandesforde Mss (1850) (N.L.I.).
3. "Letter from Mr. Wandesforde to Mr. Richard Cooke": Wandesforde Mss (N.L.I.).
4. P.P. 1835, No. 573, 17.
5. Adams, W. F. *Ireland and Irish Emigration to the New World 1815 to the Famine,* (New York 1967) 239.
6. Smith, C. W. (1974) *The Great Hunger,* (London 1974) 223.
7. Hall, S. C. and A. M. (1841-3) op. cit., 1, 39.
8. Carrick, Earl of, (1870), op. cit., 4.
9. List of people assisted to emigrate from the Wandesforde estate 1841-1855; Wandesforde Mss (N.L.I.).
10. Smith, C. W. (1974) op. cit., 209.
11. P.P. 1836, No. 35, 60.
12. Quoted in "A Reply to A Narrative of Landlord oppression and Tenant Wrong", Earl of Carrick, (Dublin 1870) 8.
13. Cullen, L. M. (1972), op. cit., 141.
14. Letter from Richard Eaton, agent of the Wandesforde estate to Mr. Cullen; Wandesforde Mss (1838) (N.L.I.).
15. O'Carroll, D. (1906), op. cit., 10.
16. Freeman, T. W. (1957), op. cit., 137.
17. Account of Collieries in Slievardagh; Irish Mining Company Mss (1846) (N.L.I.).
18. Memorial from the miners of Castlecomer to the Board of Ordnance, London; Wandesforde Mss (1849) (N.L.I.).
19. Letter to Mr. Wandesforde from Mr. Johnson, (1849), op. cit.,
20. Letter to Richard Eaton, agent of the Wandesforde estate from Mr. Patrick Purcell, landholder in Cloneen townland; Wandesforde Mss (1837) (N.L.I.).

SELECT BIBLIOGRAPHY OF SECONDARY SOURCES

Aalen, F. H. A. "The origin of enclosures in eastern Ireland", in Stephens, N. and Glasscock, R. E. (eds.), *Irish geographical studies in honour of E. Estyn Evans*, (Belfast 1970) 178-191.

Aalen, F. H. A. "Some historical aspects of landscape and rural life in Omeath, Co. Louth", *Ir. Geogr.*, (1962) IV, 256-278.

Adams, W. F. *Ireland and Irish emigration to the New World from 1815 to the Famine*, (New York 1932).

Andrews, J. H. "Geography and government in Elizabethan Ireland", in Stephens, N. and Glasscock, R. E. (eds.), *Irish geographical studies in honour of E. Estyn Evans*, (Belfast 1971).

Andrews, J. H. "Note on the historical geography of the Irish iron industry", *Ir. Geog.*, (1956) III.

Andrews, J. H. "Ireland in maps: a bibliographical postscript", *Ir. Geog.*, (1962) IV, 234-243.

Bagley, J. J. *Historical interpretation: sources of English medieval history 1066-1540*, (London 1965).

Bagwell, R. *Ireland under the Tudors*, 3 Vols., (London 1885-90) reprinted 1963.

Baker, A. R. H. and Harley, J. B. (eds.) *Man made the land.* (Newton Abbot 1973).

Baker, A. R. H. and Butlin, R. A. (eds.) *Studies of field systems in the British Isles.* (Cambridge 1973).

Baker, A. R. H. (ed.), *Progress in historical geography*, Newton Abbot 1972).

Baker, A. R. H., Hamshere, J. D. and Langton, J. (eds.) *Geographical Interpretations of historical sources: readings in historical geography* (London 1970).

Baker, A. R. H., Butlin, R. A., Phillips, A. D. M. and Prince, H. C., "The future of the past", *Area* (1969), 14, 46-51.

Beckett, J. C. *The making of modern Ireland*, 1603-1923, (London 1966).

Beresford, M. W. *History on the ground: six studies in maps and landscapes*, (London 1957).

Blacam, A. de, *Gaelic literature surveyed*, (Dublin 1929).

Black, R. D. C. *Economic thought and the Irish question, 1817-1870*, (Cambridge 1960).

Boate, G. *Ireland's natural history*, (London 1652).

Bottigheimer, K. S. *English money and Irish land*, (Oxford 1971).

Bourke, P. M. "The agricultural statistics of the 1841 census of Ireland. A critical review", *Ec. H.R.*, 2nd series, (1965), XVIII, 376-391.

Broek, J. O. M. *The Santa Clara Valley, California: a study in landscape changes.* (Utrecht 1932).

Brooks, E. St. J. *Knight's fees in Cos. Wexford, Carlow and Kilkenny in the 13th and 15th centuries,* (Dublin 1950).

Brown, R. H. *Historical geography of the United States,* (New York 1948).

Buchanan, R. H. "Rural settlement in Ireland" in Stephens, N. and Glasscock, R. E. (1971), op. cit., 146-161.

Buckley, K. "The records of the Irish Land Commission as a source of historical reference", *Ir. Hist. Stud.,* (1952-3) VIII, 28-36.

Bruen, W. E. L. "Free trade in land: an aspect of the Irish question," *T.R.H.S., 4th series, (1949) XXXI, 61-74.*

Butler, W. F. T. *Confiscation in Irish history,* 2nd ed. (Dublin 1918).

Butler, W. F. T. *Gleanings from Irish history,* (London 1935).

Butler, W. F. T. "The policy of Surrender and Regrant", *J.R.S.A.I.,* (1913) III, 99-129.

Burtchaell, G. D. *Genealogical memoirs of the Members of Parliament for the County and City of Kilkenny,* (Dublin 1888).

Caird, Sir J. *The Irish land question,* (London 1869).

Campbell, T. *Philosophical survey of the south of Ireland,* (Dublin 1778).

Carrick, Earl of. *A reply to a narrative of landlord oppression and tenant wrong,* (Dublin 1870).

Carrigan, W. *The history and antiquities of the Diocese of Ossory,* (Dublin 1905) 4 Vols.

Carte, *Life of James, Duke of Ormonde,* (Dublin 1736) 3 Vols.

Cherry, R. C. *The Irish land acts 1903 and 1904,* (Dublin 1906).

Chisholm, M. D. I. *Rural settlement and land use,* (London 1962).

Civil Survey, *Volumes of the Civil Survey,* Irish Manuscripts Commission (Dublin 1932).

Clarke, A. *The Old English in Ireland, 1625-1642,* (London 1966).

Clark, A. H. "Historical Geography" in James, P. E. and Jones, C. F. (eds.) *American Geography, Inventory and Prospect,* (Syracuse, 1954), 70-105.

Clark, A. H. *Acadia: the geography of early Nova Scotia to 1760,* (Madison 1968).

Coghlan, D. *The ancient land tenures of Ireland,* (Dublin 1933).

Collins, J. *Local government in Ireland,* (Dublin 1963).

Connell, K. H. "Peasant marriage in Ireland: its structure and development since the Famine", *Ec.H.R.,* 2nd series, (1961-2) XIV, 502-523.

Connell, K. H. "The land legislation and Irish social life, *Ec.H.R.,* 2nd series, (1958) XI, 1-7.

Connell, K. H. "The population of Ireland in the eighteenth century", *Ec.H.R.,* (1946) 16, 113-123.

Connell, K. H. *Irish peasant society: four historical essays,* (Oxford 1968).

Cooper, J. P. "Wentworth and the Byrne's Country", *Ir. Hist. Stud.* (1966) XV, 1-20.

Corkery, D. *The hidden Ireland: a study of Gaelic Munster in the eighteenth century,* (Dublin 1925) 4th impression, 1956.

Coote, Sir C. *General view of the agriculture and manufacture of the Queen's County,* (Dublin 1801).

Cousens, S. H. "Regional death rates in Ireland during the Great Famine, from 1846 to 1851", *Population Studies,* XIV, (1960-1) 55-74.

Cullen, L. M. (ed.) *The formation of the Irish economy,* (Cork 1969).

Cullen, L. M. *An economic history of Ireland since 1660,* (London 1972).

Cullen, L. M. "The value of contemporary printed sources for Irish economic history in the eighteenth century", *Ir. Hist. Stud.,* (1964) XIV, 142-155.

Cullen, L. M. "Problems in the interpretation and revision of eighteenth century Irish economic history", *T.R.H.S.,* (1967) 17.

Cullen, L. M. "The hidden Ireland: re-assessment of a concept", *Studia Hibernica,* (1969) 7-47.

Curtis, E. (ed.), *Calendar of Ormonde Deeds 1171-1603,* (Dublin 1932-43) Six Vols.

Curtis, E. and McDowell, R. B. (eds.), *Irish historical documents,* 1172-1922, (London 1943).

Darby, H. C. (ed.), *An historical geography of England before 1850,* Cambridge 1936).

Darby, H. C. "The changing English landscape", *Geographical Journal,* (1951), 117, 377-94.

Darby, H. C. "On the relations of geography and history", *Trans. I.B.G.,* (1953) 19, 1-11.

Darby, H. C. "Historical Geography", in *Finberg, H. P. R. (ed.), Approaches to history,* (London 1962) 127-56.

Davies, J. *Historical tracts of Sir John Davies, Attorney General and Speaker in the House of Commons in Ireland, 1600-1616,* (Dublin 1767).

Davitt, M. *The fall of feudalism in Ireland,* (Dublin 1905).

De Burgh, V. H. H. *The landowners of Ireland: an alphabetical list of the owners of estates of £500 valuation and upwards in Ireland . . . ,* (Dublin 1878).

Delaney, R. *The canals of the south of Ireland,* (Dublin 1966).

"Devon Commission" *Report of the Royal Commission on the law and practice in respect to the occupation of land in Ireland,* (Dublin H.M.S.O., 1847-8).

Dillon, M. and Chadwick, N. *The Celtic realms,* (London 1967).

Dineley, T. "Extracts from the Journal of Thomas Dineley, giving some account of his visit to Ireland in the reign of Charles II", *J.R.S.A.I.,* IV, V, VI, VII, IX, XXXIV, XLIII, (1856-1913).

Dineen, P. J. and O'Donoghue, T. (eds.), *The Poems of Egan O'Rahilly* (London 1911).

Dobbs, A. *Some thoughts on the tillage of Ireland,* (Dublin 1938).

Drake, M. "Population growth and the Irish economy", in Cullen, L. M., (ed.), *The formation of the Irish economy,* (Cork 1969) 65-76.

Dunlop, R. *"The plantation of Munster,* 1854-1589", *Eng. Hist. Rev.,* (1888) III, 250-269.

Dunlop, R. *Ireland under the Commonwealth, (Manchester,* 1913) 2 Vols.

Dunlop, R. "Sixteenth century maps of Ireland", *Eng. Hist. Rev.,* (1905) 20, 309-337.

East, W. G. *The geography behind history,* (London, 1938).

Edwards, R. D. and Williams, T. D. (eds.) *The Great Famine: Studies in Irish history,* 1845-52, (Dublin, 1956).

Emery, F. V. "Irish Geography in the seventeenth century", *Ir. Geogr.,* (1958) III, 263-276.

Evans, E. Estyn, *Irish folk-ways*, (London, 1957).

Falkiner, C. L. *Studies in Irish history and biography, mainly of the eighteenth century*, (London, 1902).

Falkiner, C. L. *Illustrations of history and topography, mainly of the seventeenth century*, (London, 1904).

Febvre, L. *A geographical introduction to history*, (London, 1925).

Fisher, J. *The history of land-holding in Ireland*, (London, 1877).

Fitzgerald, W. *The historical geography of early Ireland*, (London, 1926).

Flatrès, P. *Geographie Rurale de Quatre Contrées Celtiques*, (Rennes, 1957).

Ford, G. and P. *Select list of British Parliamentary Papers*, 1833-99 (Oxford 1953).

Foster, T. C. *Letters on the condition of the people of Ireland*, (London, 1846).

Freeman, T. W. "Historical Geography and the Irish historian", *Ir. Hist. Stud.*, (1946-7) V, 139-146.

Freeman, T. W. *Pre-Famine Ireland*, (Manchester, 1957).

Freeman, T. W. *Ireland: its physical, historical, social and economic geography*, (London, 1950).

Froude, J. A. *The English in Ireland in the eighteenth century*, (London, 1881) 3 Vols.

Glasscock, R. E. "The distribution of wealth in East Anglia in the early fourteenth century", *Trans. I.B.G.*, (1963) 32, 113-23.

Glasscock, R. E. "Moated sites and deserted boroughs and villages: two neglected aspects of Anglo-Norman settlement in Ireland", in Stephens, N. and Glasscock, R. E. (eds.) *Irish Geographical Studies in honour of E. Estyn Evans*, (Belfast, 1920) 162-177.

Goblet, Y. M. (ed.) *A topographical index of parishes and townlands of Ireland in Sir William Petty's MSS. barony maps c. 1655-59, and Hiberniae Delineatio c. 1672*, (London, 1932).

Goblet, Y. M. *Les noms des lieux Irlandais dans l'oeuvre de Sir W. Petty*. (Paris, 1930).

Graham, J. M. "Rural society in Connacht 1600-1640" in Stephens, N. and Glasscock, R. E. (eds.) *Irish Geographical Studies in honour of E. Estyn Evans*, (Belfast, 1970) 192-208.

Graves, J. "Ancient tribes and territories of Ossory" *J.K.A.S.*, (1849-51) 1, 230-260.

Graves, J. "The Mss notes of Dr. Thomas Molyneaux edited by the Rev. James Graves, M.R.I.A.", *J.K.A.S.*, (1860-61) 290-301.

Green, E. R. R. *The Lagan valley, 1800-1850; a local study of the industrial revolution*, (Belfast, 1963).

Griffith, R. *Report on the Leinster Coal district*, (Dublin, 1814).

Grubb, J. (ed.), *William Penn's Irish Journal 1669-70*, (Dublin, 1952).

Hall, S. C. and A. M. *Ireland its scenery, character etc.*, 3 vols. (London, 1841-3).

Hanson, L. W. *Contemporary printed sources for British and Irish economic history, 1701-1750*, (Cambridge 1960).

Hardman, E. T. *Explanatory memoir on the geology of the Leinster Coalfields*, (Dublin, 1878).

Harley, J. B. "From manpower to steam: changes in the early industrial revolution", in Baker, A. R. H. and Harley, J. B. (eds.) *Man made the* land: essays in English historical geography, (Newton Abbot 1973) 167-180.

Harris, A. The rural landscape of the east Riding of Yorkshire, 1700-1850, (London, 1961).

Harris, C. R. The seigneurial system in early Canada, a geographical study, (Madison, 1966).

Havinden, M. A. Estate villages, (London, 1966).

Hayes-McCoy, G. A. "Gaelic society in Ireland in the late sixteenth century. Historical Studies, (1963) IV, 45-61.

Hayes-McCoy, G. A. "Ulster and other Irish maps, Circa 1600," (Dublin, 1964).

Hayes, R. J. (ed.), Manuscript sources for the history of Irish civilisation, (Boston, Mass., 1966), II Vols.

Hill, Lord G., Facts from Gweedore (1846), 5th ed. (Dublin, 1887).

Hogan, W. History and Antiquities of Kilkenny County and City, (Kilkenny, 1893).

Hooker, E. R. Readjustment of agricultural tenure in Ireland, (Chapel Hill, 1938).

Hoskins, W. G. The midland peasant: the economic and social history of a Leicestershire village, (London, 1957).

Hoskins, W. G. The making of the English landscape, (London, 1955).

Hunt, C. J. The lead miners of the northern Pennines in the eighteenth and nineteenth centuries, (Manchester, 1970).

Hurst, M. Maria Edgeworth and the public scene, (London, 1969).

Inglis, H. D. Ireland in 1834. A journey through Ireland during the Spring, Summer and Autumns of 1834 . . . 2 Vols. (London, 1834).

James, F. G. Ireland in the Empire, 1688-1770, (Cambridge, Mass., 1973).

Johnson, B. L. C. "The charcoal iron industry in the early eighteenth century", Geogr. Jr. (1951) 117, 167-77.

Johnson, J. H. "Marriage and fertility in nineteenth century Londonderry", J.S.S.I.S I., (1957-58) XXI, 99-117.

Johnson, J. H. "The Irish Tithe Composition Applotment Books as a geographical source," Ir. Geogr., (1958) III, 254-262.

Johnson, J. H. "The two Irelands at the beginning of the nineteenth century" in Stephens, N. and Glasscock, R. E. (eds.), Irish Geographical Studies in honour of E. Estyn Evans. (Belfast, 1970) 224-243.

Jones-Hughes, T. "Society and settlement in nineteenth century Ireland, Ir. Geogr., (1965) 5, 79-96.

Jones-Hughes, T. "East Leinster in the mid-nineteenth century", Ir. Geogr. (1958) III, 227-241.

Jones-Hughes, T. "Landholding and settlement in the Cooley Peninsula of Louth", Ir. Geogr., (1961) IV, 149-174.

Jones-Hughes, T. "Town and Baile in Irish place-names", in Stephens, N. and Glasscock, R. E. (eds.), Irish Geographical Studies in honour of E. Estyn Evans, (Belfast, 1970) 244-258.

Lowenthal, D. and Prince, H. C. "English landscape tastes", Geogr. Rev., (1965) 55, 186-122.

Lynch, P. and Vaizey, J. Guinness's brewery in the Irish economy, 1759-1876, (Cambridge, 1960).

Lyons, F. S. L. "Vicissitudes of a middleman in Co. Leitrim, 1810-27", *Ir. Hist. Stud.* IX, (1955) 300-318.

MacLysaght, E. *Irish life in the seventeenth century*, (Dublin, 1950).

MacLysaght, E. *Irish families: their names, arms and origins*, (Dublin 1957-64) 3 Vols.

MacNiocaill, G. *Na buirgéisí*, (Dublin, 1965) 2 Vols.

Maxwell, C. *Country and town in Ireland under the Georges*, (London, 1940).

Maxwell, C. *The foundations of modern Ireland*, (London, 1921).

Maxwell, C. *The stranger in Ireland from the reign of Elizabeth to the Great Famine*, (London, 1954).

McCracken, E. "The woodlands of Ireland C. 1600", *Ir. Hist. Stud.* (1959) XI, 271-296.

McDowell, R. B. (ed.), *Social life in Ireland, 1800-1845*, (Dublin, 1957).

McGrath, M. (ed.), *Chinnlae Amhlaoibh Ui Shuilleabháin*, (Dublin, 1937).

Mills, D. R. (ed.), *English rural communities: the impact of a specialised economy*, (Bath, 1973).

Mingay, G. E. *English landed society in the eighteenth century*, (London, 1963).

Mitchell, J. B. *Historical geography*, (London, 1954).

Montgomery, W. E. *The history of land tenure in Ireland*, (Cambridge, 1889).

Moody, T. W. *The Londonderry Plantation, 1609-1641*, (Dublin, 1939).

Morley, H. (ed.), *Ireland under Elizabeth and James the First. Described by Edmund Spenser, by Sir John Davies and by Fynes Moryson*. (London, 1890).

Moryson, F. *An itinerary, containing his ten years travel through Germany . . . Ireland etc., An ed. of the itinerary published by James Maclehose and Sons.* (Glasgow, 1907-8).

Murray, R. H. *Revolutionary Ireland and its settlement*, (London, 1911).

Murray, R. H. *Commercial and financial relations between England and Ireland from the Restoration*, (London, 1903).

Nef, J. U. *The rise of the British Coal industry*, (London, 1932) 2 Vols.

O'Brien, G. *The economic history of Ireland in the seventeenth century*, (Dublin, 1919).

O'Brien, G. *The economic history of Ireland in the eighteenth century*, (Dublin, 1918).

O'Carroll, D. *Historical sketches of the parishes of Castlecomer, Ballyragget, Conahy, Muckalee and Clogh*, (Kilkenny, 1906).

O'Domhnaill, S. "The maps of the Down Survey", *Ir. Hist. Stud.*, (1942-3) III, 381-392.

O'Flaherty, R. *West Connaught, 1684* ed. by Hardiman, J., (Dublin, 1846).

O'Kelly, O. *Kilkenny, a history of the county*. (Donegal, 1969).

O'Neill, T. P. *Sources of Irish local history*, (Dublin, 1958).

O'Rahilly, C. (ed.) *Five seventeenth-century political poems*, (Dublin, 1952).

Orpen, G. *Ireland under the Anglo-Normans*, (Dublin, 1920) 4 Vols.

Orwin, C. S. and C. S. *The open fields*, (Oxford, 1929).

Otway-Ruthven, T. "The character of Norman settlement in Ireland" *Ir. Hist. Stud.* (1965) V.

Palmer, N. D. *The Irish land league crisis*, (New Haven, 1940).

Pender, S., (ed.), *Census of Ireland, C. 1659,* (Dublin, 1939).

Perkin, H. *The origins of modern English society 1780-1880,* (London, 1969).

Petty, W. *The political anatomy of Ireland,* (London, 1691).

Petty, W. *New edition of William Petty's Hiberniae Delineatio (1685),* (Newcastle-Upon-Tyne, 1968).

Phillips, W. A. (ed.), *History of the Church of Ireland* (Dublin, 1974) 3 Vols.

Pomfret, J. E. *The struggle for land in Ireland, 1800-1923,* (Princeton, New Jersey, 1930).

Power, P. (ed.), *A bishop of penal times, being the letters and reports of John Brenan, Bishop of Waterford (1671-93) and Archbishop of Cashel (1677-1693), Cork, 1932).*

Praeger, R. L. *The way that I went,* (Dublin, 1937).

Prendergast, J. P. *The Cromwellian settlement of Ireland, 3rd ed.,* (Dublin, 1922).

Price, L. *The place-names of Co. Wicklow,* (Dublin, 1945-58), 7 vols.

Prince, H. C. "Real, imagined and abstract worlds of the past", *Progress in Geography,* (1971) 1-86.

Prince, H. C. "Historical geography" in Watson, J. W. (ed.) *Congress proceedings, 20th International Geographical Congress,* (London, 1967) 169-72.

Prior, T. *List of absentees and estimate of the yearly value of their incomes spent abroad,* (Dublin, 1769).

Quinn, D. B. "Sir Thomas Smith (1513-1577) and the beginnings of English colonial theory" *Proc. Amer. Phil. Soc.* (1945) LXXXXIX 543-60.

Quinn, D. B. *The Elizabethans and the Irish,* (Cornell, 1967).

Quinn, D. B. "The Munster Plantation: problems and opportunities", *J. Cork Arch. and Hist. Soc.* LXXI (1966).

Reeves, W. "The townland distribution of Ireland", *Proc. R.I.A.* (1857-61) 7, 437-490.

Rowse, A. L. *The England of Elizabeth* (London, 1950).

Salaman, R. N. *The history and social influence of the potato,* (Cambridge, 1949).

Sauer, C. O. "Foreword to Historical geography", *A.A.A.G,* (1941) 31, 1-24.

Seymour, St. John D. *The Puritans in Ireland 1647-1661,* (Oxford, 1921).

Simington, R. C. "The Tithe Composition Applotment Books", *Analecta Hibernica,* No. 10, (1941) 295-298.

Simington, R. C. (ed.), *The Civil Survey, A.D. 1654-56, County of Tipperary,* Dublin, (1931).

Simms, J. G. *The Williamite Confiscation in Ireland 1690-1703,* (London, 1958).

Simms, J. G. "Connaught in the eighteenth century", *Ir. Hist. Stud.,* (1958), XI 116-133.

Simms, J. G. "County Sligo in the eighteenth century", *J.R.S.A.I.,* (1961) XCI Pt.ii.

Simms, J. G. "The Civil Survey, 1654-6," *Ir. Hist. Stud.* (1954-5) X, 253-263.

Simms, J. G. "Mayo Landowners in the seventeenth century, *J.R.S.A.I.,* (1965), XCV, 237-247.

Smith, C. T. *An historical geography of Europe before 1800,* (London, 1967).

Smith, C. T. "Historical geography: current trends and prospects," in Chorley, R. J. and Haggett, P. (eds.), *Frontiers in geographical thought,* (London, 1965) 118-143.

Smith, C. W. *The Great Hunger,* (London, 1974).

Spenser, E. *A view of the present state of Ireland in 1596, Renwick, W. L.* (ed.) (London, 1934).

Stephens, N. and Glasscock, R. E. (eds.) *Irish Geographical Studies in honour of E. Estyn Evans.* (Belfast, 1971).

Taaffe, N. *Observations on Affairs in Ireland, from the settlement in 1691 to the present time,* (Dublin, 1766).

Taylor, E. G. R. *Late Tudor and early Stuart Geography,* (London, 1934).

Thirsk, J. *English peasant farming,* (London, 1957).

Thomas, W. L. (ed), *Man's role in changing the face of the earth,* (Chicago, 1955).

Thomas, D. *Agriculture in Wales during the Napoleonic Wars: A study in the geographical interpretation of historical sources.* (Cardiff, 1963).

Thompson, F. M. L. *English Landed Society in the Nineteenth Century,* (London, 1963).

Thorpe, H. "The lord and the landscape: illustrated through the changing fortunes of a Warwickshire parish, Wormleighton", in Mills, D. R. (ed.), *English Rural Communities,* (Bath, 1973) 30-82.

Tighe, W. *Statistical Survey of the County of Kilkenny,* (Dublin, 1802).

Tocqueville, A. C. H. de, *Journeys to England and Ireland, C. 1835,* Meyer, J. P. ed. (London, 1958).

Trench, W. S. *Realities of Irish Life 1868,* the Fitzroy ed. (London, 1966).

Twiss, R. *A tour in Ireland in 1775,* (London, 1776).

Yates, E. M. "History in a Map", *Geogr. Jnl.* (1960) CXXVI, 32-51.

Young, A. *A tour in Ireland 1776-1779,* (London, 1780).

APPENDICES

1. Extracts from manuscript and other sources used in the Text.

(A) Four O'Brenan deeds.

(1) Donegha ne Killé mac Shane O'Brenan of Aghetobbir in Idowgh, Co. Kilkenny, Dermot mac Owen O'Brenan, Patrick alias Gilpatrick mac Donill O'Brennan, Dermot mac Donaill O'Brenan and Teig Leigh O'Brenan of the same, gentlemen, for a certain sum of money paid to them by Thomas, Earl of Ormonde, grant to Peter Butler of Graighdowske, Co. Kilkenny and Thomas Cantwell of Cantwellscourt in the same, all the messuages, lands, tenements, etc. in Aghetobbir. To hold to said Peter and Thomas, their heirs etc., to the use of the Earl of Ormonde, his heirs and assigns for ever. November 26, 1594.

(2) Owen mac Donegh Boye O'Brenan of Rathcalle in Idowgh grants to Thomas, Earl of Ormonde, all his messuages, lands and other hereditaments in Corrynshine alias Cowrefoynshin in Idowgh, to hold to said Earl, his heirs and assigns, for ever.
Witnesses: R. Shee, P. Butler, Sheriff, Piers Butler, Phillip Purcell, Oliver Seintleger, Thomas Archer. May 12, 1595.

(3) Owen McShane O'Brenan of Rathcally, Moriertagh McShane O Brenan of the same, William O'Brenane McCahir of Ballyhemekyne and Redmond Ryogh Purcell of Esker, gentlemen, grant to Thomas, Earl of Ormonde, all their messuages, lands, etc., in Corrynshine alias Cowrfoynshyn; to hold to said Earl, his heirs and assigns, for ever.
May 12, 1595.   Three seals.

(4) Doneghe ne Kille mac Shane O'Brenan of Aghetobbir and Dermot McOwen O'Brenan of the same, grant to Robert Rothe, Henry Sheeth and Thomas Archer all the messuages lands, etc., in Aghetobbir, to hold to them, their heirs, etc., to the use of Thomas, Earl of Ormonde, his heirs and assigns, for ever. Thomas Phelan of Kilkenny, clerk to deliver seisin.
Witnesses: John Rothe fitz Piers, Luke Archer fitz Laurence, Andrew Archer fitz Laurence. William Kelly.
June 26, 1595.   Two seals.
Source: Curtis, E. (ed.) Calendar of Ormonde deeds VI, 71-72.

(B) The boundaries of Idough 1635.

Territor, picinct, sive circuit' de Idough in Co. Kilkenny ab antiquo nominat' fuit Brenan, sed nunce et a longo tempore nominat et vocat fuit et est nomen de Idough-let met limitt et bond' put exprim' in his Anglican verbis viz:— First, the meares, lymitts and bounds of the said territory, precinct or circuit of land of Idough aforesaid, doe begin at Downanonugh, and soe along the mountain to a towne called Cloanbroack, and so to Garrydeny al' Deny's garden on the north, and along south-east by the meares of Slewmarge, as the bounds and meares of Croughtinecly and Confelie extends and reacheth, the which two last named towns are within Idoagh, and so along the mountayne untill you come to the Bishop of Loughlins lands in the mountayne of Slewtymare, and from thence alonge, leaving Dromroe and all that parte of the mountayne within the territory of Idough, and soe by the streame or water called Dynyn passing through the wood called Keyliffooke, and soe south-west along the ancient meares of Desert O'Leskan, leaving the said desert with the members and appurtenances thereof within Idough, and from hence north-west by the outmeares of the lands of the Earl of Ormonde called Kilmackar and Ballyooskall, and soe alonge by the lord viscount Mountgarrett's lands of Castell O'Maghan and the lands of Coolroe, and so along to the streame of Glassegall which divides Coolroe the earl of Ormond's lands and Killrush the earl of Londonderry's lands, and alonge the said water or stream until it comes to a place called Ballinagerigh, leaving the said Ballinagerigh in Idough and so to Clycoledoboy, and soe alonge to Downanonogh where the said mere first begun.

Source: Inquis. Lageniae, Com. Kilkenny 64 Car. 1, 1635 (P.R.O.).

Extract from the Down Survey of Fassadinin barony c.1654.

(C) The Parish of Conahy by Wm. Brookes.

Is bounded on the West and Northwest with the Barrony of Gallmoy on the North with the Parrish of Donaghmore on the East with Kilmaker landes on the South with Coolerahin Parrish on the Southeast with the Parrish of Mayne. The soyle is Arrable Meadowe and Pasture whereof much Heathy Shrubby and Mountaineous pasture. It containes the Ensueing forfeited townelands vizt., Ouldtowne, Grange, Knockroe and Conohye — There is a Thatcht house and some cabbins at Oldtowne and old Church and some Cabbins in the Grange and a castle in repaire and some cabbins at Conohye:—

			Arable	293.0.0.
8 Earl of Ormonde	Oldtowne	343.0.0.	Meadowe	7.6.0.
			Heat, Shrub.	
			Pasture	43.0.0.
9 The Same	Grange	449.0.0.	Arable	352.0.0.
			Meadowe	3.0.0.
			Moorish, Shr.	
			Pa.	94.0.0.

10 Lord Mountgarrett				
Ir. Papist	Knockroe	203.0.0.	Arable	155.0.0.
			Meadowe	4.0.0.
			Heat. Pas.	44.0.0.
11 Earl of Ormonde	Conohye	862.0.0.	Arable	765.0.0.
			Meadowe 2.0.0.	
			Shr. heat.	
			pas.	95.0.0.
Total of forfeited landes		1857.0.0.		1857.0.0.

Source: Mss 720 (N.L.I.).

(D) Contract between colliers and Lord Castlecomer 1755.
Agreement to work coal and culm for Lord Castlecomer.

This is to certify that we are determined to go to work wherever Lord Castlecomer tells us – on these terms that we will not expect any more than the colum and the picking of it for the use of our firing, that we will give up the pecks we formerly had and all pretensions to selling any of them and desire no more than the colum allowing his Lordship the use of what colum he wants for himself – Also that Lord Castlecomer will let us enjoy the land we now have provided we work with him and for him on the terms above mentioned paying him the rent we are now liable for it.
And it is further agreed that whatever other persons sign this paper and this article holding above four acres and his house shall only hold whatever remains over and above that quantity during Lord Castlecomer's pleasure.

9th of December 1755.

Source: Wandesforde Mss (N.L.I.).

(E) Castlecomer Estate Account 1821	£.	s.	d.
By payment to Drivers, Bailiffs woodrangers			
John Wright Aughamucky, Woodranger on Account	2.	0.	0
Servant's wages and Board wages			
Foster board and wages for himself and maid to 12 Feb.			
1822-	18.	6.	4
McDonald Coachman ½ yrs. wages	17.	1.	3
McEvoy former gate porter	7.	5.	0
Mary Martin Laundress on account	23.	0.	0
Doyle the footman	1.10.		0
George Nesbitt Park keeper a year wages	13.13.		0
Do on account as sportsman and keeping dogs	13.15.		9
Servants at C. Comer Board Wages from 25 Dec. to			
14 May 1821	58.18.		9½
By Payment of Gratuities to Town Improvement and			
Incidental Charities			

Thatching in Chatsworth Row and other assistance to poor whose houses suffered by storm	2.16. 5
Frize for coats and cloaks at C. Comer	16.19. 0
Shoe premiums for the schoolboys	2.10. 0
One years stabling for coach horses	12.10. 0
Do in advance for stages	10. 0. 0
Hyland for slates for the Shambles	21.18. 3½
Carpenter, Slator, Paving and Nailors for work at do	22. 7. 8
Iron worker for gate at do	10. 0. 0
Mrs. Carroll, cash lent to enable her to open a shop	30. 0. 0
Subscription to buy seed potatoes to be reexpended in work and provision for the poor	126. 0. 0
Do. for the distressed peasantry of Ireland	100. 0. 0
By payment of Tradesmen's Bills and other House Expenses	
McGrath in Kilkenny for flax and seed	30. 5. 6
Maxwell to buy a press bed for servants hall	1. 6. 0
Remitted to Ball's bank to pay L. Ormondes Bills	520. 0. 0
Wm. Nesbitt travelling expenses with cart to Dublin	10. 0
Thos. and Elizabeth Doyle do.	1.16. 8
Subscription to London for John Bull newspaper	17. 8
To Scotland for cart wheels	33. 0. 8
Slator, Carpenter boards and lime for work at L. Ormondes house	2.14. 6½
Handcock's Bills for Bridles, Collars and other work	7.12. 0
Brenan Butcher, Bills for meat	60.15. 9
Mr. Carpenter for medicines	7.11.10
Do. for garden materials	23.12. 2½
For his labourers	59.18. 0
Adam Smith brazier for a years work at L. Ormondes house	6. 0. 0
Clarke ironmonger, Bills for demesne gates	22.15. 9½
Do for powder and shot	5. 2. 2
George Scott to buy stock	70. 0. 0
Payment for New Buildings and other Town Improvments	
Slator, Nailor, Carpenter and Sawyer for slates, timber and chimney pieces for Arch. house	112. 7. 9
Slator, Nailor and Carpenter for Locks, Hinges	39.15. 8
Ambrose Williams on foot his general a/c	332. 3.11
Painter and Locks for Market House	1.12. 7
Making a road at Ardra £8.19. 9 and compensation to a tenant 10/-	9. 9. 0
Postage	6. 8.11

Source: Castlecomer Estate Account 1821: Wandesforde Mss (N.L.I.)

APPENDIX II

A. Inquisitions

The sources utilised in the reconstruction of the Anglo-Norman world in Fassadinin were derived mainly from Central Government records and from the great amount of data left behind by the Ormondes. The Lodge manuscripts in the Public Records Office consist of transcripts of land grants conveyed by letters patent of the King and subsequently enrolled in the great ledger books of the State. Lodge also copied down the findings of various Inquisitions and Commissions, concerned with the ownership and occupation of land in the seventeenth century. The holding of Inquisitions was a corollary of the feudal axiom that the King owned all the land in his Kingdom. On the death of a tenant-in-chief, his estate reverted to the Crown. An Inquisition post mortem was an inquiry by jury into the holdings, services and succession of a deceased person. Juries enumerated the land divisions, buildings and tenancies of the deceased's estate. They also determined who the rightful heir was. Many such Inquisitions exist for Fassadinin estates in the seventeenth century.

Another form of Inquiry by jury was Inquisition on Attainder. This was a common procedure in hybrid and peripheral regions where landowners, convicted of treason, or slain in rebellion, were attainted, and had their property escheated by the Crown. Various other legal mechanisms were contrived to expedite legal confiscation and to finance the growing expenditure of the State Exchequer. Among them was the Commission for the Remedy of Defective Titles. This Commission was empowered to issue new titles to landowners in lieu of defective ones on payment of a money fine.

Transactions concerning the ownership, occupation and transfer of land in the extensive Ormonde Lordship were faithfully recorded throughout the medieval period. The greatest single source here is the Ormonde Deeds. This great mass of documents has been edited by the historian Edmund Curtis, and published by the Stationery Office in 1943. Deeds are primarily concerned with land transfers or contracts relating to tenure. They have a uniform layout throughout the medieval period. Deeds give the date of contract and a recital of title and contract. They name the principals and the land divisions subject to transfer and, in some instances, contain stipulations which may have been responsible for landscape change.

B. The Great Surveys of the Seventeenth Century

This chapter is based on the three major documents of Central Government in the period from 1650-1700: the Civil Survey, the Down Survey,

247

and the Books of Survey and Distribution. Local documentation, in the form of the Wandesforde and Ormonde manuscript material and the Lodge transcripts of the great ledger books of the State, was also utilised. The redistribution of land was a corollary of confiscation, and led to the compilation of surveys which mapped, identified and, in some instances, described the forfeited lands. Surveys enumerated old and new landowners and some prominent items found on the lands circa 1653. The detail of the various surveys typifies the thoroughness of the conquest. Feudal law had long sanctioned the concept that rebels should forfeit their fiefs. There was a fundamental difference between these traditional confiscations and those which declared the whole nation forfeit.

(1) The Civil Survey
   The Civil Survey was by inquisition and not by mapped measurement. It was in effect a stocktaking made by the conquerors with the aid of the conquered. The survey included twenty seven counties, and excluded the Connaught counties for which the earlier Strafford Survey was available. The barony was the territorial basis of the survey and juries were empanelled to work under the direction of twenty seven county Commissioners appointed by the Government. For the Civil Survey, it is necessary to rely on copies to take the place of archives which have been destroyed. The fire of 1711 which burned down the Surveyor General's Office destroyed all of the Civil Survey that was in public custody. In 1817, however, portion of the Civil Survey consisting of ten counties was discovered in a private collection. These were deposited in the Public Record Office and a copy was made for the Quit-Rent Office. This was fortunate insofar as the Public Record Office set was destroyed in the military activity which signalled the start of the Civil War in 1922. A small portion of the Civil Survey of Fassadinin was incorporated into the Books of Survey and Distribution. This details landowners c. 1653 in the parishes of Dysert, Kilmacar and Castlecomer. The names of owners and their land divisions were the only items copied and this fragment of the survey in no way compares with the detailed account which exists for Co. Tipperary.

(2) The Down Survey
   The Civil Survey was a preliminary work in which the forfeited lands were identified and described. It therefore formed the framework for the subsequent land surveys. On the 11th of December 1654 Sir William Petty contracted with the Government to, "admeasure all the forfeited lands according to their natural, artificial, and civil bounds and to state whether the land is distinguished into wood, bog, mountain, arable, meadow and pasture." Petty pledged to perform the survey "within one year and one month, provided the weather was agreeable and the Tories quiet." The Down Survey is the mapped expression of the Civil Survey and it was by these maps and index sheets that land satisfactions were made to the soldiers and adventurers, as well as to the other interests included by the Restoration Acts of Settlement and Explanation. The instructions given to Dr. Patrick Ragget, the surveyor in charge of mapping Co. Kilkenny, reveal the cartographic terms of reference. Ragget was to inquire about previous

Surveys such as the Civil. He was to "tread the meares according to the old and civil and to take notice how the lands you have agree with the lands itself". Finally he was to mark the situation of the "present housing, buildings and other remarkable things with some character expressing their condition and repair." The Down Survey of Fassadinin covered a total of 16,309 plantation acres which was divided into eight complete, and three incomplete, parishes. The name of the local surveyor, William Brooks, is appended to the descriptive memoirs in four parishes in west Fassadinin.

The Down Survey is a mapped inventory of property ownership and items of settlement and topography. The value of the work is remarkable for its detail and accuracy considering the limitations within which it was compiled. The terms of reference of the survey precluded the mapping of unforfeited lands except where these lands were completely surrounded by forfeited lands. Therefore, it is incomplete for the barony of Fassadinin. Arable land was surveyed in 'surrounds' of fifty acres, whereas 'waste or barren mountain' land was measured in units of 500 acres. This suggests that the survey was primarily concerned with identifying 'profitable land'. The delimitation of parish boundaries in the descriptive memoirs, which complement the maps, compares very unfavourably with the more detailed information recorded in the Civil Survey. In the Down Survey, boundaries are defined in terms of the names of parishes or other territorial divisions abutting on to a given parish. William Brooks, for example, defined the boundaries of 'Donaghmore and part of Kilmenan parish' as "bounded on each other, are bounded on the north with Lewhill parish, on the west with Upper Ossory and Galmoy barony, on the south with Conohy parish and on the east with Edogh territory and Killmacker lands."

A generalised description of soil quality followed this analysis of parish location. It seems that this was a summary of the much more detailed knowledge found in the Civil Survey. The soil of 'Donaghmore and part of Kilmenan', for example, was described as: "arable meadow and pasture, some shrubby mountainous pasture and wood." The names of the forfeited townlands and a selection of settlement items found in them were then, recorded. The inventory lists a great variety of seventeenth century structures. These include castles, churches, bawns, corn mills, tucking mills, thatched stone houses, houses with chimneys, thatched houses and cabins. Castles were variously described as, "a little castle in repair", "a stump of a castle", or "a ruined castle with bawn." Churches were invariably derelict, unused or in ruins. Little attention was paid to the less substantial edifices which housed the inferior tenantry.

The connection of forfeited lands with their proprietor in 1641 followed this exposition of situation, extent, content and embellishments. The geography of ownership c. 1641 was detailed according to the same sequence for each parish. In the left hand margin of the Down Survey memoir, the 'numbers in the plott' referred to the location of the lands in the barony maps. The second column contained the name and religious affiliation of the 1641 proprietor and the forfeited land divisions. The 'acreable' content of each denomination was listed and a division of the lands into 'profitable' and 'unprofitable' followed. 'Profitable' lands were defined as arable, pasture, and meadow and 'non-profitable' land included wood, bog, and waste mountain. Pasture was further subdivided into five categories of 'common', heathy', 'rocky', 'mountain and boggy'. the acreage

249

of lands 'profitable' and 'unprofitable' and the extent of glebe or other church lands was summarised at the end of each parish memoir.

(3) The Down Survey Maps

The terms of reference and the rapidity with which the Survey was completed precluded anything but a cursory examination of landscape items. The Civil Survey gave a much more comprehensive account of the fabric of rural society. It recorded for example, the form of tenure by which various proprietors held their estates and whether they had got possession through descent, inheritance, purchase or through Crown patents. The greatest achievement of the Down Survey was the mapping of the confiscated lands and the delineation of territorial boundaries. The field work for the 'plotts' was completed between 1655 and 1657 by a diverse group which included Civil surveyors, footsoldiers and students from Trinity College. The parish maps which formed the basis of the Down Survey were generally on a scale of 1:10,000. These maps, when superimposed on the Ordnance Survey townland maps on a scale of six inches to the mile, help to identify stability and change in Fassadinin in the period from 1654 to 1840. The Down Survey map of Fassadinin barony was reproduced from the original set which is in the Bibliothéque Nationale, Paris. This is, in effect, a synopsis of the data detailed in the parish 'plotts and Bookes of Reference'. Proprietor's name engraved on the parish maps are not found on the barony charts. Parish maps do not contain a greater range of settlement items but inscriptions, which are missing from barony maps, record the type of feature and its structural condition. Unforfeited areas of Fassadinin were delimited into parish units and the names of their territorial divisions and proprietors were enumerated in the parish maps. Townland divisions in these districts were not delineated because the terms of Petty's contract with the Government excluded this.

(4) The Books of Survey and Distribution.

Two sources catalogue the impact of the restoration land settlement on ownership. Manuscript 971 in the National Library of Ireland consists of the Books of Survey and Distribution of Counties Kilkenny and Wexford. It was compiled circa 1703 and lists proprietors of lands in 1641 and grantees and lands granted in 1660 and 1668 with their acreage content. Because the process of satisfying competing claims to land was a long drawn out affair, the surveys, such as the Civil and Down, which were compiled directly after the cessation of conflict were unable to connect the lands forfeited with the adventurers and soldiers to whom they were allotted. Apart from doing this, the Books of Survey and Distribution record the names of proprietors who regained all, or portion, of their estates after the Restoration of the Monarchy. The first three columns in the Books of Survey and Distribution are exactly similar to those of the Down Survey. The fifth column indicates whether the denominations were subdivided as a result of confiscation and in some instances provides a clue as to territorial reorganisation. The sixth column listed the name of the proprietor c. 1668. This source is complemented by the Lodge Transcripts of the Records of the Rolls in the Public Record Office. Volumes XI, XII and XIII of the Lodge Mss list the lands and hereditaments granted under letters patent of King Carles II, in virtue of the Acts of Settlement and Explanation. The records of the Ormonde and Wandesforde families document the impact of the wars and land settlements on an 'Old English' and a 'New English' family. The Ormonde data paints a graphic picture of the impact of war on the great Butler family. The Wandesforde papers, on the other hand, detail the consolidation of the pre-Cromwellian colony in north-east Fassadinin and the genesis of an association that was to last over three hundred years.

(C) The Great Surveys of the Nineteenth Century.

(1) The Primary Valuation of Tenements (Griffiths Valuation)

Under the Irish Poor Law Act of 1838, commissioners were empowered to "unite so many townlands as they think fit to be a union for the relief of the destitute poor". These Unions were further subdivided into electoral divisions which were chargeable for the relief of their poor. In some instances, individual estates were recognised as electoral divisions. Under the terms of the Act, a valuation of each separate tenement was authorised to meet the requirement of the assessment of the poor rate. This valuation was entrusted to the guardians of each poor-law union and was carried out by local valuators appointed by them. In many instances, the local valuation was assigned to incompetent and dishonest valuators. The passing of the first Tenement Valuation Act and subsequent amending legislation placed the valuation on a more uniform basis throughout the country. Because of the role of Richard Griffith, mining and canal engineer and commissioner in charge of the Board of Works Relief Department during the Famine, in directing the Valuation, it is commonly referred to as 'Griffith's Valuation.'

Land and buildings were valued separately. In rural areas, the valuation was carried out on a townland basis. In towns, individual tenements were arranged according to streets. The following example taken from the General Valuation of Rateable property for the Barony of Fassadinin indicates the type of information recorded in the Valuation books.

| No. and Letters of Reference to Map | Names | | Description of Tenement | Content of Land | Net Annual Value | | |
	Parishes, Townlands and Occupiers	Immediate Lessors			Land £. s.d.	Buildings £.s.d.	Total £.s.d.
18	Mary Gorman	Thomas Kavanagh Esq.	House, Office and Land	A R P 34 2 11	28.0.0	2.0.0.	30.0.0

These books were prepared for baronies which were subdivided into townlands, civil parishes and electoral divisions of the poor law unions. The numeral in the first column referred to the location of the individual tenement on the six inch to the mile townland maps. These maps, which show the boundaries of holdings on a townland basis, can be misleading insofar as subsequent changes were often superimposed on the original valuation maps. The division of a tenement into subtenancies was indicated by the use of letters and holdings-in-common were bracketed together. This enables one to estimate the extent of these practices on a barony basis. The names of the occupiers and lessors are of great importance. They allow the historical geographer to reconstruct patterns of land owner-ship and occupation and can also be utilised as a measure of either con-tinuity or change. The Valuation Books are a more comprehensive and thorough inventory than, for example, the great ledger books of the seventeenth century. These paid no attention to the occupiers.

In the 'description of tenements', a distinction was drawn between tenements which consisted of land only, and those on which a house or other buildings were located. From an examination of this information, it was possible to determine the distribution and acreage of non-residential holdings in Fassadinin. Buildings which served religious, commercial and administrative functions were also identified. However, the com-mercial functions of buildings were not always listed. Retail outlets for basic commodities such as tea and alcoholic drink, for example, were not identified. Information on the size, distribution and number of holdings permitted an evaluation of landholding patterns in the barony. By utilis-ing these particulars it was also possible to indicate the areas in which commercial as distinct from subsistence agriculture was practised. The net annual value of a tenement was defined as "the rent for which, one year with another, the same might in its actual state be reasonably expected to let from year to year with the cost of repairs, insurance, maintenance, rates, taxes and all other public charges except the tithe rent being paid by the tenant." Land was valued at the current prices of the day, mainly with reference to the potential fertility of the soil and not according to the actual state of agriculture prevailing in 1850. 'Pasturage', for example, was to be valued at the price per acre proportionate to the number of cattle and sheep it would be capable of grazing during the year, according to the usual price per head in the neighbourhood for grazing. The quality of the 'herbage' and permanent improvements such as roads, drainage and fences were also to be taken into account.

The Valuators operated a sliding scale of allowances in respect of what were termed "peculiar local circumstances." When these circumstances such as, for example, relative location, communications, climate, elevation and shelter were favourable to agriculture, land values were correspondingly increased. On the other hand, when local circumstances were unfavourable, land values were reduced. Land valuation was, to an extent, an indication of soil fertility. It did, however, take many other aspects of site and situa-tion into account. It may be more correct to suggest that the valuation was an assessment of land potential as perceived by the valuators. The valuation of buildings was ascertained separately from land. Censuses compiled from 1851 onwards contain a summary of the total valuation of townlands and civil parishes.

(2) The Ordnance Survey Maps.

By 1842, the mapping programme on the six inches to the mile scale undertaken by the Ordnance Survey was complete. For the first time, the boundaries of all townlands, civil parishes, baronies and counties were

252

delineated. In this work, particular attention has been paid to the six-inch to the mile townland maps as well as the maps of the towns of Bally-ragget and Castlecomer on the scale of five feet to the mile. The barony map used throughout the study is based on the townland index to the six inch sheets, on the scale of one inch to one mile. Some individual maps are direct transcripts of the six-inch sheets. Man-made items such as the boundaries of territorial divisions, field outlines, roads, and settlement features, are shown on these maps. A selection of settlement items are named. These included Big Houses, churches of all denominations, police barracks, post offices and schools. The nineteenth century interest in antiquities was reflected in the care taken to mark the location of items such as castles, churches and raths. The Ordnance Survey maps are an important guide to the distribution and formal arrangement of settlement features. They show the extent of landlord demesnes. Selected items of topography such as rivers and lakes were depicted. A distinction was drawn between artificial lakes, usually found in demesnes, and natural lakes. Spot-heights rather than contours were used to indicate major variations in surface relief.

(3) Censuses

The censuses of 1841 and 1851 are of immense value to any worker in this period. The compilers of the 1841 census stated categorically that, "a Census ought to be a Social Survey, not a bare Enumeration." A great amount of information was collected and recorded. The Census territorial divisions were arranged according to townlands, parishes and baronies. At the time of the 1841 Census, the survey of Ireland on the scale of six inches to one mile was complete, except in the south-western counties of Cork, Kerry and Limerick. In the context of this study, census data is used mainly to indicate general patterns of population distribution, density and change. The Census Reports, Valuation Books and Ordnance Survey maps together provide an immense amount of detailed information on selected items in mid-nineteenth century Ireland.

254

Mountgarret Butlers, 32, 43, *45-46,* 50, 52, 59, 63, 67, 69, 71, 72, 80, 87, 154, 179, 180, 220.
Moryson, F. 25, 42.
Mossom, 90, *91,* 172, 194.
Mulhall, 98, 111.

N
Nef, 92.
Normanton, Earl of. 172, 175.

O
O'Brenans, 7, 8, 10, 17, 18, 28, *28-33,* 37, 39, 42, 58, 67, 73, 81, 94, 111, 124, 132, 168, *179-181,* 198, 208, 219, *220, 243.*
Ormondes, 7, 17, 19, 21, 25, 28, 29, 31, 43, 50, 63, 64, 69, 71, 72, 77, 80, 86, 87, 166, 169, 179.
Orpen, CH. 43.
Otway-Ruthven, J. 50.

P
Petty, W. 7, 10, 15, 17, 20, 24, 59, 66, 70, 82.
Phelan, 81, 198.
Purcell, 58, 63, *67-68,* 72, *73,* 74, 81, 82, 94, 167, 178, 179, 187, 196, 218, 220.

R
Redman, Colonel. 75, 77.
Reecks, R. 126, 139, 141, 214.
Rothes, 27, 30, 32, 41, 58, 61, 68, 73, 74, 78.
Ryan, D. 126, 131, 139, 173, 196, 201, 215.

S
Shees, 30, 32, 41, 58, 63, *68,* 73, 74, 78, 94.
Shortalls, 64, 68, 73.
Simington, RC. 73.
Simms, JG. 71.
St. George, 75, 76, 173, 174, 175.
Strangeways, 89, 166, 167, 168, 197.
Swift, 89, 91, 153, 173, 174.

T
Tighe, W. 97, 107, 143, 147, 158.

V
Vaux, Lord. 171, 196.

W
Walsh, 39, 40, 82.

Wandesforde, 9, 21, 33, 53, 55, 64, 65, 66, 67, 69, 71, 72, 77, 78, 81, 87, 91, 92, 96, 97, 121, 176, 179, 186, 187, 198, 221.
Waring, J. 166, 168.
Webbs, 24, 75, *76,* 77, 90, 91, 159, 168, 172, 174, 197.
Whitlow, JB. 3.
Williams, 78, 141, 216.
Willoughby, 168, 186.
Wilson, 103, 170.
Wright, 98, 100, 102, 145, 178, 186, 192, 193, 198.

SUBJECT-MATTER INDEX

A
Absenteeism, 74-75, 88, 97, 123, 175.
Act of Explanation, 57, 70, 174.
Act of Settlement, 57, 75, 76, 89, 174.
Administrative Divisions, *6-24.*

B
Barony unit, *7-13.*
Batwell survey, 21, *97-104,* 132, 218.
Big Houses, 89-91, 111-112, 224.
Book of ploughlands, 18, 25, 28, 34, 38, 49.
Book of Survey and Distribution, 11, 18, 21, 63, 66, 67, 74, *250-251.*

C
Castles, distribution of 63-64.
Census of population, 3, 17, *253.*
'Census' of 1659, 78-81.
Churches, distribution of 64-65.
Civil Survey, 9, 15, 17, *60-66, 248.*
Coal mining, *92-97, 142-148, 216-218.*

D
Demesnes, 90, 111, 113, 114.
Devon Commission, 200, 202, 205.
Down Survey, 9, 10, 11, 12, 15, 20, 45, 60, 62-63, 67, 68, *69-70,* 74, 77, 154, *248-250.*

E
Eaton's survey, *137-142.*
Emigration, 163, *204-209.*
Estate system, 75, 77, 84, 91, *163-176,* 225-225.

G
Great Hunger, The 121, 172, 176, 222.
Griffith's Valuation, 3, 13, 17, 22, 75, 137, *163-178,* 202, 208, *209-216, 251-252.*

H

Healy's survey, *106-121.*

I

Inquisition (1635), 8, 10, 19, 33, *39-42, 247.*
Inquisition (1630), 36-37.
Iron mining, *53-56.*

L

Land Commission, 75, 87, 89, 172, 173.
Land Occupation, *189-198.*
Land Valuation, *149-154.*
Leases, 101, 103, 107, *121-131,* 203.

M

Manors, 29, 33, 44-49.
Manorial system, *49-53,* 154, 220.
Master collier, 143-144, 217, 223.
Middleman system, 103-104.
Middlemen, 89, 121, 127-131, *131-148,* 158.

N

New English, 32-33, 38, 39, 41, *53-56.*

O

Ordnance Survey Maps, 3, 11, 13, 17, 21, 106, 164, 174, *252-253.*
Ormonde Deeds, 25, 29, 30, 50, 74, 82, 106.

P

Parish unit, *13-17.*
Physical landscape, *3-6.*
Ploughlands, 8, 10, *17-24.*
Population, distribution of *155-163.*

R

Record of the Rolls, 33, 74.
Restoration and Settlement, *74-77.*

S

Statistical survey, 95, 107.
Surrender and regrant, 30-31.

T

Territorial divisions, *6-24.*
Tithe composition books, 16, 21-23.
Toponomy, *14-24, 25-27, 34-36.*
Townlands, *17-24,* 106, 118, 181.

W

Wandesforde estate, *105-149,* 174, 183, 197, *198-218,* 223.

Wandesforde mss, 54, 84, 138, 199-200, *245-246.*
Webb estate, 89, 172-173.
Woodlands, 54, 56.

PLACES INDEX

A

Abbeyleix, 22, 159, 178, 191.
Ardaloo, 14, 15, 26, 45, 68, 73, 74, 152, 173.
Ardra, 38, 100, 113, 118, 120, 124, 125, 126, 129, 141, 203, 214.
Athy, 151, 189, 203.
Attanagh, 15, 43, 85, 159, 178, 197.
Aughamucky, 118, 126, 130, 135, 173, 195, 196, 201, 203, 215.
Aughatubrid, 8, 30, 38, 80, 82, 87, 169, 181, 196.
Aughrim, 30.

B

Ballinakill, 53, 54, 109, 116.
Ballinranke, 26, 76.
Ballycomy, 47, 100, 102, 124, 127, 129, 215.
Ballycondra, 89.
Ballyesker, 51.
Ballyfoyle, 58, 68, 74.
Ballyhimmin, 21, 36, 99, 109, 121, 135, 137, 203, 215.
Ballylinnen, 100, 111, 118, 122, 124, 125, 127, 128, 129, 130, 169, 201.
Ballymartin, 20, 26, 60, 62, 65, 67, 72, 73, 159, 192, 193.
Ballyoskill, 89, 187.
Ballyrafton, 169, 179, 187.
Ballyragget, 7, 43, 45, 49, 50, 60, 62, 63, 64, 65, 67, 69, 75, 78, 80, 91, 123, 150, 153, 154, 156, 162, 163, 169, 172, 174, 175, 181, 187, 193, 222.
Ballyroe, 93.
Barrack Street, 137, 141, 142, 212.
Barrack village, 167.
Barrow, R. 3, 53, 55, 92.
Bellmount, 172.
Borris, 23, 91, 169, 197, 225.
Borris Little, 23, 179.
Bowden's Row, 137, 213, 264.
Bridge (Main St.) 133, 135, 138, 139, 140, 214, 215.
Bullockhill, 168, 187, 196.

C

Cantwellscourt, 30.

257

Kilmacar, 14, 21, 24, 34, 45, 49, 51, 52, 63, 64, 65, 67, 69, 72, 80, 88, 91, 159, 166, 167, 178, 179, 187, 197.
Kilmademoge, 49, 60, 63, 65, 68, 73, 80, 159, 163, 168, 178, 187, 194, 196. 197.
Kilmadum, 27, 76, 80, 85, 159, 178, 190.
Kilmenan, 14, 80, 85, 159, 178, 179, 197.
Kiltown, 109, 120, 130, 131, 137, 185, 203, 214.
Kirwans Inch, 187.
Knockannadogue, 123, 124, 125, 126, 131, 139, 196, 214, 215.
Knockroe, 72, 87.

L

Leighlinbridge, 93, 94, 96, 108, 113.
Lismaine, 48, 65, 68, 73, 152, 192.
Lisnefunshin, 65, 87, 159, 172, 175, 179.
Loan, 117, 125, 126, 131, 142, 195, 206.
Loughill, 14, 21, 72, 80, 82, 89, 173.
Love Lane, 213, 214.

M

Mayne, 14, 15, 26, 51, 65, 72, 80, 159, 163, 178, 179, 190, 192.
Moneenroe, 92, 101, 103, 108, 109, 113, 118, 119, 120, 124, 125, 126, 131, 142, 152, 153, 157, 163, 181, 206, 207, 208, 214, 216.
Mount Eland, 91, 172.
Moyhora, 102, 111, 112, 115, 116, 117, 125, 127, 130, 131, 158, 174, 181, 195, 203, 208, 214.
Mothill, 14, 16, 17, 26, 49, 61, 65, 68, 76, 80, 86, 159, 168, 178, 197. ⌐
Muckalee, 14, 15, 43, 49, 64, 68, 76, 80, 85, 152, 159, 168, 178, 179, 187, 194, 196.

N

Nicholastown, 64, 68, 73.
New Ross, 47, 49, 58, 63, 92.
Newtown, 146, 156, 179.

O

Odagh, 7, 14, 15, 23, 39, 159, 178, 179.
Oldtown, 45, 65, 87.
Ouveg, 14.

R

Railyard, 109.

Rathaspick, 22, 156, 162, 178, 194.
Rathbeagh, 14, 159, 162, 178.
Rathcally, 31, 37, 196.
Rathgary, 89.
Rosconnell, 15, 21, 65, 85, 159, 162, 178, 197.

S

Shanganny, 179.
Skehana, 118, 125, 126, 130, 181, 195, 206, 216.
Slieveardagh, 6, 217.
Slievemargy, 34, 39.
Smithstown, 18, 35, 36, 66, 73, 77, 111, 112, 118, 122, 124, 125, 129.
Somerton House, 172, 175.
Springhill, 89, 168.
St. Mullins, 92, 96.
Suttonsrath, 27, 65, 68, 73, 77, 173, 187.
Swiftsheath, 24, 89, 91, 152, 153, 173, 181, 191.

T

Toortane, 187.
Tularea, 106, 110.
Tulleglass, 63, 68, 77, 173.

U

Uskerty, 118, 122, 124, 125, 129, 130, 214.

W

Waterford, 29, 93.
Webbsborough, 6, 24, 89, 91, 159, 168, 172, 181.
Woodview House, 181, 182.

LIST OF TOWNLANDS

1. Loughill
2. Rathgarry
3. Ballyoskill
4. Castlemarket E.
5. Castlemarket W.
6. Earlsgarden
7. Aghamucky
8. Ardra
9. Aughatubrid
10. Ballylinnen
11. Castlecomer
12. Clogh
13. Cloneen
14. Coolbaun
15. Coolnaleen
16. Croghtenclogh
17. Crutt
18. Donaguile
19. Drumgoole
20. Firoda Upper
21. Glebe
22. Firoda Lower
23. Gorteen
24. Kiltown
25. Loan
26. Moneenroe
27. Moyhora
28. Skehana
29. Clinstown
30. Foulksrath
31. Lismaine
32. Shanganny

33. Swiftsheath
34. Ballymartin
35. Ballynalacken
36. Ballyragget
37. Coole
38. Donaghmore
39. Finnan
40. Garrannaguilly
41. Moatpark
42. Rathduff
43. Sraleagh
44. Tinnalintan
45. Ballyrafton
46. Dunmore
47. Dunmore East
48. Dunmorepark
49. Dunmore West
50. Kirwan's Inch
51. Ballycomy
52. Clashduff
53. Coan East
54. Coan West
55. Damerstown E.
56. Damerstown W.
57. Dysart Glebe
58. Julianstown
59. Knockanaddoge
60. Smithstown
61. Uskerty
62. Ardaloo
63. Coonahy

64. Grange
65. Lisduff
66. Oldtown
67. Ballyhimmin
68. Byrnesgrove
69. Clashduff Low.
70. Clashduff Upp.
71. Commons
72. Coolnambrisklaun
73. Kilmacar
74. Maudlin
75. Moyne
76. Rathkyle
77. Sleeven
78. Tinnalintan
79. Tomakeany
80. Toorbeg
81. Toormore
82. Bullockhill
83. Kilmademoge
84. Knocknew
85. Leapstown
86. Mohill
87. Ruthstown
88. Drumerhin
89. Kilmadum
90. Gorteenara
91. Nicholastown
92. Russellstown
93. Brackin
94. Gragara

95. Inchakill Glebe
96. Jenkinstown
97. Littlefield
98. Tullowglass
99. Coolcullen
100. Coolraheen North
101. Coolraheen South
102. Corbetstown
103. Esker
104. Inchabride
105. Kilcollan
106. Lisnafunshin
107. Maudlin
108. Newtown
109. Webbsborough
110. Clogharinka
111. Coolraheen
112. Crossybrennan
113. Gaulstown
114. Knockmajor
115. Muckalee
116. Scanlansland
117. Tomascotha
118. Wildfield
119. Borris Big
120. Borris Little
121. Springhill
122. Suttonsrath
123. Kill
124. Toortane
125. Knockroe
126. Castlemarket

* See fig 1.9 on page 22.